Xenophobia and Islamophobia in Europe

Raymond Taras

EDINBURGH
University Press

Edinburgh University Press Ltd
22 George Square, Edinburgh EH8 9LF
www.euppublishing.com

Typeset in 10.5/12.5 Goudy by
Servis Filmsetting Ltd, Stockport, Cheshire, and
printed and bound in Great Britain by
CPI Group (UK) Ltd, Croydon CR0 4YY

A CIP record for this book is available from the British Library

ISBN 978 0 7486 5071 2 (hardback)
ISBN 978 0 7486 5072 9 (paperback)
ISBN 978 0 7486 5487 1 (webready PDF)
ISBN 978 0 7486 5489 5 (epub)
ISBN 978 0 7486 5488 8 (Amazon ebook)

Contents

CONTENTS

Acknowledgements

Research for this book was carried out at the Fundamental Rights Agency (FRA) in Vienna, the European University Institute (EUI) in Florence, the Institute for Studies of Migration, Diversity and Welfare (MIM) at Malmö University, and Stanford University, California. I wish to thank John Wrench at the FRA, Stefano Bartolini at the Robert Schuman Centre for Advanced Studies (EUI), Björn Fryklund in Malmö and Gabriella Safran at Stanford for providing the opportunity to make use of the excellent research resources at their institutions.

I completed the book while I was at the EUI in spring 2010 and Malmö University during the 2010/11 academic year. EUI seminars in which I took part and offered a wealth of specialised information and insightful analysis on migration and anti-immigrant attitudes included Giuliano Amato's 'Immigration and European Law', Rainer Bauböck's 'Debating Citizenship' and the Migration Working Group meetings he chaired, and Olivier Roy's 'Studying Religion'. For their original, erudite thinking which I have tapped in this book, I extend my gratitude to these experts. In Malmö, MIM's seminar series provided a forum for specialised debate on migrant integration and how its failures can produce social exclusion and xenophobia. Seminars held at Lund University's political science department also deepened my understanding of the politics of migration.

I wish to express my thanks to many academics who have given me expert advice on the subjects raised in this book. I gained immensely from the insightful, detailed, constructive sets of comments provided by two readers for Edinburgh University Press. For their valuable observations and suggestions on my interpretations of racism, xenophobia and Islamophobia, I am grateful to these colleagues from a number of universities: Tunç Aybak, Chip Berlet, Pieter Bevelander, Christian Fernandez, Alec Hargreaves, Anders Hellström, Wade Jacoby, Ayhan Kaya, Catarina Kinnvall, Nasar Meer, Cas Mudde, Delphine Perrin, Maja Povrzanović-Frykman, Anne Sofie Roald,

Hakan Yavuz and Fred Quinn. I have been enriched by discussions with researchers in Europe: Oxana Golynker, Leila Hadj-Abdou, Girish Kumar, Lamis El Muhtaseb, Ramazan Hakki Oztan, Olivia Umurerwa Rutazibwa, Alex Stummvoll, Brigitte Suter and Sayaka Törngren.

At different points in work on this book, I presented some of my key ideas to four senior political scientists. Jean Blondel, who I first met in the 1960s when he was pioneering the field of comparative politics, offered critical observations about my research design. Richard Rose, who I meet in New Orleans during his regular visits to south Louisiana, alerted me to important methodological issues affecting the analysis of citizen attitudes. Bill Safran began studying the political uses of fear and hatred decades ago, and he drew my attention to the classic literature dealing with ethnicity, religion and xenophobia. Finally, Philippe Schmitter, who introduced me to snorkelling, also introduced me to the place of big ideas in political science research. This book has, I hope, refracted some of the intellectual contributions made by this group of scholars.

I am grateful for the expert advice offered by many other colleagues with whom I have discussed the subjects of racism, religious prejudice and xenophobia. I also wish to acknowledge the intellectual stimulation provided by the many students I have taught in recent years in courses on European transnationalism, phobias and foreign policy, politics and nationalism, and phobias in contemporary Europe. They have been instrumental in inspiring, broadening and validating my interest in such inquiry.

Raymond Taras

CHAPTER ONE

Studying phobias

After she was crowned queen in 1553, Henry VIII's eldest daughter decided she was going to do something about the problem of a multicultural London. Up to 12 per cent of the city's population (10,000 strong) was made up of Protestant refugee communities and merchant-strangers. Most came from just across the English Channel – France, Wallonia, Flanders and Holland. But others originated in faraway Spain and Italy. Mary I was intent on restoring England to Roman Catholicism and sought a return to a mono-cultural England. She made it a crime to be a stranger in England without having papers of denization. All Protestant refugees were encouraged to leave.

Queen Mary faced a major obstacle in her quest to rid the country of for-eigners. Unexpectedly, 'although the English could have taken the opportu-nity of Mary I's reign to scapegoat strangers or aliens (the terms used in the period to refer to immigrants), the English more often seem to have valued and protected their immigrant neighbors'.[1] Her royal entry into London on 30 September 1553 was met by pro-stranger pageants organised by the city's mayor and aldermen 'sending the message that Londoners were inextricably linked with the strangers living among them'.[2]

This was not the end of popular protest against her anti-alien policies. A play, whose origins may date to the fourteenth century, was performed in her presence. Called *The Interlude of Wealth and Health*, it centred on a 'debate about whether Health or Wealth deserve more pre-eminence in England, and by extension whether decisions about strangers ought to be considered in light of the material or the spiritual interests of the realm'.[3] The importance to the realm of a third character, Liberty, was also discussed in this play. Exposed to the clever arguments found in the work, Mary was being enlight-ened about the trade-offs of having strangers in the country. She also was made aware of the state of public opinion on the subject.

The relevance of this disagreement in mid-Tudor England between the

1

Crown and her subjects to the study of fear of foreigners can be inflated. Scott Oldenburg has wisely cautioned that these events should be viewed

> not through the lens of a transhistorical, homogenizing 'tradition of xenophobia', but within the context of tension between the state's position on immigration and the relative failure of the [anti-alien] proclamations due to the general population's lack of enthusiasm for anti-alien activities.[4]

Marian persecutions of religious dissenters turned out to be bloodier than the hounding of foreigners. Many of Mary I's policies were undone after her death barely five years into her reign. Elizabeth I, Mary's half-sister, who succeeded her, provided a lengthier, more enlightened rule.

FRAMING MUSLIMS AS STRANGERS

It is with Britain that contemporary use of the term 'Islamophobia' is often associated. The Runnymede Trust, set up in 1968 to advise the British government on race relations, established the Commission on British Muslims and Islamophobia in 1997 to investigate discrimination against Muslims. But English anxiety about Muslims can be dated to more than 400 years earlier. So let us stay with sixteenth-century England a while longer to consider the emergence of the fear of Muslims in an all-too-overlooked context.

Henry VIII was the father of both Mary and Elizabeth but, at least as importantly, he was regarded as the godfather of the English Reformation. At the Convocation of Canterbury in 1531 he laid down a series of demands, the most significant of which were that the clergy recognise him as the 'sole protector and supreme head of the Church and clergy of England', acknowledge that the King had spiritual jurisdiction, and accept that the privileges of the church were subordinate to the Royal Prerogative and the laws of the realm. These demands were accompanied by a publicity campaign: 'A new religious imagery was constructed around the person of Henry VIII, as exemplified by the propaganda pamphlets of the era, with a constant call for English unity in an anti-Papal voice'.[5]

A leading figure in the promotion of a cult around Henry VIII was Richard Morison, author of four religious tracts between 1536 and 1539. He inveighed against the anti-Christ of the age, the Bishop of Rome, and appealed for the unity of the English: 'Let us fight this one field with english hands, and english hearts, perpetual quietness, rest, peace, victory, honour, wealth, all is ours.'[6] In this struggle Henry VIII was extolled as the Lion and Chosen One who possessed the qualities of David of the Old Testament.

The story so far is familiar. But it needs to be supplemented by consideration of an adversary of the English state that was as formidable and perhaps more menacing than the Papacy – the Turk. Morison cited Turks as

England's Other because they were loyal to their ruler: 'I am sory that they [Turkes hethen creatures] shoulde so farre excelle us, in a thynge that onely perteyneth unto us, and lytell or nothing to them. Obedience is the badge of a trewe christen man.'[7] To make matters seem worse for Henry VIII, rhetoric in Reformation England depicted the Pope as friend of the Turks.

Morison's was not a lone voice raising the fearful spectre of the Turk. After Henry's break with Rome, Thomas More sought comfort in the possibility that the looming Turkish threat would unite England and all of Europe politically and ultimately religiously:

> All Germany, for all their divers[e] opinions, yet as they agree together in profession of Christ's name, so agree they now together in preparation of a common power in defence of Christendom against our common enemy the Turk. And I trust in God that this shall not only help us here to strength us in the war, but also that as God hath caused them to agree together in the defence of his name, so shall he graciously bring them to agree together in the truth of his faith.[8]

In 1603, the last year of Elizabeth's reign, Arthur Dent published *The Ruin of Rome*, which took up the theme of Turk as threat. He warned that Christian brethren would be martyred under the twin persecution of 'the great Antichrist of Rome, and the cruel Turk'.[9] Even as the Pope brought devastation with his clergy, the Mahometan religion swept across Europe with 'martial horsemen and Turkish armies' slaughtering many 'by their cruelty and barbarous inhumanity'.[10]

There was no reason for the seminal 1997 report of the Runnymede Trust, titled *Islamophobia: A Challenge for Us All*, to make reference to these fears pervading Tudor England. Its purpose was to serve as a consultative document for the British government as well as a catalyst for social consciousness. In this latter respect the report took a back seat to a more celebrated publication citing Islamophobia that had appeared in 1985. Edward Said had compared the pathology to anti-Semitism since both were based on similar epistemological thinking. Said sought to stigmatise Islamophobia through appropriating the rhetorical strength and accusatory power of the more established pathology of anti-Semitism.[11]

The Runnymede Trust, too, tagged the term 'Islamophobia' as normative: it advanced disapproving, negative judgements about those who adopted any of a wide range of discriminatory values and practices towards Muslims, Islamic discourses and their cultural practices. Used in this way, the word had already appeared in 1918, in a French-language biography of Muhammad written by Sliman Ben Ibrahim, with illustrations by the highly regarded Orientalist painter Alphonse-Étienne Dinet.[12]

The report described Islamophobia as 'unfounded hostility towards Islam' and detailed 'the practical consequences of such hostility in unfair discrimination against Muslim individuals and communities, and to the exclusion of Muslims from mainstream political and social affairs'. It listed eight stigmatising characterisations of Islam that add up to Islamophobia: (1) monolithic and static; (2) separate and 'Other', not sharing the values of other cultures; (3) irrational, primitive and inferior to the West; (4) aggressive, violent and implicated in a clash of civilisations; (5) an ideology used to promote political and military interests; (6) intolerant of Western critiques; (7) deserving of discriminatory practices towards and exclusion of Muslims; and (8) making anti-Muslim hostility natural and normal.[13]

Islamophobia, it has been argued, 'is a much used but little understood term'.[14] I employ the term 'Islamophobia' in the normative way found in ben Ibrahim, Said and Runnymede's usage. It entails the spread of hostile public attitudes towards Muslims, in this case across Europe. The spread of Islamophobia is based in part on a conviction that Europe is in peril because of Islamisation, itself associated both with the increase in the size of Muslim communities as a result of immigration and also with the culture wars that have followed. Many politicians and observers agree that the growing presence of visible symbols of Islam – mosques, minarets, headscarves, burqas – contributes to the sense of the Islamisation of Europe. In addition, the security fears heightened by Muslim terrorist attacks often rest on the assumption of an unbridgeable civilisational divide between Western and Islamic worlds. Not least of the stigmas that are attached to Muslims is a racial frame of being of non-European stock. The category of 'brown' has increasingly become a signifier of Muslim identity distinct from Euro-Americanness.[15] Islamophobia thus entails a cultural racism that sets Muslims apart.[16] As a result, the Islamic migrant is constructed as someone burdened by alien attributes and as a carrier of antagonistic, threatening values: 'The immigrant is no longer just a classical outsider but also the terrorist within.'[17]

Islamophobia is a more complicated phenomenon than such an imaginary. The belief among some Muslim leaders, especially after the Cold War ended, that it was Islam itself that was in peril is an important consideration. Defending Islam from threats was part of a dialectical process that fed into the fears of each side about the other. Many Europeans' sense that Muslims do not like them needs to be part of an examination of the sources of Islamophobia. Those who fear or hate Muslims may believe that they merely reciprocate sentiments found among Muslim communities in their country. Some recent publications examining anti-immigrant and anti-minority attitudes and behaviour start from the assumption that many Europeans are incorrigibly intolerant, bigoted and racist. A few studies even border on reverse, anti-European racism, charging Europeans with harbouring a pervasive, endemic, whimsical hatred of foreigners that exists nowhere else.

Debate on xenophobia is often polemical and polarised, therefore. The objective of this study is to offer a comparative, data-driven, even-handed account of why many Europeans are receptive to Islamophobia. It documents Islamophobia's tortured logic and fearful consequences. Its point of departure is that prejudice is built into human nature, and it takes unusual external stimuli to turn it into a malign social pathology. A normative assumption is that just as most Europeans are hospitable, liberal minded and munificent, so most Muslims living in Europe are generous, open minded and considerate.

At the outset it is important to underline that the primary focus of this book is on receiving societies' attitudes towards Muslims; it does not systematically study Europe's Muslim communities or Islamic beliefs. I recognise, however, that in terms of relations of power a pronounced inequality exists between receiving societies and migrant communities of any kind, putting the onus on Europeans to demonstrate their big-heartedness. How fear, hostility and hate intervene to contort many Europeans' feelings towards strangers is the starting point.

CONFRONTING THE PHOBIA OF FOREIGNERS

Napoleon Bonaparte stated that there are only two forces that unite men – fear and self-interest. Hostility towards foreigners may be one of the most atavistic ways that fear and self-interest are combined.

A resurgence in research on fear of foreigners in Europe may only unintentionally reflect the importance of this Bonapartist perspective. Studying antipathy towards immigrants and, within this subset, Muslims has its own rationale. At a supranational level of governance it may serve as an indication that the European Union's ambitious, multifaceted integration project has run into difficulties. What is unexpected about the persisting public antagonism towards more profound European integration is its source. It has not been triggered by nationalistic Eurosceptic movements in recent or prospective member states expressing anxiety about surrendering sovereignty to Brussels. Instead it originates in spreading citizen hostility to strangers across Europe. Special targets are people of 'foreign' stock residing in Europe's larger cities. Political integration of the EU27, the current membership, moved forward following the implementation of the Lisbon (Reform) Treaty in 2010, though it has been set back by the financial and, in particular, eurozone crisis that fully emerged in 2008. The handful of candidate states in the Balkans that signed stabilisation and association agreements with the EU, notably Croatia and Serbia, have also been drawn into the integration process.

Two noteworthy exceptions to European integration have become lightning rods for European antipathy to its 'Others'. One is Turkey, a predominantly Muslim country which signed an association agreement with the

European Community as long ago as 1963. It applied for membership in 1987, was given candidate status in 1999, and entered into formal negotiations in 2005. With a population of seventy-five million, it would rank only behind Germany in size if admitted into the EU. Opposition to Turkey's membership application has encompassed some of Europe's best-known leaders as well as significant swathes of public opinion. It comes as no surprise that in the face of such widespread opposition, many of Turkey's leaders and much of its citizenry have lost enthusiasm for EU membership.

The second exception to the EU integration progress is constituted by a more diffuse, opaque, non-state actor sometimes described as the EU's twenty-eighth member. It is the burgeoning population of immigrant background, including third-country nationals (those not having citizenship of any EU state) living in EU countries. The vast majority of recent immigrants have no European ancestry. They speak languages, embrace cultures and customs, and often practise religions not historically associated with Europe. As a result, these populations are vulnerable to processes of Othering – an injurious emphasis on their non-European characteristics – that help Europeans describe them as 'waves' and 'tides' of foreigners, strangers and aliens – not immigrants on the road to integration and assimilation into receiving European societies. Large numbers of these Others are Muslims.

The cleavage between European nations and foreign-born migrants must be contextualised. The European project of political and economic union has been destabilised by concerns about the economic health of eurozone members; these financial and monetary problems have often been depicted as reflecting a north/south cleavage in Europe between its responsible and its profligate members. In 2011 the Schengen passport-free travel zone came under scrutiny from countries as different as France and Denmark over alleged abuse of open borders by opportunistic migrants. The 'old' and 'new' Europe division had not entirely been erased and cultural differences remained salient.[18] Big questions continued to be raised about the European credentials of Turks and other Muslims wishing to become part of the EU.

Given this broader context, is it appropriate to speak of the spectre of Islamophobia spreading across Europe? Do Europeans really dislike Muslims? Or is Islamophobia part of a more general social malaise afflicting Europe in *début-de-siècle* self-doubt? Such issues have, directly or indirectly, been addressed in numerous scholarly publications, journal articles, public opinion surveys and blogs. The terrorist attacks launched by Islamic extremists on Western targets beginning in September 2001 provided the stimulus to reflect on the salience of cultural and civilisational differences.

Researchers concerned about a possibly unjustified Western backlash against the Muslim world have been investigating the sources, nature and manifestations of Islamophobia. This research area falls within a broader field of study that can be awkwardly termed *phobiology*, the inquiry into public fears, antipathies, biases and hostilities originating in the sense of cultural differences within many countries' rapidly changing demographics.[19]

Depending on which account we read, the reassuring news may be that Europeans do not really dislike Muslims – they only object to their fanatical elements. Or we may hear a different argument based on the cliché that old habits die hard: antipathy towards Islam has a long history in Europe that, regrettably, is perfectly understandable. Such a deep structural divide assumes that Islamic civilisation was never well disposed towards such purportedly quintessentially European values as freedom of thought, tolerance, religious pluralism and gender equality. We might also be told that Islamophobic attitudes have spread and hardened but they are confined to supporters of disreputable right-wing radical movements which are removed from mainstream politics. Yet another response is sometimes advanced: anti-Muslim attitudes have become commonplace – so what? They have little bearing on domestic politics, European politics, let alone global politics.

This study examines the sources and character of Islamophobia in Europe, then, but it also focuses on its political consequences. It locates Islamophobia's distinctive character within a broader xenophobic, anti-immigrant movement that has emerged in Europe. Featuring case studies of France and Germany – though the experience of other countries is also flagged – it identifies national differences in citizen orientations towards Muslim minorities. In addition, the ways that Muslim organisations are coopted by the state are outlined. Because they represent a diversity of diaspora politics, these groups' unity, purpose, political skills and resources differ. In these conditions the effectiveness of assimilationist or multicultural models of Muslim integration will differ.

The issue of whether Islamophobia at home can affect politics abroad is important. In the West Islam has at times been depicted as both an internal and an external adversary. Not surprisingly, the fractiousness of contemporary international politics has been framed as the product of a civilisational divide. A multiplicity of factors shapes a state's foreign policy but they can be reduced to the pursuit of the national interest. This raises a series of questions centring on an understanding of that term. Is it in the national interest to promote democracy in other parts of the world, aspiring thereby to create an international democratic peace? Should the values of liberalism, toleration and human and minority rights be pressed on other societies, the holders of those rights in this way seeking to erode normative and cultural divides and the political cleavages that arise from them? Is free market reform in other countries in one's own national interest, particularly if its imposition is met with resistance abroad?

Addressing such questions requires acknowledging that the causal arrow between domestic and international variables can point in either direction. Coupled with the complexity of delimiting the national interest, a separate study is needed to assay how Islamophobia at home and abroad may be interconnected.[20] In this book, therefore, I do not examine the linkage between a domestic phenomenon such as anti-Muslim populism and its connection to developments in the international arena such as Western military interventions in Islamic states or, conversely, Islamic jihadism. In the specific case of Islam, a security dilemma has been identified as a result of hosting large Muslim communities. Security analysts have drawn up scenarios in which, under such conditions, the national state can become vulnerable to attacks by an Islamist enemy abroad.

The phenomenon of increased securitisation of immigration policy has become a major area of research. Decisions on the admission, integration and naturalisation of foreigners are being shaped by the calculus of reducing the potential threats that migrant groups pose to the domestic order. This is an 'out-in' perspective – that outsiders can affect domestic stability. But an 'in-out' approach should also be considered: relations between majority and minority groups within a country can become internationalised and shape relations between receiving and sending societies. Specifically, the existence of antagonistic relations between European nationals and Muslim migrants in EU states may be transposed to international relations between the European and Muslim worlds.

In studying Islamophobia, it is important, then, to assess whether Europeans' fear of, and even hostility towards, Muslims originates in the perceived security dilemma arising from the existence of Muslim communities at home. The radicalisation of some Muslims as a backlash to profiling and surveillance by security agencies has to be taken into account. But I do not consider the effects of securitisation on states' international politics. Nor do I examine the role of traditional and new media in legitimating and spreading Islamophobic attitudes. While important, it is perhaps an epiphenomenal feature of why many Europeans have come to fear the presence of Muslims in their societies.[21]

WHERE FEAR AND PREJUDICE COME FROM

The sources, intensity and character of any fear, especially of another religion, ethnicity or civilisation, are complex, occasionally obscure and ephemeral, and not usually concrete and tangible. Few if any studies of the contemporary politics of xenophobia begin with an examination of the origins of people's predispositions, partialities, phobias, biases, anxieties and antipathies. Part of the reason may be that breakthroughs in the scientific study of our psychological make-up have been recorded primarily in medical research. However, the social sciences and humanities have produced some important findings, for example in anthropology and psychology, cultural studies and historiography. The literature on the aetiology of fear, prejudice and hate is vast, and here we review only a cross-section of it. Particularly important to Islamophobia is discovering whether phobias and prejudice displayed by individuals and groups constitute an unusual attitude or behaviour, or whether they represent an altogether normal part of life.

It is no surprise that

> many of our political attitudes, particularly those we feel strongly about, have their source in childhood. What's wrong with that? Well, the primary problem with acting out or expressing childhood anger, pain, and fear in a contemporary political context is that it frequently results in very bad public policy.[22]

Along the way, it is a transgressive behaviour pattern that can be injurious to others.

For some psychoanalysts, our rejection of others has its earliest manifestation in stranger anxiety. While seemingly a negative personality trait – how many of us would willingly admit to being apprehensive about unfamiliar people when we are adult? – it stems from a positive quality – the assertion in infancy of a love relationship, typically with a parent. Thus attachment theory, pioneered by the psychiatrist John Bowlby and elaborated by the developmental psychologist Mary Ainsworth, underscored the importance of infant behaviour which sought proximity to an attachment figure, cultivating an affectional bond and establishing a 'secure base'.[23] Adaptive behaviour seeking out attachment can run from infancy through adolescence. Where adaptive efforts fail, a reactive attachment disorder (a widely accepted diagnosis in psychiatry) may set in and can reflect an individual's inappropriate social relatedness.

These psychiatric theories do not directly explain the appearance of xenophobia in an individual and it would be a mistake to assign them an overdetermined role. Nonetheless, infant stranger anxiety does play a key role in the predisposition to prejudice.[24] In some cases it can even produce pathological behaviour later in life. Thus, attempts to cope with anxiety may 'consist in distrust of others, projection of one's own hatred onto strangers, narcissistic rage, self-destructive tendencies, and belligerent differentiation from what is outside. Often the anxiety is linked with the narcissistic fear of a loss of self-esteem.'[25]

The repertoire of emotions towards the unfamiliar stranger who we perceive as alien and Other can range from anxiety to antipathy to hatred.[26] Admittedly, a few cultures may construct the stranger as being God in disguise, or as being sent by God.[27] More often the outsider is likely to be demonised. The Polish psychiatrist Antoni Kępiński emphasised that an

9

unfamiliar world evokes fear and aggression and the need to escape from or destroy it. Cultures produce diverse symbols and languages of fear as ways of coping with it.[28]

An initial step in examining prejudice is the recognition that it is a pervasive predisposition; no particular group has a monopoly on being prejudiced. When it is sometimes suggested that such a group does exist, it is typically to arouse prejudice against it for the suggester's prejudice. Accordingly, as American psychoanalyst Elisabeth Young-Bruehl emphasised,

> studying prejudices requires the consciousness that all peoples have prejudices, and that any group will develop customs and ways of thinking that lead the group members to form prejudgments (and often leave them unable to take the next step and see their own prejudgments).[29]

Prejudice typically rests on a perverse relationship between one group, to which the subject feels he or she belongs, and another, which is perceived as different. The terms 'in-group' and 'out-group' accurately capture the relationship. In his pioneering research on anti-Semitism, Gavin Langmuir distinguished between garden-variety prejudice, when groups simply do not like each other, and xenophobia, when a group forms a negative opinion about another. He introduced a third category to map anti-Semitism: chimera – monsters, demons, fantastical mythical creatures that become associated with an out-group. The real qualities of the out-group are conveniently ignored to make their demonisation easier.[30]

By any objective standards, demonisation should be seen for what it is – a deliberate and contrived effort by one group to stigmatise another. A well-known example is Jews cast as perpetrators of blood libel – employing the blood of Christians in certain rituals – or male Muslim martyrs ridiculed for their belief that they will have seventy-two virgins in the afterlife (the Hadith specifies seventy-two wives).[31] Of course over the course of time worse calumnies have been directed at persecuted groups.

Stereotyping and scapegoating are central to prejudice. We sometimes hear the expression 'the victim is a scapegoat'. Its intent is to make us reflect on not just the victim but the agency creating victimhood. The French philosopher René Girard elaborated:

> Scapegoat indicates both the innocence of the victims, the collective polarisation in opposition to them, and the collective end result of that polarisation. The persecutors are caught up in the 'logic' of the representation of persecution from a persecutor's standpoint, and they cannot break away.[32]

Persecution and prejudice become the fabric, therefore, of in-group identity. More than that, the persecutor claims a natural right and moral imperative to be prejudiced against others:

It is possible for the dominator to believe that he is vested with the power to establish controls, resort to physical force, and even mould consciousness, always invoking the welfare of the individuals and groups on whom he imposes his will as justification. In claiming to obey the imperatives of a responsibility that weighs more heavily upon him than anything else, he exonerates himself of any blame, when he does not simply create his own heroic reputation.[33]

Nationalist movements regularly employ acts of discrimination, hatred and persecution as evidence of heroism. One of the most notorious cases in history is the killing of Jews, gypsies, homosexuals and other 'degenerate' groups by Gestapo 'heroes' during World War II. There are even tragic cases where the chimera constructed by the persecutor produces a self-fulfilling prophecy. An in-group may direct chimerical assertions at an out-group, pressuring the latter into becoming – at least superficially and temporarily – what it has been charged with being. Young-Bruehl summarised the process by which 'over time chimeras become embedded in the in-group's culture, they sustain its social fabric, and they are widely institutionalised or legalised'.[34] A persistent case of such a chimera is the Roma population of central and eastern Europe, which has at times defined itself as the antithesis of conventional European values. As later chapters will show, most Muslims in Europe, by contrast, reject the chimera of being different.

Prejudice and chimeras are functional for the group appropriating them. They bond group members together, provide a shared psychological experience, identify markers of membership and delineate borders. They offer the necessary pretext for asserting that one's own group is better than another. Belief in a group's perfection brings elites and members together. As Young-Bruehl explained,

> Masses and elites that have nothing otherwise in common can find that the same ideology and the same organizing leadership unites them, relieves them of their rootlessness; the same apocalyptic and redemptive vision gives them a common future. They are relieved by it, enthused by it, feel swept into place by it, and they are glad to be all alike, uniform, in a historical process that asks no thinking of them but gives them the comfort of an obedience that does not feel passive to them.[35]

The product of such bonding can be the materialisation of an adversary. The sociologist James Aho outlined the circuitous process by which an enemy becomes constructed. The enemy's territory is conceived of as a series of paradoxes in which apparently unbelievable notions become true. The first paradox is of evil's inseparability from good: violence emergences from a quest for good. The second is the unifying function of enemies: 'there can be no harmony without chaos, no peace without war'. The struggle against an adversary is not just about pursuing a group's interests but cementing its social solidarity. Finally, 'the enemy is a *mysterium tremendum* . . ., a paradoxical duality that simultaneously revolts and attracts us'.[36] These three stages help consolidate an enemy for a group, and we can see the contours of this process at work in contemporary politics at both the national and the international level.

Once a foe has been identified, the question becomes whether to convert or destroy it. The second approach has an appeal justifiable by the invocation of multiple sacred texts. Redemptive violence 'promises to shatter injustice with a righteous fury, punishing the evildoers, emancipating those who have been exploited, and making the world safe for virtue'.[37] Among many sources for the need for redemptive violence is the Hebrew poem in Exodus, 'The Song of Moses and Miriam', which praises the Lord for destroying Pharaoh and his army and making the Jews' Exodus possible. Miriam sings:

> Sing to Yahweh, for he has triumphed gloriously,
> Horse and rider he has thrown into the sea! (Exodus 15:21)

The Polish sociologist Zygmunt Bauman wrote: 'What we fear, is evil; what is evil, we fear.'[38] Redemptive violence is justified in the struggle between good and evil because the world can be redeemed by annihilating evil enemies who hatch demonic conspiracies and use immoral tactics. Particularly in times of crises, biblical images of peace making through waging holy war are invoked. The combination of enemy stereotypes, the mystique of violence, an obsession with victory and worship of one's own religious symbols makes holy war a just option.[39] Religious zeal allows hatred, enmity, violence and redemption to follow each other in a logical sequence.

Prejudice and ethnicity

Gordon Allport's magisterial study *The Nature of Prejudice*, first published in 1954, surveyed various theories about the sources of discrimination. He remarked on the ordinariness of prejudice in the individual personality: Hannah Arendt's 'banality of evil' thesis appeared to spread guilt to the victims by advancing a 'structural' explanation for genocide that minimised the part played by an ordinary bureaucratic job holder like Adolf Eichmann.[40] Allport's book also reviewed the various mental illnesses related to prejudice. It concluded that 'paranoia represents the extreme pathology of prejudice'.[41]

Allport accorded special attention to the form of prejudice arising from ethnic and racial differences, national characteristics, varied types of religions and religiosity, as well as political biases. Prejudice was usually ethnocentrically organised, Allport emphasised. Individual affective and cognitive processes were important in the making of prejudice but an approach centred on social identity offered greater explanatory power. As the 2011 Friedrich Ebert Foundation report, *Intolerance, Prejudice and Discrimination*, which followed Allport, put it,

racism, sexism, anti-immigrant attitudes, anti-Semitism and many other prejudices are thus not personal traits, but social attitudes that must be understood
through the context of the person who holds them. As social attitudes, prejudices
have a cognitive, an affective and possibly also a behaviour-related dimension.
As attitudes they are learnable – and unlearnable even if this is often a long and
difficult process in cases where attitudes are deep-seated.[42]

The transformative process leading from prejudice and more general xenophobia to discrimination is complex. Xenophobia may be viewed as the
flip side of ethnocentrism. The first expresses a fear or dislike of foreigners,
the second represents an assertion of the primacy of one's own group in
ordering the world which may become the basis of discriminatory practices.
Xenophobia can be grounded in a social reality but, as suggested by the
discussion of chimeras, it may also be the product of fantasy. Young-Bruehl
sought to connect xenophobia, ethnocentrism, and chimeras this way:

> Ethnocentrism is expressed in xenophobic assertions that have at least a tangential
> relation to the characteristics of real groups or subgroups, especially to those living
> separately, preserving their distinctiveness in and by isolation, while ideologies of
> desire are expressed in 'chimeras,' or fantasies that have irrational reference to real,
> observable, or verifiable characteristics of a group or marks of difference.[43]

The French historian Pierre-André Taguieff offered his own nuanced jux-
taposition of the phenomena: 'On the one hand, then, rejection, hostility,
aversion – *xenophobia*; on the other, creating distance, cultural deafness, the
inferiorisation of "others" than us – ethnocentrism.'[44]

Where does racism fit in this taxonomy? For Taguieff, writing of the
French experience, xenophobia subsumes racism and may act as a kind of
proto-racism. The term 'race' originated in the late fourteenth century and
became widely used in the sixteenth, though it did not then have a negative
connotation. 'Natio', an older term, was employed in the Middle Ages to
refer pejoratively to foreigners.[45] In turn, 'barbarian' was less a racial than a
political and cultural concept.

It was only in the eighteenth century that Europeans began to categorise
the natural universe. The Swedish botanist Carolus Linnaeus (1707–78)
briefly turned to racial classifications, identifying the European as 'ingenious',
the Asian as 'melancholy' and the African as 'crafty, lazy, careless'. In his *On
the Natural Variety of Mankind*, Johann Friedrich Blumenbach (1752–1840),
a pioneer in the field of scientific anthropology, listed just five human races:
Caucasian, Mongolian, Ethiopian, American and Malay. With such unsci-
entific 'findings', it is not surprising that one writer concluded that 'race and
nation, far from timeless concepts, represent modern ways of understanding
and organizing human difference'.[46]

13

Racism is a multidimensional concept. As a modern phenomenon, it has produced two sweeping ideological constructs: anti-Semitism and anti-Negritude, that is, white supremacy.[47] In the first decade of the new century these two racist ideologies have been joined by anti-Arabism, frequently equated with anti-Islamism, in other words, Islamophobia. While disagreement exists on the subject, Islamophobia can be construed as a racist or, as mentioned earlier, a cultural racist construct.[48]

What these ideological constructs have in common are, for Taguieff, their origins in three principal cognitive processes. First, they advance an essentialist categorisation of individuals and groups in which people's identity is reduced to their community of origin. Second, they insist on a symbolic exclusion of select groups by stigmatising them and turning their exclusion into an imperative. Third, these racist constructs require the barbarisation of select categories of Others because they are judged to be inferior and incapable of becoming civilised, educated and assimilable.[49] Bauman summarised racism as the 'strategy of estrangement' demanding that the offender be removed from the territory occupied by the offended group.[50]

Taguieff suggested that racism operated on three levels. Primary racism was the common, even natural, reaction to the presence of a stranger. This reaction could range from mere antipathy to threatening aggressiveness. Secondary racism resulted from conceptualising reactions to the presence of a stranger into rationalised racism. Xenophobia and ethnocentrism were both rationalised attitudes. Tertiary racism was mystificatory. It assumed the existence of the two preceding levels and built upon them by invoking a quasi-biological argument for exclusion.[51] Such a form of racism was a pretext for social engineering of the kind that led to the Holocaust.

Whatever its construct, racism takes on multiple forms. It consists of hostile attitudes – opinions, beliefs, stereotypes – that lead to stigmatisation – insults, threats, hate speech. It includes behaviour and social practices that racialise relations between groups. Racism involves institutions that can perform exclusionary or discriminatory actions. Finally, it comprises ideological discourse, often in a pseudo-scientific guise, that posits opposition between groups, for example, Aryans and Semites.[52] In recent years, as terrorism and war seem to mirror a civilisational divide, it is the opposition between those of European and those of primarily Arab backgrounds that has served as the axis of racism.

THE OVERLAY OF RELIGIOUS INTOLERANCE AND RACISM

The 2001 terrorist strikes in the US triggered a backlash against the Islamic world whose centre was pinpointed as the Arab Middle East. The attacks had been carried out by Arabs, most of who were from Saudi Arabia (though a few came from the United Arab Emirates, Egypt and Lebanon). Because Islam was invoked to justify the terrorism, religious and even civilisational differences were put forward as the sources of these acts. But a more discreet racialised interpretation of 9/11 also was presented. In subsequent years, Arabophobia – though rarely called that – emerged in the West expressing popular racist stereotypes of who the terrorists were. This stereotype was belied by new acts of terror – in London, in Delhi, on transatlantic flights – that were carried out by non-Arab Muslim extremists. Explaining the scapegoating of Arabs, one British journalist noted that 'Arabophobia has been part of western culture since the Crusades'.[53] This racist framing has endured, therefore, and global jihad is still likely to be associated with an Arab signature.

To be sure, differences in national fears engender 'local' proxies for Arabophobia. In 2004 close to 200 people were killed in Madrid by bombs placed on commuter trains. The majority of the perpetrators were Moroccans, while several others were Spanish nationals of Moroccan descent. The long-existing pathology of Maurophobia – the fear of Moors – seemed to be given a new rationale in Spain. The origins of Maurophobia lay in the 711–18 conquest of most of the Iberian peninsula by Muslim armies made up mainly of Berbers – north Africans who had converted to Islam. Iberians came to refer to these invader forces – they remained on the peninsula until the Spanish *Reconquista* of 1492 – as Moors.

Strictly speaking, Maurophobia is not a racist ideology targeting one group. The term was associated not with an ethnic category but with a mixture of Muslim groups of different racial and ethnic backgrounds – Berbers, north African Arabs, Iberian converts to Islam. The word captures the protracted, conflicted Spanish experience with Muslims who crossed the Strait of Gibraltar from north Africa.[54]

The misguided use of racial categories to stereotype terrorists was driven home by the 2005 London bombings. The public transport bombs that left more than fifty people dead were detonated by three second-generation British citizens of Pakistani background along with a Jamaican convert to Islam. The terror was not the work of Arabs or even of 'foreigners'. British Muslim organisations sought to focus the public's attention on the phenomenon of terrorism – not Islam or particular ethnic groups – as the threat. Nonetheless Islamophobic groups in the United Kingdom gained mileage from associating these terrorist acts with global Islam. The mass killings of Norwegians by an ethnic Norwegian in July 2011 also was perversely utilised as a justification for Islamophobic actions.

This analysis suggests that racialised fears taking the form of Arabophobia, Maurophobia and Turkophobia – a subject addressed later in this study – are without foundation because of the spurious nature of the categorisation as well as real world events. However, they represent subsets of a more general

Islamophobia. Whether connected to racialised fears or not, religious cleavages are crucial in making sense of the politics of citizen fears in Western states.

PREJUDICE AND RELIGION

In the not-so-distant past, ideological orientations were identified as the primary foundations of citizens' values and behaviour. More recently, religious beliefs have been considered as principal determinants of political outlooks. As one scholar pointedly concluded, 'today adjectives like *communist* or *nationalist* are less likely to be associated with an army, a terrorist group, or a peace-making team than words like "Jewish militant", "Muslim fundamentalist"' or "Christian Coalition"'.[55] Who would have thought that the end of ideology, trumpeted as early as in the 1960s, would have millennium-old religions fill its vacuum?[56]

Religious constructions of political adversaries – more often, of external rather than domestic ones – have punctuated the discourse of political leaders and average citizens. But their pervasiveness goes beyond that. One might assume that military commanders, because they purportedly embrace a professional ethos, would refrain from associating enemies with religions. Yet even some of them vilify enemies by invoking their supposed diabolic nature. In 2003, US General William Boykin, deputy under-secretary of defence for intelligence in President George W. Bush's cabinet, gave a series of speeches to Christian groups. At one he asked, rhetorically, who the enemy of the United States was. 'It's not Osama bin Laden,' he stressed. 'The enemy that has come against our nation is a spiritual enemy. His name is Satan. And if you do not believe that Satan is real, you are ignoring the same Bible that tells you about God.'[57] For General Boykin it followed that God is Christian and Satan Muslim.

Islamophobia assumed political salience in the United States following the 9/11 attacks. It has formed a part of Europe's cultural baggage for much longer. This is in spite of shared beliefs within Christianity and Islam that these two religions are 'open to those beyond the original community of believers, since both [assert] the universal stature of their religions without identifying any particular people as chosen'.[58]

Beginning in the eighteenth century, European societies had come to regard Islam less as a spiritual competitor with Christianity – as had been the case in Tudor England or the Balkans – than as a religious threat to rising secularism. Islam was constructed as a negative alterity with which Christian and subsequently secular norms were contrasted, defined and valorised.

The secular–religious binary is a familiar cleavage found in many contemporary European societies. The imperative for secularism is reflected in post-Maastricht EU discourse and norms. A pragmatic rather than ide-

alistic reason explains this preference: secularism is seen as a way to tran-
scend squabbling between religions. EU discourse also shows a tendency to
downplay the part played by all religions by treating them as appendages
of cultures and ethnicities. For Mark Juergensmeyer, however, the effort to
avoid inter-religious conflicts led to a different pitfall – clashes 'between two
competing frameworks of social order: secular nationalism (allied with the
nation-state) and religion (allied with large ethnic communities, some of
them transnational)'.[59]

Specialists on Islam have spoken out against both fusing religion with
culture and juxtaposing Islam with secularism. Mahmood Mamdani identified the logical flaw in treating religion and culture as the foundation upon
which a political superstructure emerges: 'By assuming that every culture has
a tangible essence that defines it and explaining politics as the consequence
of that essence, a civilisation like Islam is reduced to a uniform universal
fundamentalist paradigm.'[60] A second fallacy was to regard Islam and secularism as mutually exclusive when they are not. For Mamdani, 'Islamic societies
were able to secularise within Islam'.[61] There is a reason why the Western tradition has not remarked upon this development: the fact that political Islam
can encompass secularism is foreign to the experience of the West, where
secularisation was carried out in opposition to Christianity.

Apart from distinguishing between religion and politics, Olivier Roy, a
French expert on Islam, also advocated decoupling religion from culture and
ethnicity. He contended that 'religions are more and more disconnected from
the cultures in which they have been embedded. Immigration and secularisation have separated cultural and religious markers.' Furthermore, 'to identify
a religion with an ethnic culture is to ascribe to each believer a culture and/or
an ethnic identity that he or she does not necessarily feel comfortable with'.
He advised, then:

> Instead of trying to pursue an elusive multiculturalism or to impose an assimilation
> based on the wrong perception of its 'common values', Europe should stick to its
> principles:
> - To deal with religions as 'mere' religions, not as the expressions of cultures or
>   ethnic groups . . .
> - To recognise the faith communities on the basis of an individual and free
>   choice . . .
> - Ethnolinguistic minorities should not be mixed up with faith communities . . .
>   freedom of religion is not the same as minority rights, although these two could
>   of course overlap (this is why I am not happy with the term 'Islamophobia'). A
>   faith is a choice, while a racial or ethnic identity is, at least in the beginning, a
>   given fact or a label bestowed from the outside. Mixing up these two does jeop-
>   ardise the way citizenship and personal freedom have been constructed as the
>   basis principles of political life.[62]

17

For Roy, the recognition of Islam as a faith, not culture, is crucial to allowing it to play a meaningful role in the private lives of European residents. In this role Islam is placed outside the public sphere in similar fashion to France's policy of *laïcité* – a religiously inspired term for, paradoxically, secularism, to be discussed in Chapter 4. In practice, this separation of religious life in the private sphere from that in the public one is more rigorously enforced in Islam than Catholicism. This differentiated treatment fulfils Roy's requirement for the presence of Islamophobia *sensu stricto*: it is discrimination against and hostility towards Islam qua religion that constitutes Islamophobia. But Roy's view can be contested, not least by Islamic clerics themselves who stress the totality of their religion, not its disconnectedness from public life. This may be why Tariq Modood, who in 1997 referred to culturally based racism directed at Muslims as Muslimophobia, subsequently refrained from using the term. Probably because of its inherent ambiguity, it is rarely cited today.

Along with anti-Semitism, Islamophobia is a rooted phobia commonly found in contemporary Europe. In my use of the term, Islamophobia bundles religious, ethnic and cultural prejudices together, just as anti-Semitism (which means more than anti-Judaism) does. Because a defining stricture of Islam is precisely the inseparability of religious life from politics and identity, any sentiment or action targeting a Muslim is necessarily anti-Islamic, even when the 'infidel' responsible for it may be unaware of this nuanced logic. In theory, Muslims themselves can be Islamophobic – self-loathing Muslims – even if they do not directly attack Islamic beliefs. It may be enough that they reject the cultural practices or political orientations that characterise Muslim communities.[63]

Systematic research into Islamophobia is a recent phenomenon.[64] By contrast, the study of anti-Semitism has a long history, it has spanned many countries, and it implicates multiple academic fields. Historians, psychologists and cultural theorists, for example, have sought to shed light on why the Holocaust happened.

Some – though not all – of the mechanisms that trigger antipathy towards Jews underlie today's hostility towards Muslims.[65] The pioneering historian of the Holocaust, Raul Hilberg, probed beyond the anti-Semitic perpetrators to identify the part played, inadvertently or not, by bystanders. Among these he included helpers and givers; gainers; and onlookers and observers, or what we might call witnesses. Hilberg also wrote of messengers who reported the annihilation taking place. Their influence on events, though minimal when compared to perpetrators, could be positive or negative – or cloaked in ambiguity, as this example illustrated: 'Polish peasants gestured to Jews on their way to Treblinka that their throats would be cut. And that is where they left it, between a warning and a taunt.'[66] In a strident variation of Hilberg's triad, another Holocaust historian asserted: 'The Holocaust is a warning. It adds three commandments to the ten of the Jewish–Catholic tradition: *Thou shalt not be a perpetrator*; *Thou shalt not be a passive victim*; and *Thou most certainly shalt not be a bystander*.'[67]

This typology has limited application to the study of European Islamophobia. While its victims are readily identifiable, its perpetrators are not. Indeed, it can be argued that the number of perpetrators of anti-Muslim violence is limited, and those few that are regularly involved, often profiled as racist skinheads, fall short of satisfying even Taguieff's second operating level of rationalised racism. However, the category of bystander takes on greater significance in the study of contemporary Islamophobia because, as data presented later in the book will suggest, there are many sympathetic onlookers who countenance the expression of anti-Muslim prejudices.

Phobias outside the West

Prejudice exists everywhere. In many parts of the world phobias identifying out-groups are constructed not along religious or racial lines but by class, caste, tribal or kinship markers (see Box 1.1). The test of who is a stranger may be more open ended.

Box 1.1 An observation about Uganda, 1962

The Langi and the Acholi treat the Kakwa superciliously, seeing them as benighted and backward. We are navigating here in the paranoid, obsessive realm of ethnic prejudice, hatred, and antipathy – albeit an intra-African one: racism and chauvinism emerge not only along the most obvious divides, e.g., white versus black, but are equally stark, stubborn, and implacable, perhaps even more so, among peoples of the same skin colour.

Source: Ryszard Kapuściński, *The Cobra's Heart* (London: Penguin, 2007), p. 78.

Of the many cases we can refer to, let us consider the case of South Africa – acknowledged as one of the continent's political success stories. In 2008 xenophobic violence exploded in the country when migrants from poorer areas of southern Africa were accused by South African citizens of taking their jobs. Particularly in townships around Johannesburg, thousands of 'foreigners' – Zimbabweans, Mozambicans, Malawians – were attacked and hundreds killed. This was a recurrence of the violence that occurred in 2005 and 2006 when Somalis living in the Eastern and Western Cape – where the international tourism industry was thriving and living standards were higher

– became the main targets of resentment by black South Africans striving to maintain existing wage levels and social benefits.

As in most Western states, the exact number of immigrants in fifty-million-strong South Africa is unknown. One estimate is between three and five million – about the same number as the country's entire white population. One report claimed that immigrants to the Rainbow Nation 'have become scapegoats for many of South Africa's social ills – high levels of unemployment, a shortage of housing and one of the worst crime rates in the world'.[68]

In 1994, as South Africa was doing away with the apartheid regime and holding its first democratic elections, President Nelson Mandela had said: 'We enter into a covenant that we shall build the society in which all South Africans, both black and white, will be able to walk tall. A Rainbow Nation at peace with itself and the world.' Fourteen years later, in 2008, he was forced to speak out against the new wave of xenophobic violence: 'Remember the horror from which we come. Never forget the greatness of a nation that has overcome its divisions. Let us never descend into destructive divisiveness.'[69]

Migrants from other countries – regardless of their race, religion or ethnicity – became an easy scapegoat for many black South Africans who remained destitute after black majority rule had been implemented. White South Africans who had enforced the apartheid system for decades were let off the hook for the continuing economic misery and violent crime affecting the lives of disadvantaged black South Africans. It was other disadvantaged black southern Africans – hardly strangers – who were perceived as the culprits.

Mandela's disappointment in seeing his ideal of a Rainbow Nation succumb to the all-too-commonplace xenophobia that is seemingly a malaise of modernity is not unique. Similar narratives detailing the backlash against migrants are told about workers from India living in the Arabian Gulf states, or labour migrants from Indonesia that come to Malaysia and other south-east Asian states with stronger economies. Religious and cultural differences may play a role in generating anti-immigrant attitudes in these regions. But class, occupational and educational differentials count heavily too. What is distinctive, then, about Europeans' propensity to be Islamophobic when expressing antipathy towards migrants and descendants of migrants?

STRUCTURE OF THE BOOK

This book focuses on the pervasiveness and strength of Islamophobic attitudes in western Europe with case studies of France and Germany. With their significant Muslim minorities – in some areas made up of large numbers of Turkish settlers and immigrants – these two countries, along with Italy, Spain, Britain and others, have experienced varying degrees of Islamophobia; we include selective data on all of them. Some of Europe's smaller states with longstanding reputations for liberalism and hospitality to strangers, such as Belgium, the Netherlands and Denmark, have equally been politically shaken by citizens' growing anxieties about immigrant and foreigner numbers. Norway and Finland, too, have elected politicians from anti-immigrant parties to their legislatures, while many in Sweden agonised about having joined their disreputable ranks after electing twenty members of an anti-immigrant party to the Riksdag in 2010. In order to test the accuracy of the perception of an insidious spreading Islamophobia across Europe, evidence about these European states will be assessed. Elsewhere in Europe, Switzerland's 2007 election result, which was largely replicated in 2011, served as dramatic confirmation that anti-foreigner political parties were on the road to governmental power. The Netherlands' 2010 election produced a doubling of legislative seats for an explicitly anti-Islamic party, which was subsequently included in a governing coalition. Hungary's overtly racist, anti-Semitic and ultranationalist Jobbik movement captured 17 per cent of the vote in the 2010 election. More than ever, fears about aliens are shaping and realigning domestic and, specifically, electoral politics in many European countries.

The book is organised in the following way. Chapter 2 explores the accepted norms and models that shape minority and migrant rights in Europe and act as preemptive measures against xenophobia and racism. It also examines EU standard setting on immigration and integration. Chapter 3 traces the process leading from the spread of anti-immigrant attitudes to the emergence of anti-Muslim ones. Chapter 4 dissects the nature of Islamophobia, looking at its religious, ethnic, cultural, customary and economic constituent parts. Chapters 5 and 6 furnish case studies of anti-Muslim attitudes in France and Germany, and what state leaders have done to counter them. Finally, Chapter 7 inquires into the point at which anti-Muslim attitudes seemed to become inevitable and irreversible, and engages in a thought experiment about how they could be unmade.

Quantitative data on phobias are extensive. We consider attitudes towards Muslims and Turks – a significant Islamic community across Europe – that have been measured in attitudinal surveys carried out by major European research centres on xenophobia: the European Monitoring Centre on Racism and Xenophobia in Vienna (which has published special reports on Islamophobia); the European Social Survey at City University, London; and the Eurobarometer (Public Opinion Analysis Sector, European Commission) in Brussels. But we also review discursive practices about Muslims – by European leaders, political party heads, public intellectuals and scholars – which also shed light on the existence and character of Islamophobia.

If Islamophobia has become pervasive in Europe, this is reason enough to investigate its sources and its consequences. Its impact extends beyond national borders and, as has been noted, helps shape international politics: concerns about a clash of civilisations and national security are often fused. Many compelling reasons exist, then, to make sense of the pathology of Islamophobia.

NOTES

1. Scott Oldenburg, 'Toward a Multicultural Mid-Tudor England: The Queen's Royal Entry Circa 1553, *The Interlude of Wealth and Health*, and the Question of Strangers in the Reign of Mary I', *English Literary History* 76 (2009), p. 100.
2. Ibid., p. 107.
3. Ibid., p. 114.
4. Ibid., pp. 114, 120.
5. Ramazan Hakki Oztan, 'Religious Uniformity and its Negotiation: The Origins of Nationalism in Early Modern England', unpublished paper (Salt Lake City: University of Utah, Department of Political Science, 2011).
6. Richarde Morysen, *An Exhortation to Styrre all Englysh Men to the Defence of Theyr Countreye* (Amsterdam: Theatrum Orbis Terrarum, 1972), p. d8r.
7. Ibid., p. a3r.
8. Thomas More, *A Dialogue of Comfort against Tribulation*, ed. Frank Manley (New Haven, CT: Yale University Press, [1535] 1977), p. 40.
9. Arthur Dent, *The Ruin of Rome or an Exposition upon the Whole Revelation* (London: T. Kelley, [1603] 1841), p. 71.
10. Ibid., p. 115.
11. Edward W. Said, 'Orientalism Reconsidered', *Race & Class* 27:2 (1985), pp. 1–15.
12. Sliman Ben Ibrahim, *La Vie de Mohammed, prophète d'Allah* (Paris: Piazza, 1918).
13. Runnymede Trust, *Islamophobia: A Challenge for Us All* (London: Runnymede Trust, 1997).
14. Ayhan Kaya, *Islamophobia as a Form of Governmentality: Unbearable Weightiness of the Politics of Fear* (Malmö: Malmö University, 2011), pp. 6–7.
15. Mehdi Semati, 'Islamophobia, Culture and Race in the Age of Empire', *Cultural Studies* 24 (2010), pp. 256–75.
16. Nasar Meer and Tariq Modood, 'Refutations of Racism in the "Muslim Question"', *Patterns of Prejudice* 43 (2009), pp. 332–51.
17. A. Sivanandan, 'Foreword', in Liz Fekete, *A Suitable Enemy: Racism, Migration and Islamophobia in Europe* (London: Pluto Press, 2009), pp. viii–ix.
18. Ray Taras, *Europe Old and New: Transnationalism, Belonging, Xenophobia* (Lanham, MD: Rowman and Littlefield, 2008).
19. A starting point for phobiology can be Pnina Werbner, 'Islamophobia: Incitement to Religious Hatred – Legislating for a New Fear?', *Anthropology Today* 21:1 (2005), pp. 5–9.
20. This is the subject of a forthcoming book which I have provisionally titled *Phobias and Foreign Policies*.
21. For an introduction, see Elizabeth Poole and John E. Richardson (eds), *Muslims and the News Media* (London: I. B. Tauris, 2006).

22. Michael A. Milburn and Sheree D. Conrad, *The Politics of Denial* (Cambridge, MA: MIT Press, 1996), p. 71.
23. For an introduction see Inge Bretherton, 'The Origins of Attachment Theory: John Bowlby and Mary Ainsworth', *Developmental Psychology* 28 (1992), pp. 759–75.
24. For a summary, see Henri Parens, 'Toward Understanding Prejudice – Benign and Malignant', in Henri Parens, Afaf Mahfouz, Stuart W. Twemlow and David E. Scharff (eds), *The Future of Prejudice: Psychoanalysis and the Prevention of Prejudice* (Lanham, MD: Rowman and Littlefield, 2007), pp. 25–8.
25. Hans-Jürgen Wirth, 'The Roots of Prejudice in Family Life and its Political Significance as Discerned in a Study of Slobodan Milosevic', in Henri Parens, Afaf Mahfouz, Stuart W. Twemlow and David E. Scharff (eds), *The Future of Prejudice: Psychoanalysis and the Prevention of Prejudice* (Lanham, MD: Rowman and Littlefield, 2007), p. 112.
26. For an overview, see Robert J. Sternberg and Karin Sternberg, *The Nature of Hate* (Cambridge: Cambridge University Press, 2008).
27. For example, Japanese folk religion sometimes regarded the outsider, who was imputed with an animal spirit, as god. Within Christianity, Marcion of Sinope (living around the second century and sometimes identified as an early Gnostic) distinguished between the Creator God who made the world and the more important, if unknowable, Stranger God who sent Christ to Earth. I am grateful to Fred Quinn and Michitaka Suzuki for highlighting these constructions of the stranger.
28. Antoni Kępiński, *Lęk* (Warsaw: Wydawnictwo Literackie, 2009).
29. Elisabeth Young-Bruehl, 'A Brief History of Prejudice Studies', in Henri Parens, Afaf Mahfouz, Stuart W. Twemlow and David E. Scharff (eds), *The Future of Prejudice: Psychoanalysis and the Prevention of Prejudice* (Lanham, MD: Rowman and Littlefield, 2007), p. 219.
30. David Norman-Smith, 'Anti-Semitism', in Richard T. Schaefer (ed.), *Encyclopedia of Race, Ethnicity, and Society* (Thousand Oaks, CA: Sage, 2008), p. 77.
31. Hadith no. 2,562, in the collection *Sunan al-Tirmidhi*, says: 'The least [reward] for the people of Heaven is 80,000 servants and 72 wives, over which stands a dome of pearls, aquamarine and ruby.' The Hadith are the oral traditions ascribed to the Prophet Muhammad's sayings and deeds. They were transmitted orally over centuries, which raises questions about their accuracy.
32. René Girard, *The Scapegoat* (Baltimore, MD: Johns Hopkins University Press, 1986), p. 39.
33. Lise Noël, *Intolerance: A General Survey* (Montreal: McGill-Queen's University Press, 1994), p. 127.
34. Elisabeth Young-Bruehl, *The Anatomy of Prejudices* (Cambridge, MA: Harvard University Press, 1996), pp. 78–9.
35. Ibid., p. 352.
36. James A. Aho, *This Thing of Darkness: A Sociology of the Enemy* (Seattle: University of Washington Press, 1994), pp. 15, 17.
37. Robert Jewett and John Shelton Lawrence, *Captain America and the Crusade against Evil: The Dilemma of Zealous Nationalism* (Grand Rapids, MI: William B. Eerdmans, 2004), p. 271.
38. Zygmunt Bauman, *Liquid Fear* (Cambridge: Polity Press, 2006), p. 54.
39. Jewett and Lawrence, *Captain America and the Crusade against Evil*, p. 8.

40. I am grateful to Bill Safran for sharing this observation. See Hannah Arendt, *Eichmann in Jerusalem: A Report on the Banality of Evil* (New York: Penguin, [1963] 2006). Arendt's own supposed prejudices against *Ostjuden* have been identified as partly explaining why she regarded Eichmann's banality as more menacing than his anti-Semitism. See David Cesarani, *Becoming Eichmann: Rethinking the Life, Crimes, and Trial of a 'Desk Murderer'* (Cambridge, MA: Da Capo Press, 2006).

41. Gordon W. Allport, *The Nature of Prejudice* (New York: Basic, 1979), p. 423.

42. Andreas Zick, Beate Küpper and Andreas Hövermann, *Intolerance, Prejudice and Discrimination: A European Report* (Berlin: Friedrich-Ebert-Stiftung, 2011), p. 28.

43. Young-Bruehl, *The Anatomy of Prejudices*, p. 77. See also Gavin Langmuir, *Toward a Definition of Antisemitism* (Berkeley: University of California Press, 1990).

44. Pierre-André Taguieff, 'Racisme, racialisme, ethnocentrisme, xénophobie, antisémitisme et néoracisme: réflexions sur des termes problématiques', in Commission Nationale Consultative des Droits de l'Homme, *La Lutte contre le racisme, l'antisémitisme et la xénophobie: année 2007* (Paris: La Documentation Française, 2008), p. 251.

45. See Ray Taras, *Liberal and Illiberal Nationalisms* (Basingstoke: Palgrave, 2002), ch. 1.

46. Eric D. Weitz, *A Century of Genocide: Utopias of Race and Nation* (Princeton, NJ: Princeton University Press, 2003), p. 17. Quotes from Linnaeus are from this work, p. 27.

47. Taguieff, 'Racisme, racialisme, ethnocentrisme, xénophobie, antisémitisme et néoracisme', p. 243. Negritude was initially associated with the cultural movement nurtured by the Senegalese president and poet Léopold Sédar Senghor beginning in the 1960s. See his *Negritude et civilisation de l'universel* (Paris: Seuil, 1977).

48. See David Theo Goldberg, 'Racial Comparisons, Relational Racisms: Some Thoughts on Method', *Ethnic and Racial Studies* 32:7 (2009), pp. 1271–82. I am grateful to Nasar Meer for sharing his critical observations on race and Islamophobia.

49. Taguieff, 'Racisme, racialisme, ethnocentrisme, xénophobie, antisémitisme et néoracisme', p. 261.

50. Zygmunt Bauman, *Modernity and the Holocaust* (Ithaca, NY: Cornell University Press, 1993), p. 65. Following Taguieff, he distinguished racism from *heterophobia*, which entails a resentment of the different. It is 'a more specific antagonism generated by the human practices of identity-seeking and boundary-drawing' (p. 64).

51. Pierre-André Taguieff, *La Force du préjugé: essai sur le racisme et ses doubles* (Paris: La Découverte, 1988).

52. Taguieff, 'Racisme, racialisme, ethnocentrisme, xénophobie, antisémitisme et néoracisme', pp. 244–5.

53. Neil Clark, 'The return of Arabophobia', *The Guardian*, 20 October 2003.

54. See Ricard Zapata-Barrero, 'The Muslim Community and Spanish Tradition: Maurophobia as a Fact, and Impartiality as a Desideratum', in Tariq Modood, Anna Triandafyllidou and Ricard Zapata-Barrero (eds), *Multiculturalism, Muslims and Citizenship: A European Approach* (London: Routledge, 2006), pp. 143–61.

55. Martin E. Marty, 'Introduction: The Role of Religion in Cultural Foundations of Ethnonationalism', in Martin E. Marty and R. Scott Appleby (eds), *Religion, Ethnicity, Self-identity* (Hanover, NH: University Press of New England, 1997), p. 10.

56. Daniel Bell, *The End of Ideology: On the Exhaustion of Political Ideas in the Fifties* (Cambridge, MA: Harvard University Press, 2000).

57. Peter Gottschalk and Gabriel Greenberg, 'Islamophobia', *New York Times*, 6 January

2008. See also their *Islamophobia: Making Muslims the Enemy* (Lanham, MD: Rowman and Littlefield, 2007).

58. Weitz, *A Century of Genocide*, p. 19.

59. Mark Juergensmeyer, *Global Rebellion: Religious Challenges to the Secular State, from Christian Militias to al Qaeda* (Berkeley: University of California Press, 2008), p. 17.

60. Mahmood Mamdani, *Good Muslim, Bad Muslim* (New York: Doubleday, 2004), p. 22.

61. Ibid., p. 47.

62. Olivier Roy, *The Mediterranean and its Metaphors* (San Domenico di Fiesole (FI), Italy: Robert Schuman Center for Advanced Studies, 2009), pp. 8–9.

63. Some observers put Ayaan Hirsi Ali, the writer and former Dutch MP, in this category. See her *Infidel* (New York: Free Press, 2008) and *The Caged Virgin: An Emancipation Proclamation for Women and Islam* (New York: Free Press, 2007).

64. Some recent books on this subject have been criticised as reproducing Islamophobic values. These include two authored by Bruce Bawer: *While Europe Slept: How Radical Islam is Destroying the West from Within* (New York: Anchor, 2007) and *Surrender: Appeasing Islam, Sacrificing Freedom* (New York: Anchor, 2010). An intellectually more ambitious study is by Christopher Caldwell, *Reflections on the Revolution in Europe: Immigration, Islam, and the West* (New York: Doubleday, 2009); it is discussed in Chapter 7. Two books written by Brigitte Gabriel for American readerships are *Because They Hate: A Survivor of Islamic Terror Warns America* (New York: St Martin's Press, 2006) and *They Must Be Stopped: Why We Must Defeat Radical Islam and How We Can Do It* (New York: St Martin's Press, 2008). Two polemical books by Mark Steyn for Canadian and American audiences are *America Alone: The End of the World as We Know It* (Washington, DC: Regnery Press, 2008) and *Lights Out: Islam, Free Speech and the Twilight of the West* (Stockade, 2009).

65. An unsatisfying, cursory introduction to the subject is Matti Bunzl, *Anti-Semitism and Islamophobia: Hatreds Old and New in Europe* (Chicago: Prickly Paradigm Press, 2007).

66. Raul Hilberg, *Perpetrators, Victims, Bystanders: The Jewish Catastrophe 1933–1945* (New York: HarperPerennial, 1993), p. 216.

67. Yehuda Bauer, *Rethinking the Holocaust* (New Haven, CT: Yale University Press, 2001), p. 67.

68. Caroline Hawley, 'Refugees flee South Africa attacks', BBC News website, 16 May 2008, http://news.bbc.co.uk/1/hi/world/africa/7404351.stm, accessed 10 February 2012.

69. Audrey Brown, 'Rainbow Nation – dream or reality?', BBC News website, 18 July 2008, http://news.bbc.co.uk/1/hi/world/africa/7512700.stm, accessed 10 February 2012.

CHAPTER TWO

Norms and models of migrant rights

Box 2.1 'Scapegoating'
gentle flocks cornered peck each other or turn to face the attacker Chip Berlet (1995)

What kind of legal and normative regimes have been set up within the framework of European institutions to promote universal rights and combat discriminatory practices, especially as they relate to immigrants? In this chapter I examine different models of accommodating immigrants and evaluate how well each of these performs in meeting the standards the EU has set. France's republican model merits special attention both because it is criticised as being tough on immigrants and because, paradoxically, it has attracted converts following a wave of elite and public scepticism about multiculturalism.

The setting of norms and standards is one of the most important functions that the EU carries out in its twenty-seven member states. We should also recognise that norms and standards also influence research on immigration. While notionally it aspires to be value free, objective and consistent with established canons of social science inquiry, much recent research on immigration reflects a normative bias that is not always transparent. This conflicted approach suggests that immigration has been a polarising issue. At the same time, there are signs that it may be developing into a valence issue – one where most people want something to be done about immigration and political leaders are persuaded they need to support the public's view.

DEBATING IMMIGRATION

In a seminal article on immigration politics published in 1995, the US political scientist Gary Freeman unpacked the character of the debate on immigration, whether joined by average citizens or academic researchers. One key characteristic of the debate was a cognitive one – how uninformed it tended to be. Freeman advanced a straightforward explanation for this:

> The most direct barrier to information about immigration is the scarcity and ambiguity of official data. Governments themselves often have only the most speculative information about the immigration intake, legal or illegal, its composition, or its effect on society and economy. Official data, such as it is, is not generally available to the public.[1]

A second principal characteristic skewing discussion of immigration was – and continues to be – its normative dimension. Strictures and taboos existed on what factors could be considered when assessing immigration politics (see Box 2.2).

Box 2.2 Normative constraints governing immigration discourse

The scarcity of information is exacerbated by the constrained discourse over immigration in liberal democracies, a constraint that may fairly be seen as a virtue. The boundaries of legitimate discussion of immigration policy are narrow, precluding, for example, argument over the ethnic composition of migrant streams, and subjecting those who criticize liberal policies to abusive charges of racism. The scholars and intellectuals who interpret and analyze immigration are with notable exceptions generally sympathetic. Indeed, immigration is one policy on which liberal sociologists and anthropologists and more conservative political scientists and economists tend to agree. What may be called the folklore of immigration – the stories, myths, and romantic images of valiant and plucky individuals seeking opportunity abroad – provides compelling resources for those seeking to shape public discussion in expansive directions and constitute daunting obstacles for critics.

Source: Gary P. Freeman, 'Modes of Immigration Politics in Liberal Democratic States', *International Migration Review* 29 (1995), p. 884.

Freeman's account identified a normative dimension that, though initially imposed on political debate, has spilled over to scholarly inquiry on immigration politics. It is the 'strong antipopulist norm that dictates that politicians should not seek to exploit racial, ethnic or immigration-related fears in order to win votes'.[2] This norm is promoted by the very nature of the policy-making process: 'Policy was typically made in administrative contexts, without public participation and with little parliamentary supervision.'[3] The anti-populist bias of academic research on immigration often means that when public opinion favours what may be construed as illiberal, discriminatory positions, it should be repudiated. In such cases, the dictum 'Change the public, not the policy' seems to apply.

By its very nature the immigration debate has drawn many polemical and passionate accounts (some of which are critiqued in Chapter 7) which have little to do with scientific objectivity. An example is a book which described Muslim immigration to Europe as an unwelcome revolution. One critic condemned it as owing 'more to tabloid headlines than to responsible research'.[4] Accordingly, then, challenging the prevailing academic values that govern the charged immigration debate without abandoning the canons of social science research would represent an ideal-type approach. Presenting and interpreting the extensive empirical data on immigration politics seems the surest way to accomplish this.

EUROPE'S COMMANDMENTS

The EU professes a strong sense of ethics. It sees itself as a values-based supranational form of governance even if its prosaic *raison d'être* originally was the promotion of unhindered trade among free-market economies. It was only a matter of time before someone compiled the unstated Ten Commandments promulgated by the EU.

Respect for democracy, human rights and the rule of law has been identified as the first commandment. The four freedoms of movement – of goods, services, capital and labour – comprise the second. Fostering social cohesion is the third, and promoting sustainable economic development the fourth. The repudiation of nationalism and support for secularism and multiculturalism are the next two interrelated commandments. The seventh entails an institutional imperative: implementing multitier governance. The next two are principles of the EU's international politics: adopting a multilateral approach and achieving consensus on the use of force. Number ten is creating an inclusive, accessible EU for both existing members and candidate states.[5]

The most important of the norms seeking to do away with xenophobia are respect for human rights, the promotion of social cohesion as well as of multiculturalism, and the repudiation of nationalism.[6] Promoting a secular social order is thought to be a way of making differences between religions irrelevant but, as I describe later in this chapter, it can add fuel to a xenophobic fire when 'strangers' insist on the freedom to practise their religion openly.

28

Standard setting is not the sole prerogative of the EU. Another pan-European institution, the Council of Europe (discussed further below), has as its primary concerns human rights and the rule of law. One of the unofficial 'commandments' it has adopted is the need for intercultural dialogue. Its 2005 White Paper stated:

> Cultural diversity is an essential condition of human society, brought about by cross-border migration, the claim of national and other minorities to a distinct cultural identity, the cultural effects of globalisation, the growing interdependence between all world regions and the advances of information and communication media.[7]

Under these conditions 'dialogue between cultures, the oldest and most fundamental mode of democratic conversation, is an antidote to rejection and violence'. The 'mainstreaming' of intercultural dialogue, especially in the political sphere, can contribute to the promotion of human rights, democracy, rule of law, social cohesion, peace and stability. If multiculturalism has furnished a model for managing diversity within a country, the ambitions of intercultural dialogue are much broader and subsume both national and transnational management of differences.

STANDARD SETTING AND STRANGERS

Not long after World War II, Europe's demographic make-up underwent a remarkable change which made the fear of foreigners salient. From being a continent that was emigrant in character – out-migration, especially to North America, had kept European states homogeneous and eased their social tensions – it was rapidly becoming a continent of in-migration. Migration into Europe was not new but its scale was unprecedented. The Swedish social theorist Göran Therborn pointed to the momentous character of this reverse flow:

> The shift from emigration to immigration represents an epochal change in European social history. Ethnic – and largely continental ethnic – conflict has substituted for intra-European nationalist rivalry. The socio-political effect has been to weaken class cleavages and politics in favour of ethnic and other non-class ones.[8]

Therborn might have added religion.

What heightened European fears about migrants was that they came from far away, bringing with them exotic languages, distinct cultural practices and non-Western religious beliefs. The stranger was not the national of a somewhat poorer European state but an alien from a remote and backward part of the world. The historian Walter Laqueur bitterly deplored the alleged differences in the attitudes and behaviour of migrants from past and present immigration waves:

> There is, to begin with, the scale of immigration. Only tens of thousands came to western Europe 100 years ago, not millions. They made great efforts to integrate socially and culturally. Above all, they wanted to give their children a good secular education at almost any price. The rate of intermarriage was high within one generation, and even higher within two. No one helped them: there were no social workers or advisors, no one gave them housing at low or no rent, and programs such as Sure Start . . . and 'positive discrimination' had not yet been invented. There were no free health-service or unemployment benefits. There were no government committees analyzing Judeophobia and how to combat it.[9]

A French demographer used a more colourful metaphor: this wave represented the revenge of the Third World.[10]

In their new countries, migrants and their children learned about, partook of and demanded rights that had been unavailable to preceding generations of newcomers – as well as in most of their countries of origin. Describing the US but applicable to other immigration societies as well, the political scientist Samuel Huntington lamented how 'previously immigrants felt discriminated against if they were not permitted to join the mainstream. Now it appears that some groups feel discriminated against if they are not allowed to remain apart from the mainstream.'[11]

As the European Community underwent economic and political integration, the cultural and linguistic diversity of its member states – even without taking into account the expanding presence of immigrant communities – presented a major challenge. As one writer put it, 'if it is to approach an "ever-closer union" of its peoples, Europe must develop a political ethos founded on intercultural empathy in which respect for linguistic diversity plays an important role'.[12] Continued in-migration complicated the quest for pan-European identity while raising existential questions about current national identities.

To be sure, the national exceptionalism of individual European states bound together within pan-European structures more probably accounts for brakes on transnational identity formation than the epiphenomenon of third-country national immigration. The migration specialist Gallya Lahav called attention to this national exceptionalism, a factor unrelated to migration, in formulating this European dilemma:

> Should the European public succumb to the threat of losing their unique cultures and identities for a viable European Union to exist or should the potential of this supranational force be dismissed for the preservation of national identity?[13]

The debate about what norms of tolerance to establish in order to accommodate immigrants at times spilled onto the streets and sparked violence.

In the 1990s German right-wing extremists bombed and burned the homes of immigrants causing significant loss of life. In the Netherlands two prominent anti-Islamic figures were assassinated during the next decade. France witnessed major riots involving marginalised minorities on two occasions in the new century. Such acts of violence seemed to resonate even louder because of the limited opportunities the public had to express their views on immigration politics.

Italy, too, was shaken by violence associated with immigrants, though these immigrants were legal and from not far away. Several brutal murders of Italian nationals were linked to Romanian citizens who had acquired the right to free movement within the EU after the country's EU accession in 2007. From discussing norms of accommodation, Italian political elites turned to debating conditions for excluding and even expelling EU immigrants. One decree declared bluntly that 'the proportion of crime committed by foreigners has increased, and those who commit most crime are the Romanians'.[14] Italian regional prefects were empowered to summarily expel citizens of fellow EU states if they were judged a threat to public security.

The increasingly hostile public reception accorded to migrants of different backgrounds, and at times to second- and third-generation citizens of immigrant background, triggered a re-examination of accepted norms of tolerance and accommodation. The concern was that 'the increasing power and visibility of ethnic minorities and the accompanying social problems which growing migration is producing, have raised concerns over what has been described as "cultural pollution", "overforeignisation", or "minorisation"'.[15]

The economic costs of receiving immigrants became a practical concern, especially after the global financial crisis that began in 2008. Fraudulence in refugee and asylum claims, together with the purported lukewarm commitment newcomers gave to their host societies, brought into question the wisdom of applying liberal standards of accommodation. The *pièce de résistance* was the terrorism in Europe that became associated with the Muslim world. These factors increased popular pressure for the use of European norms to exclude foreigners rather than to convert them to European ways.

RECONCILING IMMIGRATION AND INTEGRATION POLICIES

Standardisation – usually called 'harmonisation' in EU-speak – of policy on immigration has lagged behind that achieved in other areas. Indeed, 'policy' may be too robust a concept to use. 'Directives setting a minimum level of common standards' may be a more accurate expression, though I will continue to refer to these as policies. Thus, despite some progress, policies governing third-country nationals, asylum petitioners and citizenship applicants

31

have not become harmonised across the EU and remain inconsistent between states.

According to Terri Givens and Adam Luedtke, specialists on EU migration, crosscutting pressures stemming from the goal of European integration have led to two contradictory political developments: (1) the attempt made by the European Commission and the European Parliament, with the support of some member states, to develop a harmonised EU immigration policy and (2) the insistence by other member states of their right to control their immigration policies.[16]

At the EU governance level, a series of five-year programmes since 1999 has set out the agenda for elaborating migration and asylum policy. These programmes fall under the EU pillar of justice, liberty and security. Often termed 'justice and home affairs policy', it encompasses

> a broad grouping of policies including fundamental rights, citizenship, security and counterterrorism policies, criminal and civil law and police cooperation, as well as immigration, asylum, border management, and visa policy. In recent years, it has become one of the most prolific policy areas in terms of both cooperation and legislative output.[17]

The first programme (the Tampere programme, 1999–2004) laid the groundwork for common immigration and asylum policies and established common rules for family reunification. The most notable legacy of the second programme (the Hague programme, 2004–9) was the grandiosely titled 'Global Approach to Migration', adopted in 2005, which attached new importance to cooperation with third countries on migration flows. This had been an issue that had veered in unintended directions with unforeseen effects, as I describe below. Finally, the third programme (the Stockholm programme, 2009–14) scaled down harmonisation ambitions in the face of economic recession. It has reinstituted the individual member state as the basic level of competency, and has expressed a preference for interim measures and quick fixes rather than providing a long-term vision.

If the feasibility of harmonising immigration policy has been a contentious matter, a second one is the desirability of liberalising it. The European Commission and the European Court of Justice have generally prodded immigration authorities to adopt more liberal 'postnational' norms. At the same time, the EU has helped member states enforce tighter border controls and implement more rigorous anti-immigration measures in the name of security. These mixed messages have both reflected and reinforced member states' disagreement on who should manage immigration policy and what it should be.

There has been greater consensus on standardising policies promoting the social integration of migrants into receiving societies. Agreement on the importance of integration has led to the enactment of anti-discriminatory legislation as well as of residence rights for EU nationals moving to other EU states. Let me cite one example. The 2000 Racial Equality Directive required member states which had no national legislation governing racial discrimination to enact the directive as national law. To be sure, this did not produce sweeping cross-national reforms of laws governing discrimination. The directive concerned only race, not nationality or religion, so many immigrant plaintiffs did not qualify for the judicial remedies it set forth. But a measure of standardisation had been achieved. Similarly the EU's 2000 Employment Equality Directive prohibited discrimination in employment and occupation on grounds of religion and belief, age, disability and sexual orientation. It served as a baseline on which member states enacted additional anti-discriminatory measures.[18]

Support for standardising social integration policies is typically a partisan issue that divides political parties. In addition, a pattern of institutional support for or opposition to enacting integration policies is discernible. Generally, in any given country the finance, employment and social services ministries favour implementing integration measures. The organisational explanation for this is that the turf under their jurisdiction – and their budgetary importance – expands whenever increased efforts are made to integrate migrants. Normative considerations are usually absent.

Less policy standardisation has occurred on what can be termed control issues such as the intake and movement of non-EU citizens across EU borders.[19] As a result, the EU effectively operates on two tracks when granting freedoms of movement, residence and employment: Europeans are able to exercise these freedoms whereas the mobility of non-Europeans, including third-country nationals and illegal migrants, is restricted – and even subject to criminalisation. At the EU governance level, the institutional capacity to protect rights that migrants can theoretically exercise has been weak.[20] This is despite efforts undertaken by the European Commission, the European Court of Justice and major political groups in the European Parliament to harmonise migrant rights.

One area in which significant standardisation of policy has taken place across the EU is tightening border controls. Beginning in the 1990s European-level controls of border crossings by migrants were strengthened. Enforcement of such controls was passed to the Schengen system – a passport-free travel zone formed in 1985 which has steadily encompassed more European states (including non-EU members) and expanded its jurisdiction. While facilitating passport-free travel for citizens of most European countries, it has simultaneously evolved into a border control regime to manage and even keep out non-citizens.

Other sophisticated instruments of control that effectively regulate migrant mobility have been introduced. One key agency is Frontex, the EU's external border control force, created in 2004 at the time of eastern enlargement, whose headquarters are in Warsaw. As its official function, 'Frontex complements and provides particular added value to the national border management systems of the Member States'.[21] Its main operational objective is to ensure that all EU states that border non-EU ones exercise similar rigorous standards of efficiency and control. Another instrument of control over mobility includes the data base for Schengen, the Système d'Information Schengen. Visa-sharing information is provided by the Système Informatisé des Visas Européens. In addition, the introduction of biometric passports and transit visas has made control over the mobility of non-European citizens easier.

The coming into force in 2010 of the Lisbon Treaty, which restructured EU institutions and created the supranational posts of EU president and foreign affairs high commissioner, signalled a new stage in EU harmonisation. The treaty changed some of the institutional rules for formulating immigration policies. One of the most important is that measures determining the entry, residence and rights of legal migrants are decided in the Council of the European Union by 'ordinary legislative procedure' – that is, by a qualified majority vote rather than through unanimity. The European Parliament has been given veto power over such legislation, giving it higher visibility and allowing populist pressure to percolate upwards to shape legal migration policy.

The Lisbon Treaty did not affect member states' control over deciding the number of third-country labour migrants to be admitted. In this regard the Commission's discretion to harmonise immigration numbers remains restricted. However, the treaty did provide a legal framework for EU policies that offer member states incentives to support the integration of third-country nationals.[22] This preference for harmonising integration into receiving societies over exercising control on the scope of migration reflected the political realism that allowed the treaty to come into force. The overall impact of the Lisbon Treaty's changes to migration policy is thus more calibrated than sweeping.

Despite the rapid spread of international and intergovernmental rules, procedures and mechanisms of migration monitoring, it is at the national level that controlling in-migration is most rigidly enforced – when a national government is committed to it. Certain state institutions have vested interests in maximising sovereignty over immigration. These usually include home affairs ministries (often called ministries of the interior) along with those responsible for national security and justice. Such institutions wield more clout than pro-immigrant rights' groups, diaspora lobbies and lower courts in a country which, because they are more familiar with the plight of migrants, frequently rule in their favour. Consequently the influxes of 'traditional, poor, "ethnic", extra-European immigrants from Africa and Asia . . . continue to be framed as the legitimate concern of national societies, not the EU'.[23] In sum, national governments have generally been more responsive to calls for a restrictive immigration policy made by nationalist groups at home than to exhortations for more liberal policy emanating from the European Commission in Brussels.

Clearly which political party is in power and on which other parties it depends so as to survive in government determine whether immigration policy is restrictive or liberal. Both left-of-centre and conservative governments in European states regularly favour stricter immigration controls. Where their policy orientations diverge are on social integration policy. Governments composed of social democratic parties espouse proactive forms of immigrant integration. Even if pared down, the welfare state remains a central institutional piece in left-of-centre parties' programmes, and one of its tasks is to assist immigrants to achieve upward socio-economic mobility. For right-of-centre parties – disregarding radical right-wing ones – the general approach is *laissez-faire*, benign neglect, leaving migrants to fend for themselves.

STANDARD SETTING ON FAMILY REUNIFICATION AND ASYLUM

In spite of pressures felt within EU member states rather than at the intergovernmental level to restrict immigration, the influx of migrants has by and large remained unaffected. Two central parts of the international normative regime relating to migration have played a key role in keeping immigration numbers at unchanged levels. One is the norm of family reunification which was inserted into the Universal Declaration of Human Rights of 1948 and the International Covenant on Civil and Political Rights of 1966. These documents recognised that the family is the natural and fundamental group unit of society and is entitled to protection by society and the state. Population resettlement that results from applying this widely accepted norm underscores the priority given in a receiving society to ensuring the integrity of the nuclear family.

Two consequences of family reunification policy have evoked controversy. The first is that it may increase the number of people dependent on state welfare programmes. A dramatic statistic cited by Christopher Caldwell to illustrate this is taken from Germany. While the number of foreign residents rose steadily between 1971 and 2000 from three to 7.5 million, the number of *employed* foreigners in the workforce remained steady at two million. In 1973 65 per cent of immigrants were in the workforce; in 1983 only 38 per cent were. Caldwell believed the same pattern was discernible in Britain and France.[24]

The second contentious aspect of family unification policy is that it has often gone beyond just reuniting parents and their dependent children. It may also include reuniting an extended family whose members may include dependent minors and spouses. Sometimes derisively called daisy chain immigration, this policy promotes a steady growth in immigration figures. The increase in Europe's Muslim population is usually attributed to higher reproduction rates but it is in part the product of family reunification policy. The larger average size of the Muslim family, nuclear and extended, compared to the European one accounts for this increase.

The second norm that has enabled immigration is the right of refugees to asylum. The 1951 Geneva Convention defined a refugee as any person who is outside the country of her nationality and has a well-founded fear of being persecuted for reasons of race, religion, nationality, membership of a particular social group or political opinion. Granting asylum and protection to a person in this situation is a power reserved for the sovereign state. Few reasonably minded citizens would question the humanitarian quality of this norm.

While this norm does not confer an automatic right to asylum to the person seeking protection, the state must respect the prohibition on expulsion or forced return (*refoulement*) of the refugee that the 1951 Geneva Convention identified. This principle signifies that a refugee claimant cannot be extradited to the country of his nationality. It also means that refugee claimants cannot be ordered on a country's border to return to their home state where they are at risk of political persecution. It is permissible to send a rejected refugee claimant to a safe third country. The norm on asylum rights is widely accepted: close to 150 states have signed the 1951 convention and have adopted its principles as their national laws.

The number of asylum seekers to EU states has varied over time (as discussed in the next chapter). An increase in civil wars throughout the world has created a greater number of refugees. But there are also now fewer legal channels to enter the EU following the imposition of stricter requirements for granting the right to asylum. The so-called Dublin Regulation signed in 2003 was designed to prevent asylum claimants from submitting applications to multiple member states. It was also intended to reduce the number of 'orbiting' asylum seekers who were transferred from one EU country to another. A vivid example of its impact can be cited: Iceland (not part of the EU but a signatory of the Dublin Regulation) has virtually no asylum claimants because logistically almost all asylum seekers have to stop in an EU state – where they are required immediately on arrival to file for asylum – before they get to Iceland.

The crackdown on fraudulent refugee applicants resulted in an increase in the number of illegal immigrants, including through human smuggling. According to the Council of Europe, of about 50,000 migrants who arrived by boat in Italy, Spain, Greece and Malta in 2007, most claimed refugee status because they lacked any legal avenues to enter Europe.[25] In 2008 EU officials estimated that there were as many as eight million illegal immigrants living in the twenty-seven member states.

There is another channel open for illegal residence in a country: enrolling in educational courses to obtain a student visa, then remaining in that country after the visa has expired. Providing educational opportunities to nationals of other countries is not an international norm but more a value that a society holds dear as a way of providing equity for the disadvantaged; increasingly high tuition fees for foreign students make it economically advantageous as well. EU states vary in the degree to which exit checks are carried out to ensure that those with temporary student visas actually leave the country.

In 2010 the then British Home Secretary, Alan Johnson, reported that 30 per cent of migrants who came to the UK were on student visas, including adults registered on short courses rather than degree programmes. He was unable to say what proportion of foreign students left Britain when their visas expired (about 250,000 such visas had been issued for 2008/9), but his announcement of stricter rules on issuing student visas suggested that significant abuse had taken place. After a sudden spike at that time in applications from Bangladesh, India and Nepal, the new rules stipulated English-language competency at an intermediate rather than beginner level (as had been the case). Those registering for courses lasting less than six months could no longer bring dependants into the country, and dependants of students on non-degree courses would not be allowed to work. These new regulations complemented a crackdown on the proliferation of bogus colleges in the UK, about 200 of which had been closed down in the preceding years.[26]

Hardening policies and rules affecting would-be migrants have sometimes involved disingenuous measures. In Denmark, for example, foreign spouses of Danish citizens had to be twenty-four years of age to gain admission into the country. Foreigners were expected to buy their own health insurance for their first four years of residence in Denmark, rather than relying on the national health service.[27] As restrictive bureaucratic rules were being introduced without much fanfare in many EU states, the threat to migration had become that it would suffer death by a thousand bureaucratic cuts – not that it would be terminated by the coming to power of radical right political movements.

Norms and Practices Affecting
Irregular Immigrants

EU states have resorted to different measures to reduce the flow of irregular immigration into Europe. Variously described as illegal, clandestine, smuggled, trafficked, *sans papiers* ('without documents') migrants, they pose the most serious challenge to the EU's capacity to formulate and implement a continent-wide immigration policy.

Among EU actions to deter states from regularising the status of illegals once they have made it onto their territory is to expand the number of designated 'safe countries' outside the EU to which asylum seekers can be sent. More transit camps for refugees have been constructed outside EU borders; conversely the infamous one in Calais, France, holding refugees seeking to cross the Channel to England, was closed down in 2009. Bilateral agreements have also been signed between EU states and sending or transit countries in an effort to have illegal migrants returned and readmitted to them.

Arguably the most notorious of these bilateral accords was the one signed in 2004 by Silvio Berlusconi, the Italian Prime Minister, and Libyan leader Muammar al-Qadhafi. The perceived threat was that up to two million prospective migrants from all over Africa had hunkered down in Libya waiting for the opportunity to sail the 120 miles across the Mediterranean Sea to the Italian island of Lampedusa. Berlusconi persuaded Qadhafi to deport unauthorised sub-Saharan migrants over Libyan territory back to their origin countries and to seal off Libya's southern frontiers. In return, two months after the Libyan–Italian pact was signed and as a result of Berlusconi's lobbying, the EU agreed to lift its two-decades-old arms embargo on Libya. In addition Italian and Libyan energy companies signed lucrative contracts for the export of gas from the north African country to the EU state. This made good on the populist slogan repeated for years that what Italy needed from Libya was more gas, not immigrants. Given these background conditions, it becomes easier to understand why Qadhafi went down fighting when the Arab Spring broke out in 2011.

The inchoate EU policy on controlling illegal immigration at its source was criticised for undermining human rights. The Libyan government had not signed the 1951 Geneva Convention on refugees (though it was a signatory to the weaker African Refugee Convention regime) and was accused of brutal treatment of transit migrants and those returned from Italy. The Libyan government also expelled refugees to their origin countries (such as Sudan and Ethiopia) even though they were likely to face torture or persecution there. Not surprisingly, pro-immigration and diaspora lobbies in EU states accused political leaders of some member states of pursuing repression by proxy – by sanctioning a non-EU state like Libya to act as the agent of persecution. The intended effect was to discourage illegal migrants from attempting to arrive in the EU or trying to stay in it.[28]

The evolving EU policy of sending illegals to 'safe' third countries triggered further charges of norm violations. An entire new industry, in which European governments and companies were implicated, was organised to provide transportation facilities across the Sahara Desert for would-be migrants from sub-Saharan Africa. International human smugglers and handlers, and Libyan police and prison authorities, together with European businesses that provided container trucks, buses and utility vehicles, all profited from illegals' repeated attempts to reach Italy. The cost in human lives reached dramatic proportions. By 2010 as many as 12,000 migrants had drowned in the Mediterranean trying to cross to Europe, but many more had died in the desert before getting that far.[29]

The creation of the Mediterranean Union in 2008 represented an institutional response to the growing pathologies in bilateral arrangements among sending, transit and receiving countries. It offered a new intergovernmental channel for sending and receiving societies to work out appropriate arrangements for EU illegals. It was also an admission that the ad hoc regime of migration controls had produced legal, ethical and practical shortcomings.

The EU idea of subsidiarity has meant that without a common EU policy, immigration can be determined by member states at different levels of governance. Thus in Germany, for example, it is the subnational *Länder* that make decisions on social integration matters. The EU does not keep an 'integration index' that would measure different aspects of a country's integration policy. The closest there is is the British Council-sponsored Migrant Integration Policy Index (MIPEX).[30] Its measures are based on scores that independent scholars and practitioners in migration law, education and anti-discrimination assign for their country on each of 148 policy indicators on migrant integration. The maximum of three points is given when policies meet the highest standards for equal treatment. MIPEX rankings are not universally viewed as credible, but the EU has not attempted to develop an integration scale of its own. Nor does it offer a list of best practices that promote inclusion, citizenship, equal opportunity and anti-discriminatory measures. The result is a range of different practices across Europe in dealing with irregulars.

THE EUROPEAN PACT ON IMMIGRATION AND ASYLUM

In October 2008 the European Council took a major step towards codifying a set of norms and regulations governing irregular immigrants that were to serve as a model for individual member states. Approved by the twenty-seven national heads in Brussels, the European Pact on Immigration and Asylum, as it was called, represented a declaration of political intent more than a codex of binding laws. The pact had been a priority of the French presidency of the EU, which had run from July to December 2008. In some ways those sections of the Mediterranean Union Treaty, signed at a summit in Paris in July 2008, that concerned immigration served as a prototype of the pact.

The pact combined a liberal approach in some areas with an augmented securitisation agenda in others. Its chief objectives included combating illegal immigration, regulating legal in-migration and promoting development. It opened up borders for some groups but reinforced border controls on others. It instituted a stricter regime of protecting Europe through a shared approach ('solidarity') towards control of borders. The role of Frontex was enhanced and increased police cooperation with countries bordering EU states (such as Belarus and Ukraine) was introduced.

The process of securitisation of immigration had been set off by the 2001 terrorist attacks in the US. Adam Luedtke summarised the effects of 9/11 on EU states' migration policies: 'Not only did 9/11's aftermath shift the nature of the immigration laws that did pass, but it also warped the entire EU immigration policy agenda by shifting resources and attention away from the topic and towards terrorism and police matters.' Moreover, 'countries such as France and Belgium, which formerly had generous legislation, were able to use EU immigration law to gain the freedom to crack down on immigrant rights'.[31] Norm-driven policies were, therefore, superseded by security-relevant ones.

An important principle enshrined in the 2008 pact, championed by the French president, Nicolas Sarkozy, was that legal immigration is to reflect the welcoming capacity of each member state. Rather than drastic zero-immigration policy, selective quotas and general amnesties, each EU state could now determine how many immigrants would be admitted. The pact also set criteria for their integration into the receiving society, and it established procedures for removing foreigners who were there illegally.

The pact was premised on member states' cooperation in relocating undocumented aliens, establishing readmittance conditions with aliens' countries of origin, and adopting more severe penalties for human traffickers. For sending countries, the pact envisaged closer cooperation not just over preemptive controls on would-be illegals but on such positive areas as issuing student and work permits for qualified nationals from those countries. It set its sights on an equilibrium that would balance Europe's need for highly qualified migrants with receiving states' welcoming capacities.

The pact also introduced common asylum, detention and removal measures. Irregulars could now be detained for a maximum of eighteen months. Previously the detention limit had varied, from just thirty-two days in France to twenty months in Latvia. However, in seven other EU countries an illegal could be incarcerated for an indefinite period. The pact also set a new standard five-year ban on illegals seeking to return to an EU state.

In typical EU governance style, the new rules were to be applied in asymmetrical fashion. France's immigration minister insisted that the country's custody period before an illegal could be expelled – the shortest in Europe – would not be lengthened. Countries with periods longer than eighteen months were required to apply the EU's eighteen-month maximum, except Denmark, Ireland and Britain, which had negotiated opt-outs. The pact encouraged 'voluntary returns' that gave illegals up to thirty days to leave before they were put into expulsion proceedings.

Did the 2008 EU pact spell the end of national models of immigration and integration policy? A tentative answer is that while member states continue to enjoy discretion over immigration matters, the parameters within which policy must fit have been narrowed.[32] It is a truism that the more jurisdiction EU governance structures give themselves, the less control individual states exercise. States such as Britain had used the autonomy they had in immigration issues precisely to minimise, and even abandon, restrictive controls. They were not eager to implement a strong regulatory regime. The new pact may do this for them.

Asylum and family reunification have served as the two main normative criteria for admitting immigrants into Europe and member states have been reluctant to tamper with them. But other considerations also contributed to a largely unchecked flow of immigrants into member states. Terri Givens and Adam Luedtke asked:

> What political factors account for this loss of state control over immigration, whereby state actors were unable to prevent unwanted immigration despite solid public backing and the weakness of immigrant-representing organisations?[33]

Common answers include invoking another normative factor – the need to be attentive to transnational discourses on universal human rights. Incentives for economic globalisation have been influential. The emergence of supranational institutions and, with it, the corresponding decline in national sovereignty, is an important factor too. Consequently, the influence of norms on the making of immigration policy may be exaggerated; political and economic expediency often dictates policy. Cultural factors also play a part. EU immigration policy cannot be studied without examining who the migrants involved are. As neutral as official discourse on the ethnic and religious make-up of migrants appears to be, whether the immigration policy adopted is liberal or restrictive depends in large measure on whether it is large numbers of north Africans, south Asians or eastern Anatolians seeking residence, work permits and citizenship, or if it involves Quebeckers, Tasmanians or Volga Germans.

41

THE INSTITUTIONALISATION OF NORMS

The saying that 'hate cannot be legislated away' is being tested by EU stand-ard setting. Not only are the protections and redress a citizen can count on when experiencing bias and hostility now clearly identified, a plethora of institutions and agencies to monitor and enforce norm compliance have been established.

The EU has obtained legitimacy because, along with its earlier incarna-tions, it was able to achieve measurable progress in bringing about the eco-nomic and political integration of a steadily expanding number of member states. The EU has also recorded considerable success in the area of legal harmonisation. The *acquis communautaire*, or sum total of laws enacted by the Community, now runs to nearly 20,000 pages. It comprises thirty-five chapters that extend from the four freedoms to company law, education, environment and justice. The EU also asserts that it has become the reposi-tory of European values – a claim about normative integration. Considerable institutional growth has taken place in this area.

The European Convention for the Protection of Human Rights and Fundamental Freedoms was enacted in 1950 by the Council of Europe, itself founded a year earlier to concentrate on human rights and the rule of law across Europe. Article 14 of the convention is a prohibition on all forms of discrimination:

> The enjoyment of the rights and freedoms set forth in this Convention shall be secured without discrimination on any ground such as sex, race, colour, language, religion, political or other opinion, national or social origin, association with a national minority, property, birth or other status.[34]

In 1961 the Council of Europe adopted the European Social Charter, guar-anteeing the rights and freedoms individuals can enjoy in their daily lives. Amended in 1996, the basic rights under the charter encompass the following areas: housing, health, education, employment, social and legal protection, free movement of persons and non-discrimination. Additionally, agree-ments concluded in Turin and Paris in the 1960s committed the European Community to respecting fundamental and social rights.

The deepening integration project that led to the creation of the EU was anchored in the 1992 Treaty on European Union (better known as the Maastricht Treaty). Along with its institution-building component, the treaty affirmed the European ideals of unity, freedom, equality and justice. It was the 1997 Treaty of Amsterdam that developed the ideas of diversity and equality and extended their applicability to nationals of non-EU states. Though third-country nationals had been living in Europe for decades, their freedom of movement was limited compared to that of EU citizens. While restrictions remained, 'the language of the Treaty of Amsterdam at least began to reflect a commitment and concern for citizens and non-citizens alike'.[35]

For three decades the Council of Europe's convention and charter had served as the normative framework for Europe's citizens. A pivotal document that codified citizens' rights, including providing wider rights for non-European nationals, was the European Charter of Fundamental Rights. It was drawn up by a convention made up of diverse political representatives: members of national and European parliaments, representatives of national governments and a European Commission member. Signed at the Nice summit in December 2000, the charter's fifty-four articles spell out the EU's fundamental values and the civil, political, economic and social rights of the EU citizen – in short, a citizens' Europe.[36] It contained six telling headings: dignity, freedoms, equality, solidarity, citizens' rights and justice.

In 2005 the majority of voters in referendums held in France and the Netherlands came out against a draft of a European constitution, to which this Charter of Fundamental Rights was attached. After two years of fine tuning and repackaging this draft, EU leaders came up with the 2007 Lisbon (Reform) Treaty, which was approved by the last of the twenty-seven member states in 2009 and came into force the following year. The Charter of Fundamental Rights was attached to the Lisbon Treaty too.

For differing reasons two countries refused to be bound by the charter's provisions. Britain did not want to adhere to the charter's set of economic rights that included a liberal right to strike and a fixed-length work week. Poland feared that its social legislation, derived from Catholic social teachings, such as opposition to gay marital rights, would be superseded by the charter. Late in the process, the Czech president voiced his concern about the unrestricted right of foreigners to purchase property in his country. The Czech Republic was accordingly included with Britain and Poland as having the right to opt out of charter provisions, though it was questionable whether these opt-outs would have any legal validity after the Lisbon Treaty came into effect. The European Court of Justice (ECJ)'s legal view has been that all parts of the treaty are binding on signatories and that the Charter of Fundamental Rights constitutes an integral part, serving as the EU's human rights convention.

The institutional grounding of Europeans' rights has taken other forms. Case law deriving from the ECJ as well as from the European Court of Human Rights (ECHR) is a source of fundamental legal rights for the EU. The ECJ has increasingly referenced the body of ECHR case law and has viewed itself as bound by the ECHR's judicial precedents. The ways in which anti-discriminatory claims by EU citizens and migrants are adjudicated by the ECHR have become, therefore, an important instrument of norm enforcement.

The EU has set up a number of standard-setting agencies that do not have formal legal competence. Specifically, in its efforts to monitor and combat racism and discrimination, it has established specialised research and advisory agencies such as the European Union Monitoring Centre (EUMC). Created in 1998 and based in Vienna, the EUMC served as a research office, carrying out investigations, publishing reports and proffering expert advice to EU bodies and national governments. It was concerned with examining broad issues and trends and therefore left adjudicating individual cases to the ECHR. In 2007 the EUMC was reorganised and renamed the Fundamental Rights Agency (FRA). It continues to carry out the mission of monitoring, reporting, advising and educating European officials and publics about human rights and when they are violated. The FRA has contracted data collection on issues related to 'racism, xenophobia and related intolerances' to an agency called RAXEN. It works with 'national focal points', or research bureaus, located in all EU member states.

In spite of this elaborate institutional structure and human rights regime that it supports, the EU's normative framework still has shortcomings. The FRA's 2008 report noted how implementation of the EU's anti-discrimination legislation remained uneven. Victims of discrimination were often unaware of the legal redress open to them. Equality bodies are not always sufficiently robust to implement the Racial Equality Directive.[37] Perhaps most critically, as Michel Wieviorka, a leading French expert on xenophobia, argued, 'anti-racist legislation cannot compensate for racist-based social exclusion'.[38]

Victims of racism and discrimination often encompass minority group members who have EU citizenship, not just migrants. Minorities may be made up of communities of immigrants who arrived in a receiving European society some time ago. The term 'minority' has several different meanings. The definition provided by the European Convention on Human Rights is straightforward: 'A group inferior in number to the rest of the population and whose members share in their will to hold on to their culture, traditions, religion, or language.'[39] When the definition is disaggregated, it becomes clear that the term can subsume many groups: officially recognised minorities (Catalans in Spain), officially recognised immigrant communities (Moluccans in the Netherlands), and ethnic kin returning to the homeland (German-speaking groups in Germany who originate from outside the country, e.g. Volga Germans). Practical use of the term 'minority' identifies diverse groups: indigenous peoples and yesterday's immigrants, sojourners and settlers, guests and strangers, stranded diasporas and new migrant groups. What they share in common is living in a receiving society where they are perceived as an out-group.

Each group advances its specific claims for rights, both universal and specific. As Will Kymlicka observed, demands for collective rights by national ('autochthonous') minorities have generally carried greater weight than similar claims by ethnic groups produced by migratory movements. A key reason underlying such differentiated rights is the assumption that deciding to emigrate is a conscious and free choice made by people that implicitly or explicitly acknowledges the need to adapt to a new environment.[40] Not making an effort to adapt is sometimes seen, then, as grounds for limiting rights. But the practice in the EU has been to promote measures for the integration of migrants so that they can enjoy the full panoply of rights that minorities are accorded.

Ways of accommodating foreigners

While EU standards on minority and migrant rights – and the institutional framework to encourage compliance with them – have grown exponentially, the ways that individual member states accommodate and socially integrate foreigners differ markedly. To be sure, when the EU has held leverage, as in the case of conditionality for candidate states prior to the 2004 enlargement process, it insisted on legal compliance with its norms on minority rights.[41] From the perspective of distressed and desperate migrants, however, which states conform to EU standards is not a priority consideration. For them the bottom line is different: 'The most encouraging message all such immigrants get from their host societies is: "integrate – or else".'[42] That is because 'shared conceptions of the polity, whether as a multinational state or as an ethnic "nation", appear to remain a significant factor in how these democracies treat their resident aliens'.[43]

European receiving societies interpret integration differently from one another. The Council of the European Union defines the concept as a two-way process in which both immigrants and receiving societies have to take on particular responsibilities. The host country is required to create economic and social opportunities for immigrants while, in turn, immigrants are required to respect the basic political values of the EU, such as the democratic process and the rule of law.

Integration is generally regarded as a 'softer' approach to accommodating foreigners than is assimilation. For the German migration expert Christian Joppke, assimilation is nothing less than the negation of otherness. A politics of assimilation aims to 'eradicate the culture of the *Other* and to absorb it. It is not a matter of excluding the *Other*, but of including it to the extent that one renders it like oneself'.[44] Admittedly, the assimilation process itself is subject to different national interpretations and applications, as the race expert Liz Fekete pointed out (see Box 2.3).

Box 2.3 Different assimilations to assimilate differences

Each nation moves towards the assimilationist model in a way that is consonant with the myths upon which that nation has been built. In the Netherlands, the theme of the national debate has been 'standards and values'; in Sweden and Norway, cultural barriers to inclusion; in the UK, 'community cohesion'; in France, the principle of *laïcité* (state secularism); in Germany, the primacy of the *'Leitkultur'* (leading culture); in Denmark, the 'intolerant culture' among immigrants that prevents integration; in Spain, public safety and crime.

Source: Liz Fekete, *A Suitable Enemy: Racism, Migration and Islamophobia in Europe* (London: Pluto Press, 2009), pp. 62–3.

Accepting that assimilation can entail a number of different approaches, we can recognise two general models of accommodating migrants. One, based on social integration, which explicitly recognises and privileges diversity, pluralism and multiculturalism, has often been held up as the ideal type. The other, assimilationist, one, practised by most receiving societies for decades until the rethinking of the 1970s, has been scorned by most Western states.

Some specialists have identified a third approach, 'differentialism', which seeks to avoid ethnic conflict by keeping interactions between majority and minority groups to a minimum. The liberal variant of differentialism allows for the development of parallel institutions for majority and minorities alike. Such institutions can provide for the cultural, educational and social needs of minorities. Sometimes labelled the consociational model, this approach is frequently associated with the 'pillarisation' of institutions found in the Netherlands. The illiberal variation on the differentialist model is when the parallel institutions that have been created are not equal. They can become a mechanism to keep groups segregated, as under the former apartheid system in South Africa.

The elaborate European framework of anti-discriminatory norms, legislation and courts rules out the adoption of the illiberal differentialist model, though not the consociational one. The EU has acted in the past to thwart the emergence of institutionalised inequality. Thus in 2000, when a radical right anti-immigrant party that had done well in elections in Austria took part in a coalition government, the EU levied sanctions on the country that effectively ostracised its government. These actions were without precedent and twisted the 1993 Copenhagen criteria, which had identified the membership prerequisites for an applicant country as being the existence of a democratic system, a free market and a legal regime protecting minority rights, to include the character of the government of an existing EU state.

After imposing these sanctions against Austria, the EU sought to codify the basis for taking future action against a state not in compliance with EU norms. Article 7 of the Nice Treaty, signed by EU leaders in 2001 and taking effect two years later, stated that the European Council can declare the existence of 'a serious and persistent breach of fundamental rights' in a member state. Once such a finding was made, the Council could vote, by a qualified majority, to suspend certain membership rights of the country at fault. These procedures came into play in 2011 after Hungarian Prime Minister Viktor Orbán's right-wing government passed legislation that threatened the independence of the country's central bank, constitutional court, judiciary and media. While not directly involving a breach of fundamental rights, in the view of José Barroso, President of the European Commission, the legislation was at odds with the EU *acquis*. Moreover, Orbán's rule was becoming increasingly authoritarian and the country's minorities – Jews, Roma, Slovaks – appeared frequently to be the targets of discriminatory actions. The European Commission sent three 'letters of formal notice' to Hungary about the violation, which represented the first stage in the EU's infringement procedure. But, given the deep financial crisis that Europe found itself in, the EU's response was more muted than had been the case with neighbouring Austria in 2000.

What can be inferred from this account is that the EU is not indifferent to what model of accommodation of foreigners and minorities is adopted by a member state. The EU Commission and European Council have openly favoured the multicultural model of integration and have explicitly criticised discriminatory differentialism. EU authorities have tended to favour, and even idealise, the out-group. But there is a caveat. The EU has also idealised the model of secularism, which many of these same out-groups frequently reject. The EU's seemingly uncompromising adherence to this approach has even been labelled 'secular fundamentalism'. The simultaneous commitment to minority and migrant rights and to secularism appears to be a contradiction in terms. Politically more significant, it also runs counter to much elite and public opinion in many member states, which in turn has amplified Euroscepticism in those states.

THE MULTICULTURAL PARADIGM: THE BRITISH CASE

The distinguishing feature of the multicultural model favoured by the EU is that it is designed 'to allow the individuals and groups with different cultural backgrounds to fully join the host society without losing their peculiarities or be denied full participation into the whole society'.[45] One of the leading exponents of this model in the EU has been Britain.

An early case for promoting a multicultural society in England was put forth in 1966 by Roy Jenkins, then home secretary in Harold Wilson's Labour government. Though Jenkins did not use the term 'multiculturalism', its sense was conveyed in his statement:

> Integration is a rather loose word. I do not regard it as meaning the loss, by immigrants, of their own national characteristics and culture. I do not think that we need in this country a 'melting pot', which will turn everybody out in a common mould, as one of a series of carbon copies . . . of the stereotypical Englishman. I define integration, therefore, not as a flattening process of assimilation but as equal opportunity, accompanied by cultural diversity, in an atmosphere of mutual tolerance.[46]

The reverse anti-multicultural argument made in England is perhaps more famous. Two years after Jenkins's statement, Enoch Powell, shadow cabinet minister in the Conservative party, made his 'Rivers of Blood' speech – still today a milestone in anti-multiculturalist rhetoric. Powell described the plight of his English constituents: 'For reasons which they could not comprehend, and in pursuance of a decision by default, on which they were never consulted, they found themselves made strangers in their own country.' It would only get worse. While 'many thousands' of immigrants were willing to integrate into British society, the majority, Powell believed, were not. They had a vested interest in highlighting racial and religious differences 'with a view to the exercise of actual domination, first over fellow-immigrants and then over the rest of the population'. Citing the *Aeneid*, Powell (a classics specialist) warned of upcoming wars and of a modern-day British counterpart to the river Tiber 'foaming with much blood'.[47]

The terms of the multicultural debate had been set. Even as EU discourse continued to express a preference for multiculturalism into the twenty-first century, multicultural scepticism at the national level was growing. In his study of the practice of multiculturalism as a model for integration, Christian Joppke identified its flawed assumptions in a more insightful and less polemical way than Powell had done:

> The world of multiculturalism is populated not by individuals with a multitude of overlapping, and often conflicting, group affiliations and interests, but by groups or 'communities' that are inert, homogenous, and mutually exclusive . . . This subordination of the individual to one exclusive group runs counter to the modern principles of inclusion and fundamental differentiation, and makes multiculturalism vulnerable to fundamentalism and anti-modernist extremes.[48]

The evolution of parallel societies which interacted infrequently had facilitated the ghettoisation of minorities. These parallel societies were the product of failed multiculturalism, then, not of benign neglect by the receiving society or of insistence on community autonomy by minority leaders.

Chancellor Angela Merkel of Germany lent her political critique to multiculturalism: 'The idea of a multicultural society cannot succeed. It is prone to failure from the start. Multiculturalism is not integration.'[49] A Turkish-German scholar provided a realist explanation for the shift in the first decade of the new century away from multiculturalism: 'The singular civilisational identity of Europe demands cultural assimilation of others rather than their social, political, and economic integration. In the political vocabulary of Europe, particularly continental Europe, integration has come to mean cultural assimilation as opposed to multiculturalism.'[50] In 2010 President Sarkozy of France and Prime Minister Cameron of Britain joined in the critiques of multiculturalism. But widespread disillusionment had already been expressed, including in the academic community. A 2005 report noted that 'multiculturalism as a political ideology has helped to create a tribal Britain'.[51]

Relations between Britain's ethnic communities deteriorated in the 1990s, culminating in a series of riots in 2001 in the Midlands and Yorkshire. A detailed study commissioned by the Home Office and published at the end of that year had pointed to consistently higher levels of unfair treatment reported by Muslim groups than by other ethnic and religious communities. Muslims experienced unfair treatment across the board – in education, employment, housing, law and local government services.[52] A 2005 citizenship survey on issues of race and faith confirmed this trend. Indeed religious discrimination was worsening: 52 per cent of respondents said there was more religious prejudice than five years earlier, and Muslims were identified as the group experiencing most religious prejudice.[53]

The 2005 London terrorist attacks put the value of multiculturalism into question. The Conservative shadow home secretary wrote that 'Britain has pursued a policy . . . allowing people of different cultures to settle without expecting them to integrate into society'. The priorities had become reversed: 'often the authorities have seemed more concerned with encouraging distinctive identities than promoting common cultural values of nationhood'.[54] A year after the bombings, Ruth Kelly, the secretary of state for communities and local government, announced the setting up of the Commission on Integration and Cohesion. Her rationale rested in the weaknesses in Britain's multicultural system: 'We have moved from a period of uniform consensus on the value of multiculturalism, to one where we can encourage that debate by questioning whether it is encouraging separateness.'[55]

The commission's report was published in 2007.[56] It defined cohesion as 'the process that must happen in all communities to ensure different groups of people get on well together'. In turn, 'integration is principally the process that ensures new residents and existing residents adapt to one another'. The commission reported that most people surveyed (around 80 per cent) agreed that people of different backgrounds got on well in their local areas. This was important because Britain was on the verge of attaining 'super-diversity'. As the report noted, 'migrants come from all over the world – and not just places with historical ties to the UK'. For the commission, super-diversity now signified differing immigration routes, legal statuses and settlement patterns. Super-diversity combined with transnationalism meant that 'the UK is far more plugged in to events around the world and that cohesion in local areas can be affected by events in another country'.

But despite – or perhaps because of – the fact of super-diversity, neither the Labour government of Gordon Brown nor its Conservative–Liberal Democrat successor under David Cameron was viewed as an enthusiastic supporter of continued migration into Britain. In 2011 Cameron gave a speech to party members in which he emphasised how 'for too long, immigration has been too high'. He claimed that he wanted to get the policy right: 'good immigration, not mass immigration'.[57] He was criticised for being normative about immigration: 'It is making policies based on negative perceptions and fears rather than addressing immigration as a neutral social phenomenon that can be as beneficial or as damaging as we make it.'[58]

Cameron positioned himself, therefore, as a critic of existing immigration and multicultural policies and as an advocate of more administratively regulated policies.[59] An area where the British government had indeed much earlier adopted a managerial approach was on race relations. Whether applied to south Asians, West Indians or sub-Saharan Africans, new race boards and institutions were created to combat racial discrimination. These bodies were not always equipped to stem the process of ghettoisation, but their existence suggested that British authorities could countenance challenges to the multicultural model so long as they did not play the racist card.

It is unclear whether super-diversity in Britain is the direct result of its earlier choice, made in the late 1960s, to adopt a multicultural model. France today is also characterised by super-diversity even though it opted to pursue an assimilationist republican model decades earlier.

Assimilation: the French republican ideal?

The assimilationist model may be faulted for emphasising values directly contrary to those of multiculturalism. It 'expects minorities to adapt completely to the host society and its political system through a process of individual change, in which immigrants give up their different cultural backgrounds in order to adopt the hegemonic group culture'.[60] In Joppke's view it represents the negation of the culture of others. Because there is little give and take on mutual accommodation between host society and immigrant communities, it has not been favoured by the EU. More frequently than the multicultural approach, this model has been criticised for countenancing host society prejudices. But assimilation has historically been *de rigueur* in France, where it is associated with the republican ideal of a single people. The case of French Muslim experience under the republican model is described in Chapter 5.

Assimilationist policies have been reintroduced in European states other than France. As anti-immigration parties and movements gathered momentum in the first decade of the new century, the appeal of the hard-headed assimilationist approach grew. The spread of Islamophobic attitudes has been accompanied by calls for Muslim immigrants to integrate more fully and quickly into their new societies while downplaying a rights-based approach to their status.

In France and, to a lesser extent, Belgium and Switzerland, integration of immigrants is regarded as a social contract based on shared values. The logic of *l'assimilation républicaine* is that the values of liberty, equality and fraternity require the full insertion and inclusion of individuals in a society. In theory, then, the social, economic and political marginalisation of migrants in France represents a failure of the republican model. Paradoxically, those best positioned to be 'inserted' into French society – Maghrebis from north Africa who experienced over a century of French colonisation, including francisation – are the ones who have experienced profound marginalisation.

Assimilation of immigrants into the receiving society is the expectation of France's republican tradition because it posits an abstract universalism of rights. Minority and migrant rights fall within this universalism. The insistence on cultural assimilation follows from the principle that the French nation is based not on ethnic or racial exclusiveness but on citizenship, that is, membership in the national community. The acquisition of French values, it is understood, brings personal liberation to the individual. As a corollary, citizenship can be denied for *défaut d'assimilation*. An example is Muslim women wearing the burqa having citizenship applications rejected on the grounds that such a religious symbol is incompatible with French republican values. From this republican logic it follows that there cannot be hyphenated Frenchmen.

According to the historian Ariane Chebel d'Appollonia,

> republicanism in France consists of five key components: equality before the law; individual emancipation (commonly understood as a rejection of any form of communitarianism); a universal understanding of citizenship, based on a mix of *jus soli* and *jus sanguinis*; secularism (especially since 1905); and cultural assimilation.[61]

French republicanism has been associated with the principle of *jus sanguinis*, nationality determined by blood lines, specifically by paternity, which France introduced in 1790 and enshrined in its civil code in 1803. Much has been made of *jus sanguinis* as a racially exclusionary category that does not match up well to the more egalitarian notion of *jus soli*, citizenship of a state based on birth in it. The first supposedly produces ethnically determined nationality, the second a civic nation.

This inferential dichotomy may not be empirically grounded. As one French specialist put it, 'no necessary link connects *jus soli* with open societies and *jus sanguinis* with racist and exclusionary ones, as has been maintained by some scholars'.[62] Furthermore, the republican model contends that either being born or assimilating into the French nation produces an equality of citizenship. It is alleged to be a fairer, more democratic approach than accepting the accident of birth on French territory as the basis of citizenship.

Immigration from colonies to the metropole has been understood as the Third World's revenge on imperial Europe: 'they are here because we were there'. But the distinct colonising patterns among European nations account for some of the variation in the models of integration that were adopted. Thus 'the British ruled their imperial possessions along communal lines, dividing religious and ethnic communities, and governing in collaboration with their leaders'.[63] The Dutch ruled their colonies in similar fashion. From this Gilles Kepel, one of the leading academics holding that Islamic revivalism poses a threat to republican assimilationism, inferred that the multicultural model in which people are encouraged to stick to their own kind reflects such a colonial tradition.[64]

How colonies were administered had, in its turn, its own antecedent causes. Ian Buruma suggested that 'the colonies reflected, to some degree, the nature of the metropolitan societies, which were also divided along the lines of class, religion, and even nationhood (English, Scottish, Welsh, Ulstermen)'.[65] Whatever the case, 'imposing a common culture, at home or abroad, was seen by the British, as well as the Dutch, as impractical, illiberal, and undesirable, except for a small elite, which ruled, or helped to rule, over all this diversity'.[66]

French colonialism took a different tack. Since at least the 1789 revolution, France has regarded its political ideals as a model for an entire civilisation. French empire builders were charged with applying the republican model wherever they ventured. Chebel d'Appollonia asked, then, whether the republican model still meets the challenge of diversity. 'Does the denial of the category of "race" undermine the fight against racism?'[67] She pointed to the anachronistic origins of the model lying in the need to integrate French nationals – Bretons, Occitanes, Corsicans – not immigrants. In the Third Republic it was intended to turn those perceived as peasants – not foreigners –into Frenchmen.[68]

What constitutes Frenchness today is predicated on *not* recognising the ethnic and cultural pluralism in French society. As Karima Laachir, a cultural studies specialist, concluded, 'for "the French" it would mean to lose their "national identity" if they were to adopt the Anglo-Saxon model of multiculturalism'.[69]

THE MYTH OF THE SINGLE FRENCH NATION

The idea that a single French national identity exists has been challenged by historian Suzanne Citron. She repudiates the notion of linear national development ensconced in the country's master narrative and highlights cultural and ethnic diversity leading to *une France métissée* or 'crossbred France'.[70] Her fellow historian Fernand Braudel examined a host of factors affecting national identity, from the role of French and regional languages to national borders and Paris's dominant influence.[71] Already in 1972, when immigrant numbers were still small, the semiotician Roland Barthes underscored the importance of the French myth of a unified nation. Under it visible minorities become invisible. Recognition of minorities is superfluous because the concept of 'indifferentiation' trumps that of differential racism.[72] Twenty-five years later, philosopher Étienne Balibar contended that the French refusal to recognise foreignness demonstrates 'a profound fear of a multicultural society and cultural *métissage*'.[73] In turn, the French immigration expert Alec Hargreaves elaborated on the French prejudice against ethnic frames, often associated with supposedly misguided English and American policies (see Box 2.4).

Box 2.4 Vive la différence

In French debates over immigration and 'integration' policy during the last twenty-five years, the United States has frequently been cited as an anti-model, an example of the dreadful consequences which could follow if France were to follow so-called 'Anglo-Saxon' approaches to ethnic relations. Policies such as affirmative action and ethnic monitoring, introduced in the US to combat discrimination, are in France often blamed for producing the problems they were designed to remedy: racial discrimination, ethnic segregation, urban ghettoes, etc.

Source: Alec G. Hargreaves, 'Veiled Truths: Discourses of Ethnicity in Contemporary France', in Roland Hsu (ed.), *Ethnic Europe: Mobility, Identity, and Conflict in a Globalized World* (Stanford, CA: Stanford University Press, 2009), p. 91.

If France has appeared reticent to accept its identity as a nation of immigrants, demographics tell a different story. A study from 1988 found that one in three French people had at least one foreigner as an ancestor three generations back.[74] Today, more than 10 per cent of the French population is foreign born, higher than the EU average but in the normal range for Western receiving societies.

If the French model of integration is in theory inclusive, in practice it can be exclusionary. In the effort to be colour and ethnicity blind, it prohibited data collection on minorities that could help determine if discrimination against them exists. Only in 2009 did the French government relax this ban on compiling ethnic statistics.

To summarise, the assumption of the republican model of citizenship is that immigrants are integrated into a secular state where they are, as individuals, treated equally – no better, no worse – with the French. They acquire the same rights and obligations while obtaining respect for their culture and traditions. The idea of both injurious and positive discrimination is rejected.

The 1988 *Rapport de la commission de la nationalité* clarified what the scope of assimilation entailed. It should require assimilation into the prevailing norms of the public sphere. In their private lives, on the other hand, naturalised citizens of foreign background could hold on to their primary religious and cultural loyalties.[75] In short, even though the term 'integration' is used in French discourse on migrants, the policies are those of assimilation. In 1989 the Haut Conseil à l'Intégration (High Council of Integration) was given responsibility for monitoring cultural assimilation. In 2003 an 'integration contract' was drawn up which new immigrants were required to sign if they wished to obtain a ten-year residency permit.

Critics of republicanism point out that the public–private dichotomy is spurious. People who do not fit the definition of French citizen end up being marginalised. Referring primarily to north African immigrants, the sociologist Nacira Guénif-Souilamas cautioned that 'through a rhetorical system that claims to be universalist, an entire generation of French people suffers from a particular and illegitimate status limited to their specific origin, class, or gender, thereby ... denied equal access to citizenship'.[76] Universalism is vacuous if it cannot be applied to specific cases. How strict, then, is the application of the assimilation model today?

EXCEPTIONS TO FRANCE'S ETHNIC BLINDNESS

How exceptions to civic republican principles are made can indicate the extent to which France allows for flexibility in what is often criticised as an ossified integration model. In practice, for some time the country has followed a two-track policy on recognising difference. Officially it refuses to acknowledge difference by invoking the assimilation model. But a number of exceptions have been allowed, not all of which have led to more 'liberal' positive discrimination.

The historian Patrick Weil highlighted how the wartime Vichy regime effected a fundamental change in nationality law by introducing an ethnic quota system for immigration, similar to that created in the US by the immigration laws of 1921 and 1924. The Vichy government, seen by many as an aberration in France's political history, gave preference to immigrants coming from northern and western Europe over those from southern and eastern Europe. This provision was done away with in the postwar Fourth Republic when the American-style ethnic quotas were removed.[77]

Ethnic differentiation was also evident in a law applied in French Algeria in 1947. It conferred the title of citizen on Muslims but not on other people indigenous to Algeria; French Jews in Algeria had been made citizens already in 1870. If promoting an ethnic hierarchy represented an illiberal policy in an increasingly rebellious Algeria, in metropolitan France at that time the policy of ethnic blindness played a positive role. It served as a counterweight to racial colonialism.

The charade of maintaining ethnic and religious blindness continued into the 1960s even as state agencies were being set up to aid immigrant communities. The establishment of minority, especially Muslim, associations was promoted through funding from the Fonds d'Action Sociale (FAS). Created in 1958 together with the Fifth Republic, the FAS became an agency entrusted with administering social welfare programmes, initially for Algerians before that country achieved independence in 1962, then for all immigrants and their descendants.[78] In facilitating the integration of immigrants, the FAS was compelled to engage in ethnic categorisation.

Beginning in the 1970s, an expanding French economy needed additional workers. Importing foreign labour became a top economic priority, relegating integration policy to a secondary role. In fact, 'French officials promoted the Islamicisation of Muslim immigrants – in order to keep repatriation open – but refused to exercise control over it. As a result, the Islamicisation of Maghrebi immigration turned into the ethnicisation of Islam.'[79] However, in 1974, under the presidency of Valéry Giscard d'Estaing, legal immigration to France was ended except for family unification and political asylum programmes. This 'zero option' of a comprehensive immigration moratorium exercised by a conservative president was in part an attempt to deflect Front National leader Jean-Marie Le Pen's populist appeal to stop the 'wave' of Algerians from 'flooding' France, but it can also be interpreted as a rare case of France actually adopting a pure ethnic blindness model.

An additional step in loosening the principle of ethnic blindness came in 1981 during the presidency of François Mitterrand. A 1938 law had prohibited the formation of associations by non-citizens, in other words, recent immigrants. But a new law sanctioned the creation of ethnic associations, and the associationalist movement gathered further strength with the 1983 *marche des Beurs*. Led by North African immigrants, this march represented an unprecedented demonstration in favour of equality and against discrimination. It began in Marseilles and ended in Paris, where a delegation met with President Mitterrand and secured a major innovation in immigration policy – a ten-year residence permit. These events represented a milestone in the French state's acceptance of communitarian ethnic expression within a secular republican space.[80]

The implication was now this: 'Difference, in terms of ethnicity and later religion, would be considered acceptable by the French state if it did not challenge, but rather supported, the grand philosophies of the Republic: republican values, universal French nationhood, and . . . laïcité.'[81] The French state lent support to the Beur movement by funding and legitimating it even as it sought to channel Beur collective action into strengthening the republic while not challenging the state.

As one study concluded, then,

> since the 1980s, successive governments on both the Left and Right have tried to create a 'representative body' for the Muslim religion, seeking a single interlocutor to not only effectively manage the religious issues arising from Islam in France but also a political interlocutor.[82]

A form of state corporatism encompassing intermediary ethnic associations was in the making.

Shortly after being elected in 2007, President Nicolas Sarkozy pushed for constitutional reform which would formalise the ethnic frames and practices of the recent past. He argued for inserting the concept of diversity into the preamble of the Fifth Republic's long constitution, and established a commission to draft how such constitutional change could be implemented. Headed by a former centrist minister, Simone Veil, the commission submitted its report in December 2008. Unexpectedly, it recommended not following up Sarkozy's proposal for constitutional revision. Anticipating liberalisation of the assimilationist model, it rejected 'the ethnically-based policies of "positive discrimination" for which such a revision might have paved the way'.[83] The commission instead expressed a preference for piecemeal fine tuning of the model rather than a constitutional overhaul – an implicit recognition that its fundamental premises remained sound.

ASSIMILATION, MULTICULTURALISM AND ISLAM

The status of Muslim communities in various European countries has undergone considerable change since the 1960s. Initially in Britain and France the accepted practice was to 'define Muslims by their immigrant or citizenship status (immigrants, asylum seekers/refugees, or foreigners), by their economic function (guest workers), or by their race or ethnicity (black, Pakistani, Arab,

Turk, etc.)'.[84] In the 1970s and 1980s both countries regarded Muslims as constituting racial and ethnic minorities; by this stage, not all Muslims were immigrants and a growing number were being born in the receiving countries.

US social scientist Kathryn Gardner underlined that it was 'decades after the population's sedimentation that the category of "Muslim" gained a high level of resonance both as an identity marker for the population and as a political category'.[85] Especially in Britain, religious identity began to overshadow ethnic as the primary marker of difference. At the same time,

> an important cross-national and cross-temporal trend emerges: the government management and channelling of 'difference' into acceptable avenues. Western European governments were not passive participants, instead actively pursuing policies to construct acceptable civic racial/ethnic and, later, religious identities.[86]

Beginning in the 1990s, the dominant frame of Muslims became one whereby they constituted a religious minority. Gardner summarised:

> A younger generation of Muslims came of age in the West, often with citizenship of the Western nation in which they resided and not having a significant experience of their parents' country of origin, and were heirs to the disappointing results of the right of difference movements of the 1980s.[87]

Casting Muslims as a religious community fudged the salience of the assimilationist–multicultural distinction, and indeed the differing results produced by the two models can be overstated. Using Islamic terrorism as the outcome variable, Ian Buruma asserted that

> the fact that some of the most spectacular acts of Islamist terror have taken place in Britain and the Netherlands, and not in France, and that anti-Muslim sentiment in those countries has grown in reaction to the alleged failure of multiculturalism, cannot be denied.[88]

The assimilationist model appeared to generate no more extremist reactions than the integrationist one.

Select attitudinal data even lend support to the view that the assimilationist model performs better than multiculturalism in bringing majority and minority groups together. Gilles Kepel found that multiculturalism as practised in Britain and the Netherlands fared poorly on Muslims' perceived integration compared to the maligned French model that imposes a common secular culture. Only 20 per cent of French respondents felt that Muslims posed a threat to national security compared to double that number in Britain. Furthermore, 80 per cent of French respondents believed that being a Muslim and a French citizen were compatible while less than 60 per cent of their British counterparts accepted this view.[89] Kepel's conclusion was that imposing common values, as the French state does, benefits everybody.

Another research project compared the record of republican and multicultural policies of integration in politically mobilising migrants and their descendants. Ayhan Kaya concluded that both had failed because, whichever model was employed, 'migrants have been imprisoned in a culturalist, ethnicist and religious discourse by the states in a way that distances them from the attempt to represent themselves through legitimate political institutions like national and local parliaments'. Each approach was hamstrung by a different weakness:

> difference-conscious multiculturalism prompts migrants and minorities to mobilise themselves not along political lines but along cultural and ethnic lines, difference-blind republicanism fails in meeting identity-based claims of migrants and minorities.[90]

Political mobilisation and participation is an indicator of deeper migrant involvement in a receiving society but protection of migrant interests is more basic. Using French Muslims as a case study, Jonathan Laurence and Justin Vaisse were persuaded that a unitary French state based on republican ideals protects everyone equally, while, for them, a weak American state exploited by well-organised minority group lobbies does not.[91] Their evidence from France can be summed up this way:

> Most statistics are moving in positive directions: better command of French, more intermarriage, more successful careers, and declining birth rates among immigrant families. Religious practice is not more widespread among Muslims than in other religious groups in France.[92]

Despite this, few would disagree that 'Muslims in France endure daily acts of hostility and rejection in the workplace and job market, in house-hunting, and in ordinary social interactions'. This experience can lead to the 're-Islamisation' of younger Muslims: they 'are not returning to the "family Islam" of their parents, born in North or West Africa, but to a new "globalised Islam" that gives them an identity that a grudging French society has not furnished'.[93]

Are these shortcomings produced by the assimilationist model rather than global events occurring outside France? For Ariane Chebel d'Appollonia, French integration policy was indeed to blame: France had moved from recognising the 'right to be different' (*le droit à la différence*) to applying a 'difference in rights'. She caricatured the approach in this ironic slogan: 'Down with the Republic of the Oppressed, Long Live the Democracy of the Ghettos'.[94]

The riots in the *banlieues* in 2005 and 2007 have generally been presented as the protests of young marginalised Muslim migrants and children of migrants. But they brought together Africans, Arabs and Berbers, Muslims and non-Muslims to remonstrate against being excluded from French society through discriminatory practices in employment and education. The riots were not 'anti-French' or a demand for migrant groups' independence from French society. On the contrary, 'the rioters seemed to be saying, "We're here! Notice us! Let us in!"'[95]

A landmark case applying the assimilationist premise governing French citizenship occurred in 2008 when the French Council of State rejected an application for citizenship filed by a Moroccan woman. She had appeared at the naturalisation interviews wearing the burqa – the head-to-toe veil commonly associated with Salafism, a conservative Sunni Islamic movement which is sometimes disparaged as Wahhabism. The citizenship rejection was based on the grounds that she accepted 'a radical practice of her religion incompatible with the essential values of the French community and notably with the principle of equality between the sexes'.[96] The woman, married to a French citizen and mother of three French-born children, had argued that wearing the burqa, leaving her home infrequently and giving full submission to the authority of her husband represented the practice of Salafism. But the Council of State ruled that these practices were incompatible with French values.

As part of an official debate on French identity launched by President Sarkozy, in a political address to Parliament at Versailles in 2009 he proposed banning the wearing of the burqa. Such legislation, he argued, would constitute a 'law of liberation, not a ban', because it involved securing a woman's freedom and dignity and was not about freedom of religion. In 2010 the National Assembly voted in favour of a partial ban to be applied in public places such as hospitals, schools and public transport. The decision did not make wearing the burqa illegal, it only gave public officials the authority to have it removed. In 2010 the Constitutional Council ruled that the law did not create disproportionate punishments, and upheld it.

President Sarkozy framed the burqa issue as not religious but cultural, yet this distinction is problematic, as this chapter has highlighted. For example, in Britain both the wearing of the hijab and Islamic instruction are allowed in state schools. France's tradition of laïcité (discussed below) rules out religious instruction or symbols in public educational institutions. German policy falls somewhere in between these cases. These different approaches may reflect contrasting histories of church–state relations in these countries.[97]

For Muslim communities the nature of church–state relations – and in practice, the relationship between religion and politics – entails both opportunities and constraints. Where states provide funding for religious instruction, Muslims may become beneficiaries. But church–state arrangements can also confine the range of claims that Muslims can make, as the partial French ban on the burqa shows.

Islam adds complexity to the prevailing model of church–state relations in France because of its colonial and postcolonial policies which actively promoted 'moderate' Islam.[98] Paradoxically, then, 'a different kind of Islam is being privileged within the state'. It is defined as a national or even a European Islam, 'one which is moderate, civic-minded, and oriented to harnessing positive faith capital'. It is to be

> a Western Islam that would embrace liberal values, particularly those of human rights, democracy, and gender equality. The agenda was concerned with the 'moderate' content of the message as well as encouraging Muslims to 'opt in', taking part in and also taking pride in the host society and its democratic process.[99]

Strict separation of church and state, then, was negotiable and could be relaxed if it provided an opportunity structure to coopt moderate Euro-Islam.

LAÏCITÉ AND FRENCH ISLAM

The core of the republican model remains robust if eroded in places. One of its five fundamental principles, which recently underwent rethinking, is laïcité, the premise of a secular society. Originating in the 1789 Revolution, which sought to protect the independence of the French state from the Catholic church, the principle was codified in the 1905 law on the separation of church and state. It has been argued that 'in polities in which some form of church–state separation has been adopted, fundamentalism seems less likely to dictate the course of national self-definition'.[100] Few in the West today question the advantages of the separation of politics and religion.

France has embraced the model of secularism and has become one of the most secularised states in Europe. Catholicism, the religion of the majority, has been in decline for decades and church attendance is low. Polls suggest that 30 to 40 per cent of the country's population are non-believers. After Turkey, France has the most restrictive laws restricting the public display of religious symbols. While Belgium, too, appears to be a stridently secular state, its constitution proclaims the state 'neutral' in religious matters, not *laïc* as in France.

In these circumstances, why has the virtue of secularism become questioned? Islam is part of the answer. France is home to one of the largest Muslim communities in Europe. If the Jewish idea of the supremacy of civil law – *dina de-malkhuta dina* – can be employed to accept secular rules, Islamic practices contain many visible norms and codes which directly conflict with a secular ban on religious symbols. Negotiating a middle way between religious belonging and strict secularism is a political imperative in a paradoxically less secular twenty-first century.

Islam is not the only religious actor interested in obtaining a wider presence in public space. The interests of the Catholic church were at the centre of President Sarkozy's keynote speech in 2007, which set out his idea of 'positive laïcité'. Given in the Lateran Palace of the Vatican in the presence of the Pope and cardinals, he claimed that no one challenges laïcité today precisely because it has proved to be successful: 'It is a liberty: the liberty to believe or not, to practice a religion or change it . . . the liberty to not be discriminated against by the state because of one's belief.'[101] The virtue of secularism is, then, that it undercuts the salience of the border between believing and not believing, in much the same way that each individual internalises in himself both belief and non-belief.

Sarkozy contended that as France had become more diverse, laïcité had become both a necessity and an opportunity – a condition that ensures civil peace. It also provides historic continuity and not a negation of the past or severance of France from its Christian roots. The President affirmed that

> Like Benedict XVI, I believe that a nation which ignores its ethnic, spiritual and religious heritage commits a crime against its culture, against this historical mixture, its patrimony, its art and popular traditions, which deeply permeate our manner of living and thinking. Pulling out roots is to lose meaning, to weaken national identity, to further impoverish social relations which have such a need for symbols of memory.[102]

Sarkozy contended that it was time for France to openly recognise its Christian origins while defending the principle of laïcité. Such a positive laïcité is 'one which, while protecting the right to think freely and to believe or to not, regards religions not as a threat but a strength'. The key message in Sarkozy's rethinking went beyond Catholicism's place in France. His liberal interpretation of laïcité promised a platform for encouraging dialogue between France's great religions while, as he put it, promoting rather than constraining their spiritual growth.

Making good on his cautious idea to reinsert the religious into the public sphere, in 2009 Sarkozy announced his intention to appoint religious officials to the Economic, Social and Environmental Council. He insisted, though, that this would not change the institution's equilibrium, which was based on secularism.[103] That same year France's foreign minister, Bernard Kouchner, set up a section on religion in the bureaucracy he oversaw. He explained it as the effect of globalisation and a necessary modernisation of ways of thinking in the diplomatic corps.[104] These moves, overseen by Sarkozy, the self-styled *l'homme de la rupture* – the man who breaks from the past – seemed to offer a more advantageous opportunity structure for French Muslims, whom much of this rethinking implicitly concerned.

NORMS AND FEARS

This comparison of different models of integration standard setting may be misguided. The damning verdict of one academic study is that 'absolute assimilationism has failed in France, but so has segregation in Germany and multiculturalism in the Netherlands and the United Kingdom'.[105] For some immigrant communities, then, the conclusion is 'a pox on all your models'.

Elites and publics have disagreed over policies concerning migrants: how many to admit into a country, how to integrate them into society, what to do about irregular migrants, how to preserve migrants' cultural heritage but also their own, how to reconcile religious differences. More so than the public, political elites tend to believe that they can make over the social fabric of a country without evincing a popular backlash. Public fear is important to them largely in terms of how they can capitalise on it.

The moralising discourse of political elites can be especially alienating because it implies that non-compliant groups deserve to be stigmatised. Thus the term 'xenophobic' is polarising when used by one group about another, for instance, by establishment politicians describing the view of a marginalised economic class. Use of the word 'Islamophobic', tellingly, is less polarising and therefore worrying, as evidence presented in the next chapter will indicate.

EU leaders deserve credit for taking up the struggle against public fears. Would xenophobia in Europe be worse if the EU, with its elaborate norms-based institutions, policies and discourse, did not exist? In all probability, yes. Given established standards on inclusion and tolerance, why do European citizens nevertheless express fears about strangers, and what is the place of Islamophobia among them?

NOTES

1. Gary P. Freeman, 'Modes of Immigration Politics in Liberal Democratic States – Comment/Reply', *International Migration Review* 29 (1995), p. 883.
2. Ibid., p. 885. For a more recent critique, see Freeman's 'Does Politics Trump the Market in Contemporary Immigration?', in Marco Giugni and Florence Passy (eds), *Dialogues on Migration Policy* (Lanham, MD: Lexington, 2006), pp. 109–18.
3. Freeman, 'Modes of Immigration Politics in Liberal Democratic States', p. 891.
4. Malise Ruthven, 'The Big Muslim Problem!', *New York Review of Books*, 17 December 2009, p. 64. The target of the attack was Christopher Caldwell's *Reflections on the Revolution in Europe: Immigration, Islam, and the West* (New York: Doubleday, 2009).
5. Michael Emerson, 'What Values for Europe?', in Pamela Kilpadi (ed.), *Islam and Tolerance in Wider Europe* (New York: Open Society Institute, 2007), pp. 9–13.
6. For groundbreaking introductions to the subject, see Seyla Benhabib, *The Rights*

of Others: Aliens, Residents and Citizens (Cambridge: Cambridge University Press, 2003); Yasemin Nuhoğlu Soysal, *Limits of Citizenship: Migrants and Postnational Membership in Europe* (Chicago: University of Chicago Press, 1995).

7. Council of Europe, *White Paper on Intercultural Dialogue* (Strasbourg: Council of Europe, 2005).
8. Göran Therborn, *European Modernity and Beyond: The Trajectory of European Societies, 1945–2000* (Thousand Oaks, CA: Sage, 1995), p. 51.
9. Walter Laqueur, 'So Much for the New European Century', *Chronicle of Higher Education*, 11 May 2007, p. B7. Excerpted from his *The Last Days of Europe: Epitaph for an Old Continent* (New York: Thomas Dunne, 2007).
10. Jean-Claude Chesnais, *La Revanche du Tiers-Monde* (Paris: Robert Laffont, 1987). See also Alfred Sauvy, *La Vieillesse des nations* (Paris: Gallimard, 2001).
11. Samuel Huntington, 'The Erosion of American National Interest', *Foreign Affairs*, September–October 1997, p. 33.
12. Peter A. Kraus, *A Union of Diversity: Language, Identity and Polity-Building in Europe* (Cambridge: Cambridge University Press, 2008), p. 192.
13. Gallya Lahav, *Immigration and Politics in the New Europe: Reinventing Borders* (Cambridge: Cambridge University Press, 2004), p. 104.
14. John Hooper, 'Italian woman's murder prompts expulsion threat to Romanians', *The Guardian*, 2 November 2007.
15. Madeleine Demetriou, *Towards Post-Nationalism? Diasporic Identities and the Political Process* (Aalborg: Center for International Studies, Aalborg University, 1999), p. 9.
16. Terri Givens and Adam Luedtke, 'The Politics of European Union Immigration Policy: Institutions, Salience, and Harmonisation', *Policy Studies Journal* 32 (2004), p. 149.
17. Elizabeth Collett, 'The European Union's Stockholm program: less ambition on immigration and asylum, but more detailed plans', Migration Information Source website, January 2010, at http://www.migrationinformation.org/Feature/display.cfm?id=768, accessed 24 January 2012.
18. Nasar Meer, 'The Impact of European Equality Directives upon British Anti-discrimination Legislation', *Policy and Politics* 38 (2010), pp. 197–215.
19. See the pioneering work by Christian Joppke, *Immigration and the Nation-state: The United States, Germany, and Great Britain* (Oxford: Oxford University Press, 1999).
20. Givens and Luedtke, 'The Politics of European Union Immigration Policy', p. 159.
21. http://www.frontex.europa.eu, accessed 24 January 2012.
22. Collett, 'The European Union's Stockholm program'.
23. Adrian Favell, 'Immigration, Migration, and Free Movement in the Making of Europe', in Jeffrey T. Checkel and Peter J. Katzenstein (eds), *European Identity* (Cambridge: Cambridge University Press, 2009), pp. 171–2.
24. Christopher Caldwell, *Reflections on the Revolution in Europe: Immigration, Islam, and the West* (New York: Doubleday, 2009), p. 49.
25. 'EU approves illegal migrants plan', BBC News website, 18 June 2008, http://news.bbc.co.uk/1/hi/world/europe/7460007.stm, accessed 10 February 2012.
26. 'Tougher rules to stop abuse of student visa system', BBC News website, 7 February 2010, http://news.bbc.co.uk/1/hi/uk/8502640.stm, accessed 10 February 2012.
27. See for example 'Welfare prescription: make immigrants pay', *Copenhagen Post*, 8–14 April 2011, p. 14.

28. Catherine Wihtol de Wenden, *Démographie, immigration, intégration* (Paris: Fondation Robert Schuman, 2008).

29. An excellent overview of the politics of the migrant journey from sub-Saharan Africa to Europe is provided by Hein de Haas, 'Trans-Saharan migration to north Africa and the EU: historical roots and current trends', Migration Information Source website, November 2006, http://www.migrationinformation.org/feature/display.cfm?id=484, accessed 24 January 2012.

30. In the 2010 index, Sweden had the best score followed closely by Portugal. Latvia had the lowest score just ahead of Cyprus. See http://www.mipex.eu

31. Adam Luedtke, 'Fortifying Fortress Europe? The Effect of September 11 on EU Immigration Policy', in Terri E. Givens, Gary P. Freeman and David L. Leal (eds), *Immigration Policy and Security: U.S., European, and Commonwealth Perspectives* (New York: Routledge, 2009), p. 144. Christina Boswell, in the same volume, argues that immigration policy was not significantly affected by 9/11; see her 'Migration, Security and Legitimacy: Some Reflections', pp. 93–108.

32. Hubert Peres, 'Towards the End of National Models for the Integration of Immigrants in Europe? Britain, France and Spain in Comparative Perspective', in Adam Luedtke (ed.), *Migrants and Minorities: The European Response* (Newcastle upon Tyne: Cambridge Scholars, 2010).

33. Givens and Luedtke, 'The Politics of European Union Immigration Policy', p. 148.

34. Council of Europe, Convention for the Protection of Human Rights and Fundamental Freedoms, http://conventions.coe.int/Treaty/Commun/QueVoulezVous.asp?NT=0 05&CL=ENG, accessed 24 January 2012.

35. Alessandra Beasley Von Burg, 'Muslims and Multiculturalism in the European Union: Putting Diversity, Acceptance and Equality to the Test', in Adam Luedtke (ed.), *Migrants and Minorities: The European Response* (Newcastle upon Tyne: Cambridge Scholars, 2010).

36. The Charter of Fundamental Rights of the European Union, http://www.europarl. europa.eu/charter/default_en.htm, accessed 10 February 2012.

37. European Union Agency for Fundamental Rights, *Annual Report 2008*, http://fra. europa.eu/fraWebsite/attachments/ar08p2_en.pdf, accessed 24 January 2012.

38. Michel Wieviorka, 'Contextualizing French Multiculturalism and Racism', *Theory, Culture, Society* 17:1 (2000), pp. 157–62.

39. European Convention on Human Rights, art. 29, para. 1. Cited by Riva Kastoryano, 'Transnational Networks and Political Participation: The Place of Immigrants in the European Union', in Mabel Berezin and Martin Schain (eds), *Europe without Borders: Remapping Territory, Citizenship, and Identity in a Transnational Age* (Baltimore, MD: Johns Hopkins University Press, 1999), p. 83.

40. Will Kymlicka, *Multicultural Citizenship: A Liberal Theory of Minority Rights* (Oxford: Clarendon Press, 1995), p. 96.

41. Judith G. Kelley, *Ethnic Politics in Europe: The Power of Norms and Incentives* (Princeton, NJ: Princeton University Press, 2004), pp. 174–95.

42. Favell, 'Immigration, Migration, and Free Movement in the Making of Europe', p. 175.

43. David C. Earnest, 'Neither Citizen nor Stranger: Why States Enfranchise Resident Aliens', *World Politics* 58 (2006), p. 268.

44. Christian Joppke, 'Beyond National Models: Civic Integration Policies for Immigrants in Western Europe', *West European Politics* 30 (2007), p. 3.

45. Enric Martínez-Herrera and Djaouida Moualhi, 'Predispositions to Discriminatory Immigration Practices in Western Europe: An Exploration of Political Causes', *Portuguese Journal of Social Science* 5 (2007), p. 222.

46. Roy Jenkins, quoted by Christian Joppke, 'Multiculturalism and Immigration: A Comparison of the United States, Germany, and Great Britain', *Theory and Society* 25 (1996), p. 480.

47. 'Enoch Powell's "Rivers of Blood" speech', *Daily Telegraph*, 6 November 2007 (delivered 20 April 1968).

48. Joppke, 'Multiculturalism and Immigration', p. 449.

49. Quoted in Vivienne Walt, 'Life on the front lines', *Time*, 20 February 2005.

50. Hasan Kösebalaban, 'The Permanent "Other?"' Turkey and the Question of European Identity', *Mediterranean Quarterly* 18:4 (2007), p. 107.

51. Congressional Research Service, *Muslims in Europe: Integration in Selected Countries* (Washington, DC: Congressional Research Service, 2005).

52. Paul Weller, Alice Feldman and Kingsley Purdam, *Religious Discrimination in England and Wales* (Home Office, 2001).

53. Sarah Kitchen, Juliet Michaelson and Natasha Wood, *2005 Citizenship Survey: Race and Faith Topic Report* (Department for Communities and Local Government, 2006).

54. David Davis, quoted in 'Davis attacks UK multiculturalism', BBC News website, 3 August 2005, http://news.bbc.co.uk/1/hi/uk_politics/4740633.stm, accessed 10 February 2012.

55. Speech by Ruth Kelly at the launch of the Commission on Integration and Cohesion, 24 August 2006.

56. Commission on Integration and Cohesion, *Our Shared Future* (Commission on Integration and Cohesion, 14 June 2007).

57. David Cameron, 'Speech on immigration to party members', *New Statesman*, 14 April 2011.

58. Zrinka Bralo, 'Immigration is neither good nor bad', *The Guardian*, 15 April 2011.

59. Nasar Meer and Tariq Modood, 'The Multicultural State We're In: Muslims, "Multiculture" and the Civic Re-balancing of British Multiculturalism', *Political Studies* 57, pp. 473–97.

60. Martínez-Herrera and Moualhi, 'Predispositions to Discriminatory Immigration Practices in Western Europe', p. 222.

61. Ariane Chebel d'Appollonia, 'Race, Racism and Anti-discrimination in France', in Sylvain Brouard, Andrew M. Appleton and Amy G. Mazur (eds), *The French Fifth Republic at Fifty: Beyond Stereotypes* (Basingstoke: Palgrave Macmillan, 2009), p. 269.

62. Robert O. Paxton, 'Can you really become French?', *New York Review of Books*, 9 April 2009, p. 52.

63. Ian Buruma, 'Living with Islam', *New York Review of Books*, 14 May 2009. This argument is developed further in Gilles Kepel, *The War for Muslim Minds: Islam and the West* (Cambridge, MA: Belknap Press, 2004).

64. See Gilles Kepel, *Allah in the West: Islamic Movements in America and Europe* (Cambridge: Polity Press, 1997). See also his *Beyond Terror and Martyrdom: The Future of the Middle East* (Cambridge, MA: Belknap Press, 2008).

65. Buruma, 'Living with Islam'.

66. Ibid.
67. Chebel d'Appollonia, 'Race, Racism and Anti-discrimination in France', p. 268.
68. Eugen Weber, *Peasants into Frenchmen: The Modernisation of Rural France, 1870–1914* (Stanford, CA: Stanford University Press, 1976).
69. Karima Laachir, 'Crossing the "Threshold of Intolerance": Contemporary French Society', in Stefan Herbrechter (ed.), *Cultural Studies: Interdisciplinarity and Translation* (Amsterdam: Rodopi, 2002). See also Karima Laachir, 'French Muslims and the Politics of *Laïcité*', *Maghreb Review* 33 (2008), pp. 21–35.
70. Suzanne Citron, *Le Mythe national: l'histoire de France revisitée* (Paris: Atelier, 2008).
71. Fernand Braudel, *The Identity of France: People and Production* (New York: Perennial, 1992).
72. Roland Barthes, *Mythologies* (London: Jonathan Cape, 1972).
73. Étienne Balibar, *La Crainte des masses: politique et philosophie avant et après Marx* (Paris: Galilée, 1997), pp. 327–8.
74. Gérard Noiriel, *Le Creuset français: histoire de l'immigration XIXe–XXe siècles* (Paris: Seuil, 1988), p. 10.
75 Rapport de la Commission de la Nationalité, *Etre français aujourd'hui et demain*, 2 vols. (Paris, Christian Bourgeois, 1988).
76. Nacira Guénif-Souilamas, 'The Other French Exception: Virtuous Racism and the War of the Sexes in Postcolonial France', *French Politics, Culture & Society* 24:3 (2006), p. 24.
77. Patrick Weil, *How to Be French: Nationality in the Making since 1789* (Durham, NC: Duke University Press, 2008).
78. Amelia H. Lyons, 'Social Welfare, French Muslims and Decolonisation in France: The Case of the Fonds d'Action Sociale', *Patterns of Prejudice* 43 (2009), pp. 65–89.
79. Chebel d'Appollonia, 'Race, Racism and Anti-discrimination in France', p. 273.
80. Catherine Wihtol de Wenden and Remy Leveau, *La Beurgeoisie: les trois âges de la vie associative issue de l'immigration* (Paris: CNRS, 2001), pp. 9–10.
81. Kathryn L. Gardner, 'The Politicisation of Religion in the West: Assessing the Effects of Policy Legacies and Government Construction on a European Islam', in Adam Luedtke (ed.), *Migrants and Minorities: The European Response* (Newcastle upon Tyne: Cambridge Scholars, 2010).
82. Gardner, 'The Politicisation of Religion in the West'.
83. Alec G. Hargreaves, 'Veiled Truths: Discourses of Ethnicity in Contemporary France', in Roland Hsu (ed.), *Ethnic Europe: Mobility, Identity, and Conflict in a Globalized World* (Stanford, CA: Stanford University Press, 2009).
84. Erik Bleich, 'The Legacies of History? Colonization and Immigrant Integration in Britain and France', *Theory and Society* 34 (2005), pp. 171–95.
85. Gardner, 'The Politicisation of Religion in the West'.
86. Ibid.
87. Ibid.
88. Buruma, 'Living with Islam'.
89. Gilles Kepel, *Beyond Terror and Martyrdom: The Future of the Middle East* (Cambridge, MA: Belknap Press, 2008). The data were taken from a 2007 *Financial Times* poll.
90. Ayhan Kaya, 'Age of Securitization: Challenging Multiculturalist and Republicanist Policies of Integration', Migration Citizenship Education website, 2011, http://www.

migrationeducation.org/28.1.html?&rid=189&cHash=1f962e3839d6f3a33cb8584ce 49a8935, accessed 25 January 2012.

91. Jonathan Laurence and Justin Vaisse, *Integrating Islam: Political and Religious Challenges in Contemporary France* (Washington, DC: Brookings Institution Press, 2008).

92. Paxton, 'Can you really become French?', p. 55.

93. Ibid.

94. Ariane Chebel d'Appollonia, *Les Racismes ordinaires* (Paris: Presses de Sciences Po, 1998), pp. 89, 91. On le droit à la différence see Henri Giordan (ed.), *Démocratie culturelle et droit à la différence: rapport au Ministre de la Culture* (Paris: Documentation Française, 1982). This report proposed a national commission on minority cultures which would promote ethnic cultural revival.

95. Buruma, 'Living with Islam'.

96. Bruce Crumley, 'Too Muslim to be French?' *Time*, 12 July 2008.

97. Joel S. Fetzer and J. Christopher Soper, *Muslims and the State in Great Britain, France, and Germany* (Cambridge: Cambridge University Press, 2005).

98. John R. Bowen, *Why the French Don't Like Headscarves: Islam, the State, and Public Space* (Princeton, NJ: Princeton University Press, 2007).

99. Gardner, 'The Politicisation of Religion in the West'.

100. Martin E. Marty and R. Scott Appleby, 'Conclusion: Remaking the State – The Limits of the Fundamentalist Imagination', in Martin E. Marty and R. Scott Appleby (eds), *Fundamentalisms and the State: Remaking Polities, Economies, and Militance* (Chicago: University of Chicago Press, 1993), p. 640.

101. Nicolas Sarkozy, speech at the Lateran Palace, Vatican City, 20 December 2007.

102. Ibid.

103. Stéphanie Le Bars, 'Les limites de la "laïcité positive"', *Le Monde*, 20 December 2008.

104. Stéphanie Le Bars, 'Bernard Kouchner vient de créer un pôle religions au Quai d'Orsay, une première en France', *Le Monde*, 25 July 2009.

105. Robert S. Leiken, 'Europe's Angry Muslims', *Foreign Affairs*, July–August 2005.

CHAPTER THREE

From fears about immigrants to prejudices against Muslims

Displaying prejudice is generally regarded as a damning sin, or at least a humiliating *faux pas*. Modernity has come to be defined by the converse: 'The ideal of life without prejudices, stereotypes, preconceptions, and pre-existing authority is . . . regarded as a proper, indeed, a noble one.'[1] Prejudice reduction has become a vital objective in modern societies. The sum total of EU norms of inclusion and accommodation of diversity, as well as the supranational institutions and national models constructed to promote these, attest to this fact.

There are good reasons to be prejudiced against prejudice. The British psychiatrist Theodore Dalrymple noted how 'there have been so many negative stereotypes that have been false, demeaning, and cruel, and that were made a justification for injustice or barbarity, that the very idea of stereotyping any group negatively has been discredited'.[2] A French counterpart concurred, albeit with a hint of irony. Patrick Declerck believed that as a result of 'programmatic tolerance . . . "to hate" is not done anymore. It is even practically illegal.' He explained: 'Democracy has located man in exactly the same place occupied in the earlier architecture of Christian theology by a divinity. Our political and religious dogmas forbid us to think of, conceive of, or imagine an enemy. In short, to hate.'[3]

In logical terms, prejudices cannot be eliminated (see Box 3.1). Accordingly,

> to overturn a prejudice is not to destroy prejudice as such. It is rather to inculcate another prejudice. The prejudice that it is wrong to bear a child out of wedlock has been replaced by the prejudice that there is nothing wrong with it at all.[4]

This means that 'no system of ethical propositions, or any other system of propositions, can exist without presuppositions, that is to say, prejudices'.[5]

Box 3.1 A syllogism on the human condition

The distinction between good and evil is both inevitable and necessary for the exercise of virtue.
The distinction between good and evil can be based only on prejudice.
Therefore, prejudice is necessary for the exercise of virtue.

Source: Theodore Dalrymple, *In Praise of Prejudice: The Necessity of Preconceived Ideas* (New York: Encounter, 2007), p. 122.

FROM HOSPITALITY TO HOSTILITY

Hostility to strangers is, as suggested in Chapter 1, a common form of prejudice and may originate in childhood experience. Anti-immigrant attitudes are a manifestation of this hostility but they are not a 'natural' stage in human development, instead refracting social biases. Antipathy towards migrants has become more widespread as the sheer scope of international migration has expanded worldwide. One estimate is that some 200 million people today are migrants of whom one-tenth (twenty million) have an irregular status. As the movement of peoples has become globalised, migrants exhibit more diverse backgrounds. They represent not just rural poorly educated populations seeking to escape poverty and lack of opportunity in underdeveloped regions; sections of the well-educated urban middle class who wish to better their socio-economic, political and professional conditions have also become geographically mobile. Some traditional out-migration countries have become receiving societies; in Europe this includes Greece, Italy and Spain among others. South-south migration, between countries in the southern hemisphere, has also expanded enormously.[6]

Few citizens in Western societies envy the plight of the vast majority of immigrants seeking to improve their living conditions. Still, a perception persists that immigrants who have reached the affluent West have improved their lot; by contrast many host society members continue to feel trapped in their socio-economic status and geographic location with little occupational mobility available. This sense of relative deprivation has hardened following the 2008 economic crisis.

Projecting the frustration of an unavailable longing – mobility – upon a target – migrants – can produce unsettling effects. Their very freedom to be mobile sparks envy. As an example, ethnic Germans living in the Federal Republic may feel that Turkish settlers and immigrants have acquired more freedoms and special rights than they have. Envy may produce what French thinker René Girard described as mimetic desire. It is 'a kind of nonconscious imitation of others' which is shaped by an appropriative (or acquisitive) instinct. Release from this appropriative instinct, which sometimes takes a violent form, is possible by resorting to scapegoating – 'nonconscious convergence upon a victim' that brings relief from violence proneness.[7]

Why citizens come to fear, then often hate, foreigners has been the subject of much research. Mimetic desire is just one possible explanation. A metaphorical one has it that Europe is haunted by its inner demons.[8] A philosophical paradigm advanced by the French-based philosopher Tzvetan Todorov asserts that any critique of the Other is really a critique of the self,[9] a view eloquently supported by the cultural theorist Julia Kristeva (see Box 3.2).

Box 3.2 The foreigner within us

Foreigner: a choked up rage deep down in my throat, a black angel clouding transparency, opaque, unfathomable spur. The image of hatred and of the Other, the foreigner is neither the romantic victim of our clannish indolence nor the intruder responsible for all the ills of the polis. Neither the apocalypse on the move nor the instant adversary to be eliminated for the sake of appeasing the group. Strangely, the foreigner lives within us: he is the hidden face of our identity: he is the hidden face of our identity . . . He disappears when we all acknowledge ourselves as foreigners, unamenable to bonds and communities.

Source: Julia Kristeva, *Strangers to Ourselves* (New York: Columbia University Press, 1991), p. 1.

Many creative writers have made attempts to understand the sources of Othering. The majority of Salman Rushdie's novels grapple with the issues of identity, assimilation, belonging and borders. The Indian-born novelist was in an unenviable position to give expert commentary on identity markers and their consequences: he had been at the centre of a controversy – and the target of a fatwa ordering his killing – over supposedly blasphemous anti-Islamic passages in *The Satanic Verses*, which appeared in 1988.[10] In a more romantic novel, *The Enchantress of Florence*, published two decades later, he reflected on the nature of foreignness: 'Was foreignness something to be embraced as a revitalizing force, bestowing bounty and success upon its adherents, or did it adulterate something essential in the individual and society as a whole?' In a commentary Rushdie ventured an answer:

There are two kinds of people in the book. There are people who draw their sense of themselves and their sense of being in the world from movement between places. And there are other people who find that to be absurd – who think that all the meaning they have of the world arises from the place they belong.[11]

It is this eternal clash of ideals that brings about the confrontation between strangers and home dwellers.

Some cultures have nuanced understandings of the native–foreigner dichotomy. For instance, to be Japanese involves satisfying a set of cultural, linguistic, ethnological, social and political criteria. By contrast, *gaijin* are generally Westerners, and *gaikokujin* are people from the outside world. However subtle such distinctions may be, 'we' and 'others' have been constructions since time immemorial (see Box 3.3)

Box 3.3 The ever-present Other

Our contemporary suspicion of and antipathy for the Other, the Stranger, goes back to the fear our tribal ancestors felt towards the Outsider, seeing him as the carrier of evil, the source of misfortune. Pain, fire, disease, drought, and hunger did not come from nowhere. Someone must have brought them, disseminated them. But who? Not my people, not those closest to me – they are good . . . The guilty are therefore the Others, the Strangers. That is why, seeking retribution for our injuries and setbacks, we quarrel with them, enter into conflicts, conduct wars.

Source: Ryszard Kapuściński, *The Cobra's Heart* (London: Penguin, 2007), p. 94.

The fear of strangers is not always self-induced: it has been regularly incited by those in authority to serve their interests. Almost a century ago the Russian critic Mikhail Bakhtin broached the idea of 'official fear', which he understood as a by-product of a cosmic fear sensed by humanity.[12] Political elites are skilled in the art of spreading fear among citizens, though not all resort to it.

The contingent nature of hospitality to strangers is an additional explanatory framework for the rise of fear of the foreigner. In a controversial book on Muslim immigrants, the American journalist Christopher Caldwell even suggested that 'hospitality is related to xenophobia. In fact, it is one of the faces of xenophobia.'[13] Phobias shape the limits on hospitality offered by a host society to strangers. In 1908 the German sociologist Georg Simmel observed how 'a stranger is not one who comes today and goes tomorrow, but rather as the person who comes today and stays tomorrow'.[14] A century later French philosopher Jacques Derrida highlighted the conditional nature of hospitality: it is circumscribed by a country's laws, especially those regulating immigration. The legal system places restrictions on the immediate, infinite and unconditional welcoming of the Other.[15] Caldwell was blunter: 'Hospitality is meant to protect travellers in hostile territory; it is not meant to give large groups of visitors – who may include militants, freeloaders, and opportunists – the run of the place.'[16]

The sociologist Meyda Yegenoglu concurred with this interpretation: 'Conditional hospitality is offered at the owner's place, home, nation, state, or city – that is, at a place where one is defined as the master and where unconditional hospitality or unconditional trespassing of the door is not possible.' She elaborated:

> The *law of hospitality* is the *law of oikonomia*, the law of one's home. Offered as the law of place, legal-juridical hospitality lays down the limits of a place and retains the authority over that place, thus limiting the gift that is offered . . . In this way, the foreigner is allowed to enter the host's space under conditions determined by the host.[17]

Let us consider one somewhat obscure example. One of the world's oldest parliaments, the Alþingi in Iceland, decided around 1431 that no foreigners (*útlenskir menn*) could remain in Iceland after 8 September – the feast of the Blessed Virgin, when the last ships were permitted to sail from the country. The 1490 Píningsdómur ('Píning's Verdict') provided some leeway: foreigners could overwinter in Iceland if sick, injured or shipwrecked but they were not allowed to engage in fishing or trade during this period. The main purpose of this verdict was to keep seasonal work seasonal. 'Outlanders' were expected to return to their native countries, then, coinciding with the time set in the *Jónsbók* legal codebook when Icelandic farmers returned livestock to their home pastures from summer grazing lands.[18] Parameters of hospitality to strangers were etched in stone even in a remote, inaccessible periphery of Europe.

It follows that

> because they trespass over the allowed borders of guest status, migrants engender uncertainty and ambivalence. By refusing to accept the termination of their allowed period of stay and thereby turning their temporary status into an unexpected permanency, they remain 'stubbornly and infuriatingly indeterminate'.[19]

It is migrants' indeterminacy which in part produces a transition from hospitality to hostility on the part of receiving society members.

Yet it is not as if receiving societies countenance such indeterminacy. Sustained and multifaceted efforts are undertaken by receiving governments to 'brand' migrants consistent with accepted national typologies. As a specialist on comparative immigration highlighted,

> the categorisation system that public policy actors adopt to define migrants strongly shapes the degree and the form of claims made by migrants . . . The labels adopted also tell us about the threshold to be passed to be considered a full-fledged member of the majority society's imagined community.[20]

The interactive character of the relationship between hosts and strangers has a marked effect on both sides and goes a long way to determining whether antagonism or agreement will prevail.

THE ALLEGED WRONGDOINGS OF MIGRANTS

European phobias about migrants feed on the perception that strangers have overstayed their welcome. But there are tangible grievances as well. Many of society's pathologies are blamed on this group:

> Immigrants, and particularly foreigners, are presented as the persons responsible for the deterioration of security conditions, terrorism, unemployment and increased public expenditure. This process of stigmatisation and criminalisation provides a breeding ground for racial discrimination towards this part of Europe's population.[21]

Eloquent voices have been heard seeking to check such stigmatisation. The Moroccan-born writer Tahar Ben Jelloun has argued for a 'politics sustained by a philosophy, a thought that puts the self and the other in a face-to-face relation that is creative, healthy, without rancour and without resentment'.[22] In *L'Hospitalité française*, he argued that such encounters were particularly important given France's colonial history and the rising presence of migrants from postcolonial states.

Immigration phobia entails more than the belief that strangers are trespassing on the conditions of hospitality. A popular myth about recent migrants is that they have become harder to assimilate when compared to earlier groups. An ethnic and even racial component is invoked to explain this difference. The 1960s wave of immigration was in great part intra-European, bringing south-eastern Europeans, like Yugoslavs and Greeks, to the industrial economies of the west. With hindsight, these Europeans are viewed as having been more assimilable than their more recent counterparts.

A racialised component to immigrant phobia has lurked under the surface – when it has not been openly displayed. One of its principal sources is Eurocentrism, and the European conception and construction of Otherness involve the following logic:

> Paradigmatic Eurocentrism views putative European arrogance vis-à-vis non-Europeans by and large as understandable, if not ultimately justifiable. Indubitably acting as history's protagonists, Europe's elites naturally, if unconscionably, developed supercilious attitudes toward those for whom they paved the path of progress.[23]

Ayhan Kaya was blunter about the role played by racism in typecasting migrants: 'The way migrants and Muslims are recently being perceived in the

73

West takes me to suggest that the road from national purity and genius to racism is relatively direct.'[24] The explanation is straightforward: migrants are seen as challenging the purity of the state. In turn, popular views about migration have become 'discourses of danger' alienating migrant communities from the mainstream of majority society.

The construction of immigrant identity has increasingly entailed an association with someone of non-European background, a category that is racially and culturally loaded. One study found, predictably, that 'racial cues alter immigration opinion. Group cues (invoking ethnic identities/stereotypes) change beliefs about the severity of the immigration problem, and they trigger emotions (not beliefs about severity), which then drive opposition.'[25] Americans have felt more threatened by Latino than European immigration, and this perceived threat has triggered greater opposition to any type of immigration. In Europe it is the non-European migrant that triggers the chain reaction resulting in anti-immigration sentiment.

But there are caveats. The Sri Lankan writer and pioneering theorist of race Ambalavener Sivanandan regarded the new xenophobia emerging in Europe as 'bearing all the marks of the old racism without the genetic underpinnings. It is '"xeno" in form. It is a racism that is meted out to impoverished strangers even if they are white. It is xeno-racism.'[26] He contextualised this concept: 'Racism never stands still. It changes shape, size, contours, purpose, function, with changes in the economy, the social structure, the system and, above all, the challenges, the resistances, to that system.' An example of xenoracism – xeno in form, racist in content – that Sivanandan cited was British xenophobic attitudes towards migrants from other EU states, the largest group being made up of Poles. They were constructed as migrant strangers even though they were white and physically indistinguishable from their hosts.[27] The original aspect of Sivanandan's approach is that categories of Europeans can be targets of xeno-racism by other European groups.

The term 'migrant' contains a synthesising power allowing heterogeneous groups to be categorised together. These include people who were born, lived and obtained citizenship in a European country but remained identified as strangers. Thus, children of non-European migrants have been described as second-generation immigrants by *les français de souche* ('French with roots'). Again, racialisation lies just under the surface in developing such a typology.

Most of the time, the stranger is associated with someone from far away. As the Dutch sociologist Saskia Sassen has underscored, the stereotype of the immigrant as typically a person fleeing persecution and poverty in the developing world helps heighten fears of a 'mass invasion' of Europe.[28] She disputed the assumption that migration is a random event:

Migrations do not simply happen. They are produced. And migrations do not involve just any combination of countries. They are patterned . . . In brief, international migrations are produced, they are patterned, and they are embedded in specific historical phases. Acknowledging these traits opens up the immigration policy question beyond the familiar range of border control, family reunion, naturalisation and citizenship law.[29]

Patterns of labour migration are embedded in broader social, economic and political structures. They are shaped by the increasing transnationalisation of immigration policy making, especially among EU member states (as outlined in the previous chapter). They also encompass the categories of circular migrants, or sojourners who work in a country temporarily before returning home, and permanent settlers who remain in the receiving society.

The division of labour in which immigrants take on lower-skilled employment while the higher-paying skilled jobs are reserved for 'nationals' contributes to the racialised perspective. The racialisation (or ethnicisation) of the division of labour may be reflected in lower production costs brought about by the employment of cheap labour from Africa and Asia. Better paid 'nationals' not only look down on immigrant labour but ensure it is politically kept in check. The US sociologist Immanuel Wallerstein and Étienne Balibar term this 'racism typical of the era of "decolonisation"'. Its defining characteristic is that

it is a racism whose dominant theme is not biological heredity but the insurmountability of cultural differences, a racism which, at first sight, does not postulate the superiority of certain groups or people in relation to others but 'only' the harmfulness of abolishing frontiers, the incompatibility of life-styles and traditions.[30]

Fear of the foreign is, then, a particularly diffuse and complex phobia with different sources, rationales and pretexts. Economic insecurity is just one part of a deeper anxiety composed of a proprietary feeling that the material standards of a society are the achievement of its current members and are not to be shared with new arrivals. The economist Mario Nuti suggested that one of the sources of resistance to immigration was 'the refusal to allow current and future generations of outsiders to take part of the social capital that has been provided and paid for by society for the benefit of future generations of national children'.[31]

EUROPE'S MULTIPLE INSECURITIES

The multiple sources of anxiety about migrants elude holistic treatment. That they are not always based on tangible factors makes analysis even trickier. In a study of supporters of the Front National in France, Michel Wieviorka suggested that instead of 'objective insecurity' based on French workers' direct

75

contacts with immigrants, they experienced a general social malaise about and perception of crisis in the existing social order. They were concerned about a process of disintegration thought to be fracturing the traditional national community, and about a breakdown of national institutions.[32] This is similar to what Elisabeth Young-Bruehl, in *The Anatomy of Prejudices*, contended: 'For an obsessional prejudice to emerge as a commanding social force it must galvanise a widespread feeling in a society that the political institutions are corrupt.'[33] If not corrupt, then these institutions were seen at least as unresponsive to public opinion.

Europe's fears of its inner demons and its hatred of the strangers within are complex subjects with various consequences. The philosopher Cornelius Castoriadis disentangled the origins of these complexes by contending that hatred had two sides. One was the obverse side of self-love, or narcissism. European colonial power had inflated self-worth and self-ascribed moral superiority: in France it had been *la mission civilisatrice*, in Britain the white man's burden, and in Germany the belief that *am deutschen Wesen soll die Welt genesen* ('the German spirit shall heal the world'). Consequently affirmation of the value of white Europeans had led to emphasis on the non-value of non-white Europeans. The second side of hatred of others was what Castoriadis termed 'unconscious self-hatred'. The presence of the Other developed into a cipher for self-doubt and ontological insecurity.[34] One interpretation of this reasoning is as follows:

> the production of otherness within . . . animates the psyche with an elemental self-hatred that always lies in ambush even in the most extreme manifestations of primary narcissism (self-love). For Castoriadis, the radical hatred of the other, observed indicatively in racist affect, leans precisely on this outmaneuverable psychical self-hatred.[35]

More tangibly, European insecurity and self-hatred can be identified in attitudes to neighbouring states and regions. Fabrizio Tassinari, an expert on security issues at the Danish Institute for International Studies and author of *Why Europe Fears its Neighbors*, sets out this argument:

> Europeans are alarmed by their neighbors. Recent polls suggest that two out of three Europeans are concerned about Russia as an energy provider and about Moscow's behaviour towards its neighbours. About 70 percent in Germany and France believe that Turkey has such different values that it cannot be considered a Western country. Two-thirds of the population in Italy, the Netherlands, and Spain think that greater interaction between the Muslim and Western worlds constitutes a threat. Name one of the countries neighboring Europe, and it is quite likely that the average European citizen will at best associate it with gaping cultural or economic differences and at worst with the barbarians at the gate.[36]

To sum up, Europe's insecurity encompasses not just migrants, neighbouring countries and Islamic civilisation but parts of entire continents – Eurasia (led by Russia), north Africa and even the United States.

Fear of strangers is caused by factors ranging from our own personal anxieties about status and well-being to the nature of the society we live in. In theory, xenophobia may have little to do with immigrant numbers, racist ideologies or radical-right movements. Instead it may be 'based on prejudice which is fuelled by dissatisfaction with national governments, low confidence in national political leaders and institutions, and distrust in EU policies'.[37] Politics can be the cornerstone of this phenomenon: 'Xenophobia is the product of a deep "democratic disenchantment" fuelled by social distrust and economic pessimism.'[38] It is surprising how infrequently politicians and academics identify such disenchantment as explaining the rise of xenophobia today.

Zygmunt Bauman is an example of this trend. He blamed the spread of xenophobia less on politics and more on the replacement of structures of solidarity with new forms of competition:

> Xenophobia, the growing suspicion of a foreign plot and resentment of 'strangers' (mostly of emigrants, those vivid and highly visible reminders that walls can be pierced and borders effaced, natural effigies, asking to be burned, of mysterious globalizing forces running out of control), can be seen as a perverse reflection of desperate attempts to salvage whatever remains of local solidarity.[39]

The creation and enlargement of the EU has been shaped by the principle of economic competition and the free market, even if regional integration, harmonisation and unification have acted as the political mantras. Following Bauman, we can ask whether local solidarities that have crumbled under globalisation have resulted, together with democratic disillusion, in the recent increase in xenophobia.

EVIDENCE OF XENOPHOBIC ATTITUDES

Public opinion is capricious and can become focused on frivolous issues. But it can also reflect a calculated personal cost–benefit analysis of a policy issue that parts ways with the prescriptive norms advanced by public officials. Gary Freeman's cost–benefit analysis suggested who the principal beneficiaries of large-scale immigration were: employers in labour-intensive industries, those dependent on an unskilled workforce, and businesses that profit directly from population growth (real estate, construction and the like). By contrast,

> the immediate costs of immigration fall disproportionately on that minority of the population competing with immigrants for scarce jobs, housing, schools and government services, but these groups, the least advantaged in the society, lack the resources to make their voices heard.[40]

Public opinion may represent an attitudinal snapshot of those adversely affected by immigration. For Freeman, because immigration produces concentrated benefits and diffuse costs, those who benefit from immigration have greater incentives to organise than those who absorb its costs. In this context unease about immigration, reflected in public opinion, may represent a rational response to a cost–benefit calculus.

Survey results of public attitudes towards migrants may suggest whether rational considerations – as Freeman's logic would suggest – or irrational ones shape citizen responses. Eurobarometer surveys from 1988 to 1997 found low levels of xenophobia among Europeans: no more than 15 per cent of respondents asserted that the presence of people of other nationalities was disturbing to them personally. But a pecking order existed of desirable and undesirable migrant groups. Respondents generally favoured northern and southern Europeans and cared least for Turks, with north Africans and Asians not much more popular.[41]

Members of the European Parliament (MEPs) had similar views to the public on the subject of ethnic hierarchies. One study found that they too regarded Turks, north Africans and Asians as the least attractive migrants. National variations were apparent, however. While German MEPs identified eastern Europeans as least desirable, Greek MEPs classified Turks in this category.[42] In a 2007 survey, MEPs and EU officials both placed Turkey in the middle of a 'thermometer reading' that measured feelings towards others. 'Warm' feelings were registered towards the EU, cool feelings towards Iran.[43]

Explaining such ethnic preferences, Gallya Lahav underlined that 'elites in general preferred the more economically competitive, yet culturally more similar Eastern European immigrants to those from developing countries'. Those who supported less immigration from eastern Europe were more concerned with unemployment; those who believed immigration from the Third World should be restricted were more alarmed by racial differences.[44] A counterintuitive finding of one Eurobarometer survey was that no significant correlation existed between being unemployed and harbouring xenophobic attitudes.[45]

A cross-national study of discrimination in the EU published in 2008 asked respondents if they felt that discrimination on religious grounds was widespread or not. Forty-two per cent reported that it was fairly high or high in housing matters and 35 per cent in the educational sphere. The encouraging news was that less than one-fifth of EU citizens claimed that they had been discriminated against on any basis – religion, disability, age, gender, sexual orientation, race or ethnic origin, although the most common grounds cited for experiencing discrimination (by 19 per cent) were race or ethnic origin.[46]

There were significant variations in the country data. Almost one-third of

French respondents (31 per cent, the highest figure in the EU27 and a full 12 percentage points above the EU27 average) stated that they or someone close to them had experienced discrimination because of their race or ethnic origin. Twenty-seven per cent of respondents in Luxembourg and 26 per cent in Denmark also asserted this. At the other end of the scale were countries where less than one in ten respondents claimed to have personally experienced racial or ethnic discrimination. The lowest proportions were in Malta (5 per cent) followed by Lithuania and Poland (both 7 per cent).

A full 10 percentage points separated the average of felt discrimination in old compared to new member states. About two in ten citizens (21 per cent) from the EU15 stated that they had personally experienced racial or ethnic discrimination, compared to just over one in ten in the twelve new member states (11 per cent).

Religion and belief system as the basis for being discriminated against were cited comparatively infrequently, by just 11 per cent of respondents. Only sexual orientation was less frequently reported as the basis of felt discrimination. France again led countries in having the highest reported levels of personal experiences of discrimination based on religion or belief (19 per cent); this was 8 percentage points above the EU27 average. At the other end of the continuum, the lowest proportions of respondents reporting being discriminated against on the basis of religion or belief were in largely Orthodox Bulgaria (4 per cent) and Romania (5 per cent), as well as predominantly Catholic Lithuania and Italy (6 per cent each).[47]

It is significant that that two mainly Orthodox nations followed by two largely Catholic ones reported the least religious discrimination. Secular France, by contrast, had the highest reported level of discrimination based on religion or belief system. The presence of a large Muslim minority that may believe that French *laïcité* discriminates against Islam could be a contributing factor to the country's elevated level of felt discrimination. The notion that a secular state may contribute to greater felt religious discrimination than a confessional one runs counter to the received wisdom of EU elites. But it is a hypothesis that should not be dismissed.

The political scientists Richard Rose and Kenneth Newton suggested a different way to approach relations between, on the one hand, nationals of a country and, on the other, minority and migrant communities. Rather than use the concepts of fear, hatred, racism and discrimination, their comparative survey of social tensions in European societies published in 2010 listed the rank order of the perceived level of tensions along six different axes. First came perceived tensions between different racial and ethnic groups: 40 per cent of respondents claimed there were 'a lot' of tensions. The next three poles were clustered together: tensions between management and workers (32 per cent), between different religious groups (31 per cent) and between poor and rich (30 per cent). Tensions between old and young (18 per cent) and men and women (12 per cent) were significantly less marked.[48]

The study reported large differences between countries in the level of perceived tensions between ethnic and racial groups. At least half of the sample in the Czech Republic, France, Hungary, Italy and the Netherlands believed that racial and ethnic differences in their societies caused a lot of tension. Italians, as well as French and Dutch (again), most often identified high tension between religious groups in their countries (over 40 per cent of respondents). Significantly, in Europe's stronger economies, where Muslim immigrants are concentrated, higher levels of perceived racial or religious tension were recorded. Thus in the EU15 countries, where Muslims make up over 3 per cent of the population, 33 per cent of respondents claimed there was a lot of religious tension. In stark contrast, there was no significant flagging of religious tension in the new EU member states, where Muslims account for less than 0.1 per cent of the total population. Rose and Newton contended that the heightened sense of tension in societies where there were more Muslims was related to the extent to which the majority population perceived Muslims as aliens who are 'not like us'.[49]

It is difficult to make the case that sensing greater social tension when Muslims are present amounts to a form of discrimination. It is, as the authors of the report note, tied more closely to a sense of identity – who is like us and who is not. It may well be that perceived difference leads ultimately to differential and even discriminatory treatment of Muslims. The actual effects of fear are elusive to measure.

PATTERNS OF MIGRANT SETTLEMENT

Immigration became a politically salient issue in the 1970s. Apart from Europe's need for migrant labour to spur economic growth, the 1973 oil crisis set into motion population movements from countries adversely affected by the sharp increase in energy costs. Specialists adopted a wide range of approaches to study migration patterns. In 1975 the leading English art critic John Berger published *A Seventh Man*, an insightful and prescient profile of Europe's guest workers.[50] A decade later, in his best-selling *Ganz unten* ('Lowest of the Low'), German journalist Günter Walraff went under cover, as a Turkish guest worker, to expose the systematic exploitation of labour migrants in his country.[51] In France in turn, three years later, Julia Kristeva concluded, probably oversimplistically, that 'the foreigner is the one who works'. In her groundbreaking and introspective *Strangers to Ourselves*, she affirmed that 'you will recognise the foreigner in that he *still* considers work as a value'.[52]

Sympathetic, even sentimental reflections on guest workers by writers and artists have been offset by hard-hitting, candid assessments provided by social scientists. In his iconoclastic 1995 article, Gary Freeman described the insidious legacy of the guest worker era: general scepticism about state capacity to manage immigration policy, control borders and reconcile migration with national interests. Both public officials and average citizens shared the unease about migration trends.[53]

Since the turn of this century about three million immigrants have entered Europe legally each year. Diffuse reasons explain the increase in the size of the foreign-born population in individual European countries (see Table 3.1). The demographics of a number of European states – France, Britain, Portugal, Spain, Belgium, *inter alia* – have been profoundly shaped by their colonial past, in particular when migration from the periphery to the postcolonial metropole accelerated. The demographics of other European societies were shaped by processes of globalisation after the Cold War. Following the collapse of the Soviet bloc intra-European mobility rose as well: Italy and Greece, for instance, became homes for large numbers of eastern European migrants.

Table 3.1 Number of foreigners in select European states, 2005

State	Number	% population
Germany	6.7 million	8.8
France	4.0 million	8.0
United Kingdom	3.0 million	5.2
Spain	2.7 million	6.2
Italy	2.6 million	4.6
Switzerland	1.5 million	20.3
Belgium	900,000	8.6
Austria	810,000	9.7
Netherlands	690,000	4.2
Greece	550,000	5.2
Sweden	480,000	5.3
Portugal	430,000	4.1
Czech Republic	280,000	2.7
Denmark	270,000	5.0
Ireland	260,000	6.3
Norway	220,000	4.8
Luxembourg	180,000	39.0
Hungary	150,000	1.5
Finland	110,000	2.2

Source: Catherine Wihtol de Wenden, 'Demography, Immigration, Integration (First Part)', *European Issues* 111 (2008).

Patterns of ethnic settlement across Europe differ in many ways. Some immigrant populations are concentrated in particular states: 95 per cent of all Algerians and 70 per cent of all Tunisians living in Europe reside in France; two-thirds of all Turks in Europe live in Germany. Most Albanian migrants have chosen Italy or Greece for their host society. Some migrant groups, meanwhile, develop into major diaspora communities scattered across several countries. They become influential transnational networks in their own right, often independent of their country of origin. Diasporas establish economic, cultural, religious and familial ties across borders. There are approximately three million Turks in Europe – two million in Germany but also significant numbers in France, Belgium, Switzerland, Austria and Nordic states. There are half a million Moroccans in France, but they also represent either the largest or the second-largest foreign community in Spain, Italy and the Netherlands. In earlier decades this status was one most often held by 'fellow Europeans' – Italians and Yugoslavs.

Migration of ethnic kinfolk is another distinctive phenomenon. Two million *Aussiedler* – Germans who had lived outside the *Heimat* – returned to their homeland and acquired German citizenship after the fall of the Berlin Wall. About 350,000 members of the Turkish minority in Bulgaria returned to that country after having fled during an anti-Turkish campaign in the late communist period. Up to 30,000 Finns moved from Russia to Finland after the Cold War. Large numbers of Transylvanian Hungarians and Romanians in Hungary exchanged national homes after 1989.

Historically mobile groups became even more mobile as Europe liberalised border controls. The Roma community, making up 10 per cent of the population in Romania (two million) and Bulgaria (700,000), now travel to western European states. And nationals from distant lands – Sri Lankans, Pakistanis, Chechens – have established a significant presence in France, as have Filipinos in Italy.[54]

The migrant group in Europe receiving greatest attention over the last decade has been loosely connected Muslim communities. Their presence in Europe has accelerated exponentially (see Table 3.2): 'between 1950 and 2000, the number of Muslims in Western Europe rose from 800,000 to 15 million. It is now [in 2008] 20 million.'[55] At the start of 2011, there were just over 44 million Muslims, representing 6 per cent of the total population, in all of Europe (including Russia and Turkey).[56] These 'growth' and 'global' figures appear to be functions of immigration flows, but they are also products of net reproduction rates among longtime as well as recently settled Muslims in Europe. Writer John Bowen exposed the facile logic linking immigration growth to Muslim population increases in the public mind: 'Complaining of too many "immigrants" has been a relatively safe way of complaining of too much Islam.'[57]

One of the more polemical blogs documenting the status of Muslim com-

Table 3.2 Muslims in Europe

Country grouping	Number of Muslims (millions)		% total population	
	1982	2003	1982	2003
EU15	6.8	15.2	1.9	4.0
EU15 plus new EU member states	7.0	15.5	1.6	3.4
Other European states incl. Turkey and Russia	56.0	74.8	50.0	56.0
All European states incl. Turkey and Russia	62.9	90.3	11.6	15.0

Source: US Department of State, *Annual Report on International Religious Freedom*, *2003*; 1982 estimates from M. Ali Kettani, *Muslim Minorities in the World Today* (London: Mansell, 1986).

munities in Europe and apparent manifestations of discrimination against them belongs to Daniel Pipes.[58] A journalist and Middle East specialist at the Hoover Institution, he remarked on the rapid growth of Muslim populations in European cities (see Table 3.3): 'It is striking to note that many of the continent's largest cities – London, Paris, Berlin, Moscow – also have its largest Muslim populations; also, the capital cities are disproportionately represented. Also noteworthy is how, other than Marseilles, they are all northerly.' Pipes hazarded a guess about future growth: 'Given the proportionately higher influx into Sweden than other countries, I'd put my money on Malmö or Stockholm being the first west European city with a Muslim majority, with Moscow as a wild card.'[59]

In an eight-country survey whose results were reported in 2011, agreement with the statement 'There are too many Muslims in this country' ranged from 61 per cent in Hungary to between 49 and 42 per cent (in descending order) in Italy, Poland, Germany, Britain and the Netherlands, to 36 per cent in France and only 27 per cent in Portugal. Yet Portuguese respondents were most likely to agree that 'Islam is a religion of intolerance' (62 per cent) compared to under half in Britain and the Netherlands.[60] The study also combined six surveyed dimensions of prejudice – anti-immigrant attitudes, anti-Semitism, racism, anti-Muslim attitudes, sexism and homophobia – to arrive at a Group-Focused Enmity Index (GFE). Calculated as the mean value of the six individual GFE elements, it expressed the enmity's overall intensity. Here Hungary and Poland had significantly higher GFE ratings than the cluster made up of Italy, Germany, Britain and France, with the Netherlands lowest. The explanation for this hierarchy was straightforward: lower incomes had a statistically significant effect on higher GFE.[61]

Table 3.3 Estimated Muslim population in select European cities

Malmö	c. 25%
Marseilles	25%
Amsterdam	24%
Stockholm	20%
Brussels	17–20%
London	17%
Moscow	16–20%
Birmingham	14%
The Hague	14%
Copenhagen	13%
Aarhus	c. 10%
Antwerp	7%
Paris	7%
Berlin	6%
Hamburg	6%

Source: 'Muslim Population in European Cities', Islam in Europe website, 23 November 2007, at http://islamineurope.blogspot.com/2007/11/muslim-population-in-european-cities.html, accessed 26 January 2012.

Fear of the Muslim presence in Europe has become an issue that right-wing populist groups have dramatised and it is not always easy to distinguish fact-based accounts from normative, even polemical ones. It is a small step from reflecting on which European city will be the first to have a Muslim majority population to speculating about the consequences this will have. As Ayhan Kaya observed, it has become commonplace that 'Muslims are increasingly represented . . . as members of a "precarious transnational society", in which people only want to "stone women", "cut throats", "be suicide bombers", "beat their wives" and "commit honour crimes"'.[62] In some respects, this is a caricature of a caricature, providing a pastiche of Islamophobe thinking.

The fallout, nevertheless, from the immanent fear of Islamisation of Europe is that it feels a need to protect itself from 'the enemy within' and seeks to relocate the origins of the threat to beyond national borders. In part *raison d'état* explains why Islamophobic narratives come into being:

> The fear of migrants and Muslims prevalent in the West cannot have material sources; it is in fact a constructed and fabricated fear, serving the interests of nation-states which are no longer equipped with the tools to redistribute justice and peace relatively equally.[63]

There is uncertainty among European publics over how to respond to political successes recorded by Muslims living on the continent. In 2009 the first 'veiled' elected representative in Europe, a young woman of Turkish background, took her seat in the Brussels regional assembly. She had gained much of her support from the 30 per cent of the Brussels regional population that is Muslim. Wearing a headscarf to the swearing-in ceremony was controversial enough. But those who insisted that this was in keeping with Belgian multiculturalism nevertheless found a reason to object to her politics: it lay in her denial that Turks had committed genocide against Armenians in 1915.[64]

The interwoven complexity of demographic and political trends across Europe evokes both uncertainty and insecurity. Sociologist Adrian Favell posed this existential question about Europe: what will its identity look like in a decade or two? In speculating about its future, he felt compelled to reference Europe's Muslim populations. Identity would hinge on

> whether or not Moroccans and Turks – by far the largest immigrant populations in Europe, and the closest 'ethnic' neighbours – are also mobile Europeans by the logic of regional integration. The politics currently do not look good: Europe may choose to heed nativism and treat its Moroccans and Turks in the same dismal fashion in which the US treats its Central American 'alien' workforce.[65]

In other words, for Favell, these two groups are likely to be denied the geographic and occupational mobility that citizens of new EU member states have recently come to enjoy. A 'two-track Europe' originating along the axis of migration policies – not economic ones – is, then, a distinct possibility.

INTEGRATION CHOICES AND MIGRANT STRATEGIES

The integration of migrants is an issue distinct from immigration policy.[66] Migrants arriving in Europe with many different collective identities are presented with a set of norms on integration that they are under pressure to adhere to. Accepting these norms involves choices about future identity. Five sets of alternatives confronting migrants seeking to adapt to EU norms can be identified.

First, the collective identities that migrants arrive with are likely to undergo mutation in Europe. Whether the changes are profound or shallow depends to a large degree on the strength of migrant group solidarity. Receiving societies expect that strangers' identities should become less associated with the country of origin as they integrate into that new society. How quickly this occurs depends on differences in integration policy from one country to another. Chapters 5 and 6 will describe how the French model calls for comprehensive and rapid identity transformation when compared to the multicultural approach adopted in Germany.

Migrants also have to choose whether their identities will remain coherent or become fragmented. Which alternative is preferred is shaped by the degree of unity within a group. Host European societies typically encourage a shift from coherent sending-society identities to hybrid, fragmented ones that reflect European values of diversity. Identity coherence is difficult to maintain for migrant groups seeking upward mobility in new receiving societies.

Migrant identities, like those of the receiving society itself, can be inclusive or exclusive, determined by the type of gatekeeping applied towards prospective members. Accordingly the third choice arriving groups have is whether to keep their community homogeneous or become more inclusive and open up to other groups, even at the cost of a loss in cultural and religious uniformity.

Choice four is about whether an open or closed identity will characterise a migrant community. Receiving societies generally pressure groups to display greater cognitive reflexivity and questioning of community identity. They are more likely to object to an uncritical dogmatic assertion of it. Yet some migrant communities, especially Muslim ones in contemporary Europe, are perceived as uncompromising in their retention of traditional religious practices and rejection of secular values.

The final choice is whether migrants should engage in cooperative or assertive behaviour when negotiating group interests with non-members, specifically, with host society representatives. In many ways the willingness to adopt a cooperative strategy is the crucial litmus test that outsider groups need to pass if they wish to be accepted in their new country.[67]

We can hypothesise, then, that migrant communities striving to maintain a collective identity by prioritising rootedness, coherence, gatekeeping, rigidity and resoluteness are likely to engender hostility in host society members. Not adhering to the informal European normative regime is likely to elicit a xenophobic backlash among some sections of the host society. So it is no coincidence that the 'loyalty' of Muslim communities to their new homes in Europe is under scrutiny. Often they are stereotyped as having a deep-seated, homogeneous, exclusionary, inflexible and combative identity. Islamophobic attitudes are based in part on the perception that on the five identity-and-integration questions they are faced with, Muslim minorities make politically incorrect choices.

The migration specialist Christina Boswell has stressed that 'much of the recent literature on international migration has focused on patterns of social interaction between migrants and communities of origin'.[68] So far I have been theorising about interactions between migrant and receiving communities. I noted that the way migrants negotiate their own group identity in their new society helps determine the reaction, positive or negative, of the majority. Boswell has proposed three distinct theoretical approaches to study the character of intra-group interactions.

The first framework is cultural embeddedness. It identifies the distinct cultural norms and beliefs in the community of origin that shape emigrants' subsequent social ties. Ideas about the desirability of migration and which types of people should migrate are pivotal here. Expectations about loyalty, solidarity and mutual support among people from the same place of origin are significant, too. As a result, migration decisions

> cannot be explained in terms of generalisable features common to all individuals (rationality, utility maximisation), but emerge as a response to quite specific historical and cultural conditions. These can evolve into a culture of migration, a set of norms and beliefs that influence patterns of cross-national ties.[69]

The second approach entails transnationalism, understood as the retention of social, economic, political and symbolic bonds between emigrants and their communities of origin. Transnational interactions often turn emigrants into bilingual residents of two countries. They develop dual lives. The influence of the socio-cultural characteristics of sending communities is balanced by the social and political conditions obtaining in receiving societies. The transnational model holds that the cultural baggage of migrants may be less of a factor in determining their status in a new society than the imperatives that that society imposes on them.

The third approach is centred on migrant networks. Interactions between emigrants and communities of origin are the product of individual calculations of costs and opportunities. The breadth of migrant networks adjusts in tandem with changes in opportunities in the place of destination. Rational choice theory can explain why migrants retain established social ties and build new networks. Social ties are utilitarian, based on a rational calculation of expected costs and benefits and an interest in utility maximisation. In turn, migrant networks serve as a set of social connections that can reduce the costs of migration and integration.

Network theory has become an attractive framework for explaining patterns of social interaction among migrants. The retention of ties with fellow emigrants helps ease economic and social integration in the receiving society, thereby reducing the costs of migration. Networks left behind in the place of origin can channel investment, diffuse risk and even prepare for a migrant's eventual return home. Ties are determined, therefore, not by shared norms but by the opportunity structure in the place of destination. In short, as Douglas Massey and his collaborators have contended, 'networks make international migration extremely attractive as a strategy for risk diversification or utility maximisation'.[70]

In the case studies of France and Germany we will see in greater detail how host society reactions to Muslim communities are shaped by their intra-group interactions. But one problem to be noted at the outset is the possibility that, however strategically sophisticated the choices made by

Table 3.4 Population of Turkish descent, circa 2000

Germany	2,470,000
Netherlands	300,000
France	220,000
Austria	180,000
Belgium	110,000

Source: Maurice Crul and Hans Vermeulen, 'Immigration, Education, and the Turkish Second Generation in Five European Nations: A Comparative Study', in Craig A. Parsons and Timothy M. Smeeding (eds), *Immigration and the Transformation of Europe* (Cambridge: Cambridge University Press, 2006), p. 237.

Muslim migrants may be, they may nevertheless come under attack from the receiving society. Pursuing cultural embeddedness opens up migrants to the charge of a refusal to integrate. If they emphasise transnational interaction they run the risk of being seen as reflecting divided loyalties. Networking so as to maximise benefits and minimise risks can be stigmatised as blatant opportunism. We will see whether specific Muslim communities and different national differences matter. Do Maghrebi communities in France prefer cultural embeddedness, leading to their social exclusion? Does Turks' steadfastness of opting for transnational networks in Germany, or elsewhere in Europe (see Table 3.4), produce a backlash that raises questions about their loyalty? Are migrant communities in Britain motivated by a personal cost–benefit analysis that places in doubt the cohesion of British society? In short, have diaspora identities of immigrant minorities and the supporting institutions they construct help promote or impede their integration and acceptance? Or is it a case of 'damned if they do, damned if they don't'? Migrant communities are never sure of obtaining a sense of belonging to their receiving societies.

How gatekeeping functions

Anti-immigration sentiments have been expressed in different ways since the guest worker programmes of the 1960s were launched. Extensive empirical research has been devoted to measuring the attitudes of citizens in receiving countries to migration. Here we focus on recent research, though many of the findings reflect continuity with earlier results.

A key research objective has been to explore the connection between the increase in immigrant numbers and economic growth. One possible answer was provided by the global economic recession that emerged in 2008. The argument that increased migration fuels economic growth was refuted: continued high immigration numbers did not stave off recession. It seems more plausible to contend that both the recent economic decline and earlier economic growth were unconnected to immigration trends.

A major study of pre-economic-crisis attitudes towards immigrants in Europe was published in 2007. The author, Eva Green, contextualised the issue the following way:

> Some nations have a long history of immigration, which has resulted from both colonial and labour importing policies. Other countries, in turn, have remained fairly homogenous until recently ... Hostile and xenophobic attitudes towards immigrants remain common, notwithstanding the context of expansion of the European Union to the East, and harmonizing of immigration and asylum regulations within the Union.[71]

Green pointed to 'new more covert and acceptable ways of expressing xenophobia and prejudice. Defence of traditional values is one of the key components of these new subtle and symbolic forms of prejudice.'[72] Support for a mythic national identity is a common way of trying to make foreigners unwelcome.

We can identify two general levels at which European migration gatekeeping operates. The first, individual level is based on an applicant's language and working skills. The second level is categorical, where race and religion serve as the salient factors. Individual immigration criteria are more inclusive than categorical ones since they are colour blind and assume that with time all immigrants can become like their hosts. Green pointed out that individual-level factors betray a subtle form of prejudice because migrants are expected to adopt host country values and to conform to its practices. Expectations of assimilation can reflect expressions of prejudice. Thus 'technical' considerations operating at the individual level may result in a selection process that favours well-educated, high-status, Westernised immigrants.

Using European Social Survey (ESS) data from 2003, Green ranked the importance to European respondents of particular characteristics of migrants that favoured or hindered their admission to the receiving country.[73] Forty-one per cent of respondents were classified as individualist gatekeepers: they endorsed individual entry and expulsion criteria while rejecting categorical ones. Another 36 per cent were strict gatekeepers who opted for a categorical basis for excluding migrants. The remaining 23 per cent were lenient gatekeepers who did not emphasise either set of criteria. For Green, this typology approximated the distinction between subtle racists, bigots and egalitarians.[74] In summary,

> the notions of blatant and subtle prejudice are helpful in conceptualizing categorical and individual immigration criteria. The endorsement of categorical criteria is explicitly xenophobic or prejudiced, since it is directed towards the rejection of entire categories of people, for example, non-Whites. Categorical entry criteria

are particularly harsh because they are absolute in nature, they imply absence of individual control, and they leave no option to satisfy the required criteria. The support for these criteria is thus akin to traditional or blatant prejudice.[75]

When the type of gatekeeping was matched with a particular region of Europe, western European countries such as the Netherlands and Germany fitted the individualist gatekeeper cell as fairly liberal on migrant entry and expulsion. Britain, Belgium and France were slightly more anti-categorical than categorical, and slightly more individualistic than collectivist. As might be expected, the Scandinavian countries were clustered together as lenient, anti-categorical gatekeepers. By contrast, the strict gatekeeper cell, endorsing categorical criteria, encompassed a number of eastern and southern European states: Poland, Italy, Spain and Portugal in particular, followed by the more individualist Greece, Hungary, Czech Republic and Slovenia.[76]

The endorsement of stricter gatekeeping in eastern and southern Europe was partly explained by their recent experience of shifting from emigrant, labour-exporting nations to receiving societies. Green added that 'illegal immigration is also greater in [countries in] Southern and Eastern Europe due to their position on the borders of Europe'. Finally,

> restrictive immigration attitudes emerge as a result of competition for scarce resources. The subordinate low-status position of South and East Europe compared to West and North Europe in terms of wealth, for example, could thus explain a greater degree of strict gatekeeping.[77]

Another major quantitative study utilising ESS data about immigration was carried out by John Sides and Jack Citrin. Published in 2007, it concluded that opposition to immigration was motivated by one of two reasons: an interests-based one ('immigrants are taking my job'), or a values-based one related to national and political identities ('immigrants are taking my country').[78] Self-interest and fear, as Napoleon Bonaparte had proclaimed, were motivators of men.

The authors examined the preferred qualities that people in receiving societies wanted in immigrants. Respondents were asked to choose from among three factors: (1) they should have close family already living here, (2) they should be able to speak the national language and (3) they should be white. Language skills were deemed most important and, across all surveyed countries, white racial background was considered unimportant. Swedish respondents were less insistent on the need for any of the criteria to be present while the Greek sample pressed most for the presence of all three.[79]

Citrin and Sides also addressed the pivotal question of why a gap existed between citizen and elite attitudes towards immigrants. As Gary Freeman had highlighted, 'the central puzzle of the politics of immigration in liberal democracies is the large and systematic gap between public opinion and public policy'.[80] Citrin and Sides did not examine the validity of the 'capitalist conspiracy' argument that immigrants keep labour costs down. Their analysis centred instead on the weight that the better educated sections of society, which generally are supportive of continuing immigration, carried with political elites:

> The effect of education suggests one reason why immigration policies tend to be more permissive than the public is itself: if educated people are simultaneously more supportive of immigration and more likely to participate in politics, then the 'signal' being received by policy makers may be skewed somewhat toward opening the 'golden door'. The effects of both [cultural and religious] measures of homogeneity, especially when compared to the notable but less robust effects of financial insecurity, suggest that attitudes toward immigrants depend more on 'symbolic' attitudes toward cultural unity than the material circumstances of respondents.[81]

The authors' conclusion confirmed that in most countries a disjunction had emerged between public opinion and the dominant view of political elites, which was more favourably disposed towards immigration.[82] A significant corollary of this finding was that hostility towards immigration expressed by survey respondents had little impact on immigration policy since citizens were not the decision makers.

Further evidence of the more liberal orientations of better-educated social strata was furnished by a different comparative study of Europe. This one reported that better-educated respondents with higher occupational skills were significantly less racist than other groups and placed greater value on cultural diversity. These respondents also believed that immigration generates benefits for the host economy as a whole.[83]

Another cross-national study concluded, conversely, that individuals from lower education strata, occupational groups and income levels opposed immigration most. It found that the better the economic conditions prevailing in a European country, the less its residents were disposed to exclude immigrants from it. In addition, the degree to which a country had ethnic diversity was correlated with attitudes to migrants, so that ethnically heterogeneous societies exhibited stronger resistance to migrants. Finally, the higher the number of asylum seekers, the stronger the resistance to refugees.[84] This study lent support to the theory of ethnic competition, which holds that perception of ethnic threat shapes attitudes.

What factors may contribute to resolving the political divisiveness over immigration? Several large-scale studies have concluded that cultural integration occurs most smoothly when the acquisition of citizenship is held up as a realistic possibility for immigrants. The logic is that migrants have an incentive to absorb the dominant values of receiving societies when they are sure there is a concrete payback – citizenship.[85] Accordingly, when this process of integration is perceived to be occurring, the expectations of the public are met and, as a consequence, conflict over immigration is likely to wane. But if integration appears to founder, then many European countries, especially those with various anti-immigrant political parties, and a proportional representation electoral system that makes it easier for them to win seats, will continue to experience significant political conflict about their huddled masses.[86]

In sum, demographic gatekeeping in Europe is influenced by an array of calculations going beyond the issue of race and religion. Ways of integrating migrants affect them directly, of course, but they also shape popular attitudes within receiving societies, sometimes in counterintuitive ways. For example, a study of citizen attitudes in Japan found that advocates of deeper immigrant assimilation were far from xenophobic: 'Japanese people who want immigrant assimilation are more supportive than multiculturalists are of increasing immigration and giving equal rights to immigrants.'[87] It is within this complex, sometimes contradictory set of attitudes that Islamophobia is situated.

NATIONAL DIFFERENCES IN ATTITUDES TO IMMIGRATION

European societies, and democracies generally, differ in their approaches to immigration. Images of the national self may play a significant role in determining immigration policy. One study on twenty-five Western countries reported that 'shared conceptions of the polity, whether as a multinational state or as an ethnic "nation", appear to remain a significant factor in how these democracies treat their resident aliens'.[88] The test of good treatment was, in this study, whether non-citizens were enfranchised locally.

Election results indicating rising support for radical right parties in different countries are another political indicator highlighting different responses to immigration. They complement the numerous cross-national academic studies mapping differences in national publics' attitudes to migrants. Variance in the capricious, often irrational nature of immigration phobia can be the *explanandum* for contrasting party performances and electoral outcomes. Let us consider some of the principal findings from this literature.[89]

We noted that ethnically diverse societies oppose immigration more than homogeneous ones; this is largely due to exposure to ethnically based competition. Diversity does not invariably lead to virtuous attitudes, therefore, and developing into a diverse society is itself a contested goal. One study on the desirability of religious diversity reported that European countries were evenly split between those for and against it. Of the EU states surveyed, France gave least support for religious homogeneity; Poland and Greece lent most support for it. By contrast, cultural homogeneity was endorsed by most of the twenty European countries surveyed. Respondents in eastern (the Czech Republic and Poland) and southern (above all Greece but also Portugal) European countries offered the highest level of backing for cultural homogeneity.[90]

An external factor – whether migrants come from richer or poorer countries – also differentiated European publics' attitudes towards immigration. ESS data from 2002/3 for twenty-one countries indicated that 'people coming from wealthy countries are more warmly welcomed than those coming from poor countries',[91] although the degree of support varied, from 43 per cent in Portugal to 79 per cent in Sweden. Correspondingly, support decreased in almost all countries when immigrants came from European countries that were poorer than the receiving society. The continuum again extended from Portugal to Sweden: support for such immigration was just 39 per cent in the former but 87 per cent in the latter. Swedes thus proved to be an anomaly, approving of in-migration of poorer Europeans more than of richer Europeans.

When attitudes to immigration from poorer non-European countries were measured, support declined everywhere other than in Germany, Italy and the United Kingdom. The overall pattern showed that Sweden represented 'the only country whose citizens express a preference for people from poorer countries. Conversely, Italian preference for citizens of wealthy countries is more unadorned.'[92] In their favour, the 'wealth bias' of Italian respondents was not based on race: 'Italians and Portuguese do not notice any difference whatsoever between citizens from wealthy European or wealthy non-European countries.'[93]

In judging immigrants, European respondents attached the greatest importance to their willingness to adopt 'the way of life in the country'. The next most important criterion was more utilitarian: possessing work skills 'needed in the country'. One of the least important qualities for European respondents was 'coming from countries with a Christian background'. Again, significant differences were found across European publics. Citizens in Germany and Sweden attached much more importance to the immigrant's disposition to adapt to 'the way of life in the country' than those in south-western European countries.[94] A sense of civic- – perhaps even civilisational – pride informed these social-market and social-democratic countries. Alternatively, normative and moral smugness might have swayed these respondents to expect outsiders to adapt to their way of life.

We return to the question of dissonance between citizen attitudes and elite-driven policy. The survey of European attitudes to immigration found that respondents in two predominantly Catholic societies, Italy and Spain, paid little importance to the religious background, Christian or otherwise, of migrants. Nevertheless Italy has established a generous quota for Filipino migrants, who are largely Roman Catholics. Would-be immigrants from Albania, Morocco and Tunisia, on the other hand, have to compete for a limited number of residency visas. Similarly the Spanish state has adopted admission policies that favour people from countries with Roman Catholic traditions such as the Philippines: Filipinos may apply for Spanish citizenship after living in the country for just two years. By contrast, Moroccans are required to fulfil a ten-year residency period before becoming eligible for citizenship even though northern Morocco was a more recent Spanish colony. As the authors of this study conclude, 'despite the nominal secular character of the states concerned, the Roman Catholic Church has a strong influence – either direct or indirect – on their immigration policies'.[95] A corollary may be inferred that Muslims become relegated to second-class immigration candidates.

Attitudes to Turks are significant for at least three reasons: (1) Turkey has applied for EU membership, (2) its diaspora in Europe is extensive and (3) it constitutes a Muslim-majority country. The degree of hostility towards minorities, migrants and Muslims may be captured in European perceptions of Turks. In 2008 feelings towards Turkey (where 100 represented very warm feelings, 50 neutral feelings and 0 very cold feelings) varied from just 42 on the part of the EU public to 52 for MEPs and 59 for EU officials. Conversely, the thermometer reading of Turks' feelings towards other Europeans in 2008 remained generally cool, at 33 (though up 7 from 2007).

With regard to Turkey joining the EU, 42 per cent of the European public called it neither a good or a bad thing. By contrast, 60 per cent of European Commission officials viewed it as a good thing. MEPs were split between seeing it as good or bad. As for citizens, 57 per cent of European respondents agreed that Turkey has such different values that it is not really part of the West. The national breakdown was 76 per cent of Germans, 68 per cent of French, and 61 per cent of Italians. A majority of Turkish respondents (55 per cent) also agreed that Turkey's values make it not part of the West.[96] In sum, Europeans and Turks themselves are divided about the supposed civilisational divide between them.

ANTI-IMMIGRANT POLITICAL PARTIES

When parties with xenophobic agendas become a force in a country's parliament, help shape its legislation and even take part in a governing coalition, they may attempt to fuse state nationalism with discriminatory and exclusionary values. Within the EU, nationalist and/or anti-immigrant movements have grown in influence in the first decade of the new century. Cases include Austria, Belgium, Denmark and the Netherlands in the west, and the Czech Republic, Hungary and Slovakia in the east. Radical right-wing parties have emerged, even in Sweden, and they emphasise the urgency of defending national culture and traditions, in this way seeking to raise an emotional backlash against foreigners. 'Immigration remains tinged with cultural or societal considerations that correlate with more affective than instrumental evaluations of policy preferences.' Indeed 'the primacy of cultural values is particularly pertinent to issues related to identity, such as immigration, asylum, and citizenship'.[97]

Highlighting the centrality of culture is consistent with findings from the political scientist Ronald Inglehart's massive empirical study showing how culture underpins societies which have achieved freedom and modernisation.[98] It is no surprise that identity politics have assumed a higher profile in newer democracies, as they are associated with an expansion of freedom. But even established democracies have faced risks when creating space for identity politics. Especially when it involves migrant groups, 'identity is the dangerous area where the [integration] project can destruct if it challenges the nations in an overly confrontational manner'.[99] Right-wing parties have often framed such challenges as threats to the organic existence of the nation.

In his search for an antecedent cause for the rise of ultranationalist movements, Wayne Cornelius, an American specialist on Mexico, and his co-authors cautioned against unmanaged immigration even if courts backed rights-based immigrant claims. 'Judicial activism [on immigration] has helped spawn a plethora of political parties . . . of the extreme right.' The authors pointed to examples from Europe: the German skinhead movement of the 1990s represented a backlash against alleged judicial backing for Turkish immigrant claims, while in France Jean-Marie Le Pen benefited politically from being fined in 2005 on a charge of inciting hatred towards immigrants.[100]

One comparative study (which excluded eastern Europe) focused on how political parties exploited voters' xenophobic attitudes for electoral gain. Beginning in the 1970s, right-wing politicians capitalised on voter resentment of ethnic minorities to win legislative seats. They stirred up citizen xenophobia to advance another agenda as well – to limit welfare programmes for all disadvantaged groups, migrant or not. By targeting voters who held conservative views on race and immigration but were liberal on economic issues, right-wing parties were able to piece together a regressive social agenda. One study was able to quantify this effect: if all voters held non-racist views, liberal and conservative parties alike would have pushed for levels of income redistribution 10 to 20 per cent higher than they did under current levels of xenophobia.[101]

This raises the question of how xenophobic contagion may spread from single-issue right-wing parties to established mainstream ones, thereby crossing what has been called the *cordon sanitaire* between the two. In 2005 the European Commission against Racism and Intolerance warned that xenophobia as a 'type of argument is no longer confined to the sphere of extremist political parties, but is increasingly contaminating mainstream political parties'.[102]

Identifying a party's stance on a subject like immigration is not as straightforward as it may appear. Several different approaches can be taken, not always leading to consistent findings.[103] One simple way is to take what parties say their policy is, for example in their manifestos, at face value. Another approach is to look at how parties behave, for example, how their members vote in the legislature. Further insight into policy preferences can be gained by conducting surveys of party leaders, members and supporters.

An innovative framework was developed by Kenneth Benoit and Michael Laver. They asked academic experts on particular countries to rate the policy orientations of parties in their country of specialisation. Employing this method, in 2002–3 387 political parties in forty-seven countries were given ratings by these experts. These expert responses were then located on scales that measured thirty-seven policy dimensions.[104] Specialists evaluated the importance of a particular policy dimension to each party on a twenty-point scale. Looking at the specific dimension of immigration policy, experts assessed whether parties supported the full integration of immigrants and asylum seekers into their societies (which was assigned a score of 1), or supported returning immigrants to their countries of origin (given a maximum score of 20). A high score on the salience of immigration combined with a high score on removing immigrants signified a party strongly committed to an anti-immigration policy.

With few exceptions, at the time of the survey (2002) economic policies (taxes/spending, regulation/deregulation) were given the highest salience scores in most western European countries. Immigration policy was ranked of highest importance in Belgium, Denmark, Luxembourg and the Netherlands (Table 3.5, column 2). The highest mean xenophobic score for all parties combined in a particular country was recorded in Denmark (column 1).

Benoit and Laver identified a number of party-specific findings. The most anti-immigrant parties in western Europe were Vlaams Belang (Flemish Interest) in Belgium and the Nationaldemokratische Partei Deutschlands (National Democratic Party) in Germany (column 4). The largest vote-getting party that had the highest xenophobic rating (column 3) was Switzerland's Schweizerische Volkspartei (Swiss People's Party). Anti-immigrant parties that made up part of governing coalitions at the time of the experts' survey were found in Austria, Greece, Italy, Malta and Switzerland. By contrast, the largest vote-getting parties having the lowest xenophobic scores were found in Spain and Sweden.

These results tell us little about the status of parties emphasising explicitly anti-Muslim programmes. Campaign rhetoric, slogans and posters would need to be examined for the frequency of anti-Muslim references. Benoit and

Table 3.5 Experts' ratings of importance of immigration policy, support for repatriating immigrants and anti-immigrant political parties in western European states, 2002

State	Mean score on issue	Rank in importance	Score of party with most votes	Party with highest score
Austria	14.0	2	13.6 (ÖVP, Austrian People's Party)	18.5 (**FPÖ, Freedom Party of Austria**)
Belgium	14.1	1	12.9 (VLD, Flemish Liberals and Democrats)	19.8 (VB, Flemish Block)
Cyprus	11.9	6	7.5 (AKEL, Progressive Party of Working People)	14.8 (NEO)
Denmark	15.7	1	15.1 (Venstre, Left)	19.4 (DF, Danish People's Party)
Finland	10.9	9	12.3 (KESK, Centre Party)	18.8 (PS, True Finns)
France	13.7	3	12.4 (RPR, Rally for the Republic)	19.3 (FN, National Front)
Germany	14.1	2	7.7 (SPD, Social Democratic Party) / 14.6 (CDU/CSU, Christian Democratic Union/Christian Social Union)	19.8 (NPD, National Democratic Party)
Great Britain	13.3	5	9.0 (Labour Party)	13.8 (Conservative Party)
Greece	13.5	4	14.6 (ND, New Democracy)	14.6 (ND, New Democracy)
Iceland	8.1	5	9.6 (**XD, Independence Party**)	9.6 (**XD, Independence Party**)
Ireland (Rep. of)	11.6	6	14.7 (**Fianna Fáil**)	14.7 (**Fianna Fáil**)
Italy	14.3	2	14.4 (**Forza Italia, Forward Italy**)	19.3 (Lega Nord, Northern League)
Luxembourg	15.0	1	14.5 CSV (Christian Social People's Party)	17.5 (ADR, Alternative Democratic Reform Party)
Malta	8.1	8	14.0 (**PN, Nationalist Party**)	14.0 (**PN, Nationalist Party**)

Table 3.5 (continued)

State	Mean score on issue	Rank in importance	Score of party with most votes	Party with highest score
Netherlands	14.0	1	11.4 (CDA, Christian Democratic Appeal)	18.3 (LPF, Pim Fortuyn List)
Northern Ireland	9.1	8	15.4 (DUP, Democratic Unionist Party)	15.4 (DUP, Democratic Unionist Party)
Norway	12.7	6	9.3 (Arbeiderpartiet, Labour Party)	19.1 (FrP, Progress Party)
Portugal	13.0	6	12.2 (**PSD, Social Democratic Party**)	15.3 (**CDS-PP, Democratic and Social Centre – People's Party**)
Spain	14.3	4	7.4 (PSOE, Spanish Socialist Workers' Party)	16.6 (PP, People's Party)
Sweden	12.4	6	7.4 (SAP, Social Democratic Workers' Party)	11.0 (Moderata Samlingspartiet, Moderate Coalition Party)
Switzerland	14.7	4	18.8 (**SVP, Swiss People's Party**)	19.7 (Schweizer Demokraten, Swiss Democrats)
Turkey	9.5	9	10.4 (AKP, Justice and Development Party)	15.9 (MHP, Nationalist Movement Party)

Source: Kenneth Benoit and Michael Laver, *Party Policy in Modern Democracies* (Abingdon: Routledge, 2006). Compiled from Appendix B, pp. 178–271. Anti-immigrant right-wing parties that were in government at the time the research was carried out are listed in bold font.

Laver did not extend their research to the study of xenophobic parties in post-communist states but instead introduced a different set of policy dimensions which produced counterintuitive results. Nationalism, often seen as a major problem in central and eastern Europe, was ranked the most important policy dimension only in Bosnia – a fragile state held together with the assistance of Western peacekeepers, not a common identity. Nowhere in the region was religion ranked highest. These findings did not necessarily contradict Cas Mudde's more pessimistic evaluation of eastern European xenophobia published a few years later.[105] But they do suggest that many observers have exaggerated the salience of religious and nationalist politics in the region.

How have right-wing politics changed since these findings were recorded in 2002? The most important development is that anti-immigrant parties have increased in electoral strength in many western European states. In Denmark after the 2001 parliamentary elections the Dansk Folkeparti (Danish People's Party) became the third largest party and was pivotal in supporting the governing conservative–liberal coalition. In three subsequent elections it maintained a 12–14 per cent share of the popular vote, though it lost parliamentary influence in 2011 when a Social Democrat-led coalition formed the government. Swiss elections have reflected a similar pattern: the anti-immigrant Schweizerische Volkspartei captured 27–29 per cent of the national vote in the three elections between 2003 and 2011 and has been in the governing coalition.

National elections held in Austria in 2008 led to significant gains by two far-right parties, the Freiheitliche Partei Österreichs (Austrian Freedom Party) and the Bündnis Zukunft Österreich (Alliance for Austria's Future) (whose leader, Jörg Haider, was killed in a car accident a short time later). In neighbouring Hungary, the far-right party Jobbik (The Better One) won 17 per cent of the vote in the first round of the 2010 parliamentary elections and ended up with the third most seats. Anti-Semitic and anti-Roma, it was the radical face of the right, whose main standard bearer, Fidesz, which also embraced Magyar nationalism, won a two-thirds parliamentary majority. In the Netherlands, the Partij voor de Vrijheid (Party for Freedom), campaigning on an explicitly anti-Islamic platform – its leader, Geert Wilders, had even promised to ban the Qur'an in the country – made major gains in 2010 national and regional elections.

Also in 2010 the Sverigedemokraterna (Sweden Democrats), recommending voluntary repatriation of immigrants, won twenty seats in the Riksdag. They were subsequently instrumental in defeating several key pieces of legislation proposed by the governing coalition by voting together with the left-of-centre parliamentary bloc. In 2011 it was the turn of the anti-immigrant populist Perussuomalaiset (True Finns) party to make a dramatic electoral breakthrough: they won thirty-nine seats and captured nearly 20 per cent of the vote – improving their support over their previous showing by fifteen per cent. The True Finns became the largest opposition party in the Finnish parliament.

In a number of respects Italy presents a special case of anti-immigrant politics. National elections held in 2008 led to the return to power of Silvio Berlusconi for a third time. His right-wing Popolo della Libertà (People of Freedom) party was allied with the Northern League (Lega Nord), which supported anti-immigration policies. For a decade Berlusconi, caught in a number of controversies, enjoyed a special place in European anti-Islamic discourse. Just two weeks after the 9/11 attacks, while most other Western leaders were still cautious about blaming Islam for inspiring the terror, the Italian leader was outspoken. On a trip to Germany he asserted 'the superiority of our civilisation which . . . guarantees respect for human rights and religion'. He added that 'this respect certainly does not exist in the Islamic countries'.[106] In 2008, while completing the so-called Berlusconi IV government, the prime minister appointed the controversial Northern League politician Roberto Calderoli as a cabinet minister. Calderoli had courted controversy in 2006 when he wore a T-shirt emblazoned with one of the Prophet Muhammad Danish cartoons. When Italy defeated France in the 2006 World Cup final, he inveighed that France had 'sacrificed its identity for results by fielding blacks, Muslims and Communists'.[107] After the 2009 Swiss referendum rejection of further minaret building, Calderoli announced: 'Yes to church towers, no to minarets,' and recommended that Italy adopt Switzerland as a model society.[108] Contemptuous public discourse in Italy characterised the Berlusconi era, which ended in 2011.

Three exceptions to the rise of nationalist politics can be cited. Poland, a leader of xenophobic high politics in Europe in 2006–07 when Lech Kaczyński was president and his brother Jarosław was prime minister, voted in a more moderate government in 2007. Not only did the Catholic nationalist Prawo i Sprawiedliwość (Law and Justice) party lose that election, the far-right Samoobrona Rzeczpospolitej Polskiej (Self-Defence of the Republic of Poland) movement lost all six of its seats. Poland's 2011 election confirmed the marginalisation of the nationalist right. That same year the Spanish election resulted in the return of the conservative Partido Popular (People's Party) to power. Though critical of immigration, its victory had less to do with this issue and more with the country's economic difficulties including massive unemployment.

In the United Kingdom in 2010, the anti-immigrant British National Party (BNP) polled less than 2 per cent of the national vote (an increase nevertheless of 1.2 percentage points on its previous showing). Its leader, Nick Griffin, a member of the European Parliament, suffered a lopsided defeat in an east London constituency. If in Britain support for radical-right parties at the national level appeared to be unrelated to ethnic diversity, an individual voter's hostile attitude towards immigrants, refugees and multicultural policies did predict a vote for a right-wing party.[109]

Elections to the European Parliament in 2009 provided one other indication of the increasingly sturdy support base of the political right. Turnout (43 per cent) was lower than in the past, itself a possible sign of protest against politics as usual. Not all incumbent parties were punished and support for mainstream centre-right parties, like the Union pour un Mouvement Populaire (Union for a Popular Movement) in France, President Sarkozy's party, held steady. Left-of-centre parties failed to gain from the economic crisis and if anyone did it was the populist right. The most noteworthy feature of the 2009 European parliamentary elections was that 'a chunky protest vote went to populist and far-right outfits vowing to close borders, expel immigrants or dismantle the European Union'.[110] These groups made up what Richard Rose termed 'drawbridge parties' – those which want to defend national borders against alien influences, whether those influences derive from Brussels or immigrant communities. Wilders's anti-Muslim Partij voor de Vrijheid in the Netherlands is an example.

Radical right anti-immigrant parties also elected more MEPs in Austria, Denmark, Greece, and Italy, reflecting previous trend lines in national elections. They made a breakthrough in Britain, where the BNP won its first two seats. The Perussuomalaiset party unexpectedly won one seat in generally liberal Finland, and Slovakia elected one right-wing MEP as well. The right in Bulgaria and Romania repeated its surprising electoral successes of five years earlier: the anti-minorities Bulgarian Natsionalen Sayuz 'Ataka' (National Union 'Attack') movement won two seats while in Romania the Partidul România Mare (Greater Romania Party) – an anti-Roma, anti-Magyar, anti-Semitic movement – took three seats. Hungary's xenophobic Jobbik also won three seats in Strasbourg.

On several occasions right-wing parties have formed parliamentary blocs in the European Parliament making them eligible for funding (more than five million euros over the five-year term), staffing, a party office, committee assignments and agenda-setting rights. After 2007, a right-wing bloc called Identity, Tradition, Sovereignty (ITS) was formed and claimed the backing of twenty-three million Europeans. But internal disputes led to its disintegration: chief among these was the rift between right-wing Italian MEPs who supported the expulsion from their country of Romanians who committed crimes there, and right-wing Romanian MEPs who defended their compatriots. Following the 2009 elections a new far-right bloc was set up. Anchored by the Eurosceptic (but non-racist) United Kingdom Independence Party and Italy's Lega Nord, the new Europe of Freedom and Democracy bloc crossed the minimum threshold of twenty-five MEPs from seven member states. The exclusion of far-right parliamentarians from Austria, Bulgaria and Romania made this bloc's orientation less xenophobic and more Eurosceptic than its predecessors in Strasbourg.

The importance of the creeping, far-flung rise of xenophobic parties cannot be overestimated. Anthony Messina thinks of them as game changers:

When political longevity (i.e., the tendency of anti-immigrant groups to endure as central actors in the political and/or party system) is juxtaposed with the variable of ideological/political commitment (i.e., the level or intensity of the commitment of a group to an anti-immigration and immigrant policy agenda), the new radical right emerges as the most consequential, and potentially the most influential, anti-immigrant actor within Western Europe.[111]

The positive news is that the influence exerted by enraged xenophobic parties is largely contingent:

> Only *some* anti-immigrant groups threaten domestic politics and policy; moreover, even these groups do so only *under very specific political circumstances*. The overwhelming majority of these illiberal actors are currently and indefinitely confined to the fringes of governmental and political power.[112]

Until recently, most governments in European states were relatively immune to the pressures exerted by anti-immigrant forces. But the strength of anti-immigrant politics can be measured in ways other than the electoral performance of far-right parties. The mainstreaming of xenophobic discourse has represented an alarming development as centrist and centre-right parties borrow anti-migrant and anti-multicultural narratives of the far right to campaign for more votes and gain power sharing. If, as a result of the successes of right-wing parties, illiberal, anti-democratic rhetoric becomes more 'centred', the stress arising between the democratic process and the populist politics of fear may deepen and shake Europe's stability.

Notes

1. Theodore Dalrymple, *In Praise of Prejudice: The Necessity of Preconceived Ideas* (New York: Encounter, 2007), p. 100.
2. Ibid., p. 104.
3. Patrick Declerck, 'Je haïs l'Islam, entre autres', *Le Monde*, 11 August 2004. See also his *Garanti sans moraline* (Paris: Flammarion, 2004).
4. Dalrymple, *In Praise of Prejudice*, p. 25.
5. Ibid., pp. 122–4.
6. Catherine Wihtol de Wenden, *Atlas mondial des migrations* (Paris: Autrement, 2009). See also Catherine Wihtol de Wenden and Sophie Body-Gendrot, *Sortir des banlieues* (Paris: Autrement, 2007) and Bertrand Badie, Guillaume Devin, Rony Brauman, Emmanuel Decaux and Catherine Wihtol de Wenden, *Pour un autre regard sur les migrations: construire une gouvernance mondiale* (Paris: La Découverte, 2008).
7. René Girard, *The Girard Reader*, ed. James G. Williams (New York: Crossroad Herder, 1996), pp. 290, 293.
8. See Robert Wistrich, *Demonizing the Other: Anti-Semitism, Racism and Xenophobia* (London: Routledge, 1999).
9. Tzvetan Todorov, *Conquest of America: The Question of the Other* (New York: Harper and Row, 1984).
10. Salman Rushdie, *The Satanic Verses* (New York: Viking Press, 1988).
11. Salman Rushdie, *The Enchantress of Florence* (New York: Random House, 2008). See also Mukund Padmanabhan, 'Imagining the Self and the World', *The Hindu*, 13 April 2008.

12. Mikhail Bakhtin, discussed by Zygmunt Bauman, *Wasted Lives: Modernity and its Outcasts* (Cambridge: Polity Press, 2003), pp. 46–53.

13. Christopher Caldwell, *Reflections on the Revolution in Europe: Immigration, Islam, and the West* (New York: Doubleday, 2009), p. 72. He refers to the Gothic tribes' peace settlement with the Roman empire in 382 as based on *hospitalitas* (billeting on profitable lands) but not *connubium* (the right to marry Romans). Xenophobia arose because 'the accordance of the former privilege was linked to the denial of the latter'.

14. Georg Simmel, 'The Stranger', in *The Sociology of Georg Simmel* (New York: Free Press, 1964), p. 402.

15. Jacques Derrida, *Adieu to Emmanuel Levinas* (Stanford, CA: Stanford University Press, 1999).

16. Caldwell, *Reflections on the Revolution in Europe*, pp. 71–2.

17. Meyda Yegenoglu, 'From Guest Worker to Hybrid Immigrant: Changing Themes of German-Turkish Literature', in Sandra Ponzanesi and Daniela Merolla (eds), *Migrant Cartographies: New Cultural and Literary Spaces in Post-colonial Europe* (Lanham, MD: Lexington, 2005), pp. 141–2.

18. Katelin Marit Parsons, 'Integration in Iceland: What Can We Learn from the (Distant) Past?', paper presented at Conference on Integration and Immigrants' Participation, University of Iceland, Reykjavik, 15 November 2011. See also Kirsten Hastrup, *Island of Anthropology: Studies in Past and Present Iceland* (Odense: Odense University Press, 1990), p. 231.

19. Yegenoglu, 'From Guest Worker to Hybrid Immigrant', pp. 143–4; Zygmunt Bauman, *Modernity and Ambivalence* (Ithaca, NY: Cornell University Press, 1991), p. 65.

20. Sarah Scuzzarello, *Caring Multiculturalism: Local Immigrant Policies and Narratives of Integration in Malmö, Birmingham and Bologna* (Lund: Department of Political Science, Lund University, 2010), p. 241.

21. 'Annual Report on ECRI's Activities Covering the Period from 1 January to 31 December 2005', European Commission against Racism and Intolerance website, May 2006, http://www.coe.int/t/dghl/monitoring/ecri/activities/Annual_Reports/Annual_Report_2005_en.asp#TopOfPage, accessed 25 January 2012.

22. Tahar Ben Jelloun, *L'Hospitalité française* (Paris: Seuil, 1997), p. 24. For an introductory academic study, see Karima Laachir, 'Hospitality and the Limitations of the National', in Jennie Germann Molz and Sarah Gibson (eds), *Mobilizing Hospitality: The Ethics of Social Relations in a Mobile World* (Aldershot: Ashgate, 2007).

23. Peter O'Brien, *European Perceptions of Islam and America from Saladin to George W. Bush: Europe's Fragile Ego Uncovered* (New York: Palgrave Macmillan, 2009), p. 157.

24. Ayhan Kaya, *Islam, Migration and Integration: The Age of Securitisation* (Basingstoke: Palgrave Macmillan, 2009), p. 24.

25. Ted Brader, Nicholas A. Valentino and Elizabeth Suhay, 'What Triggers Public Opposition to Immigration? Anxiety, Group Cues, and Immigration Threat', *American Journal of Political Science* 52 (2008), pp. 959–78.

26. Ambalavener Sivanandan, 'UK Commentary: Racism 1992', *Race and Class* 30:3 (1989), pp. 85–90.

27. Ambalavener Sivanandan, 'The contours of global racism', IRR News website, 26 November 2002, http://www.irr.org.uk/2002/november/ak000007.html, accessed 25 January 2012.

28. Saskia Sassen, *Guests and Aliens* (New York: New Press, 1999), p. 2.

29. Ibid., p. 155.
30. Étienne Balibar and Immanuel Wallerstein, *Race, Nation, Class: Ambiguous Identities* (London: Verso, 1991), pp. 34, 21.
31. D. Mario Nuti, 'Immigration is economically intractable', 18 May 2009, http://www.dmarionuti.blogspot.com/2009/05/immigration-is-economically-intractable.html/, accessed 25 January 2012.
32. Michel Wieviorka (ed.), *La France raciste* (Paris: Seuil, 1992), p. 160. This argument has much in common with the effects of modernisation described in Daniel Lerner, *The Passing of Traditional Society: Modernizing the Middle East* (New York: Free Press, 1968).
33. Elisabeth Young-Bruehl, *The Anatomy of Prejudices* (Cambridge, MA: Harvard University Press, 1996), p. 353.
34. Cornelius Castoriadis, 'Reflections on Racism', *Thesis Eleven* 32 (1992), pp. 1–12.
35. Stathis Gourgouris, 'On Self-alteration', *Parrhesia* 9 (2010), p. 9.
36. Fabrizio Tassinari, *Why Europe Fears Its Neighbors* (Santa Barbara, CA: Praeger, 2009), pp. 2–3.
37. Ariane Chebel d'Appollonia, 'Race, Racism and Anti-discrimination in France', in Sylvain Brouard, Andrew Appleton and Amy G. Mazur (eds), *The French Fifth Republic at Fifty: Beyond Stereotypes* (Basingstoke: Palgrave Macmillan, 2009), p. 279. See also Ray Taras, *Europe Old and New: Transnationalism, Belonging, Xenophobia* (Lanham, MD: Rowman and Littlefield, 2009).
38. Chebel d'Appollonia, 'Race, Racism and Anti-discrimination in France', p. 280.
39 Zygmunt Bauman, *Europe: An Unfinished Adventure* (Cambridge: Polity Press, 2004), p. 99.
40. Gary P. Freeman, 'Modes of Immigration Politics in Liberal Democratic States – Comment/Reply', *International Migration Review* 29 (1995), p. 885.
41. Standard Eurobarometer 30 (1988), 37 (1992), 39 (1993), and 48 (1998), at http://ec.europa.eu/public_opinion/archives/eb_arch_en.htm, accessed 26 January 2012. Eurobarometer 60.1 (Autumn 2003) was the last to ask EU15 respondents about whether 'immigrants contribute a lot to our country or are a threat to our way of life'. This choice, which served as a measurable indicator of xenophobia, was subsequently dropped from the survey.
42. Gallya Lahav, *Immigration and Politics in the New Europe: Reinventing Borders* (Cambridge: Cambridge University Press, 2004), p. 116.
43. Centre for the Study of Political Change, *European Elites Survey: Key Findings 2007* (Siena: Centre for the Study of Political Change, 2007), pp. 12, 15.
44. Lahav, *Immigration and Politics in the New Europe*, pp. 91–3.
45. Standard Eurobarometer 47 (Spring 1997), http://ec.europa.eu/public_opinion/archives/eb_arch_en.htm
46 Gallup Organisation, *Discrimination in the European Union: Analytical Report* (European Commission, 2008), pp. 5–6.
47. Ibid., pp. 17–18.
48. Richard Rose and Kenneth Newton, *Second European Quality of Life Survey: Evaluating the Quality of Society and Public Services* (Dublin: European Foundation for the Improvement of Living and Working Conditions, 2010).
49. Ibid., pp. 8–9.
50. John Berger, *A Seventh Man: Migrant Workers in Europe* (New York: Viking, 1975).

51. Günter Walraff, *Ganz unten* (Cologne: Kiepenheuer und Witsch, 1985).
52. Julia Kristeva, *Strangers to Ourselves* (New York: Columbia University Press, 1991), pp. 17–18. It was originally published as *Étrangers à nous-mêmes* (Paris, Fayard, 1988).
53. Freeman, 'Modes of Immigration Politics in Liberal Democratic States', p. 890.
54. Catherine Wihtol de Wenden, 'Demography, Immigration, Integration (First Part)', *European Issues* 111 (2008).
55. Bassam Tibi, *Political Islam, World Politics and Europe: Democratic Peace and Euro-Islam versus Global Jihad* (London: Routledge, 2008), pp. 203, 194.
56. *The Future of the Global Muslim Population*, Pew Research Center website, 27 January 2011, http://pewresearch.org/pubs/1872/muslim-population-projections-worldwide-fast-growth, accessed 13 February 2012.
57. John R. Bowen, 'Nothing to Fear: Misreading Muslim Immigration in Europe', *Boston Review*, January–February 2010.
58. These apparent manifestations are documented at the following websites:
http://www.euro-islam.info/
http://islamineurope.blogspot.com/
http://www.islamophobia-watch.com/
http://www.einnews.com/news-Racism-Xenophobia
59. Daniel Pipes, 'Muslim Populations in European Cities', 29 December 2007, http://www.danielpipes.org/blog/2007/11/muslim-populations-in-european-cities.html, accessed 26 January 2012.
60. Andreas Zick, Beate Küpper and Andreas Hövermann, *Intolerance, Prejudice and Discrimination: A European Report* (Berlin: Friedrich-Ebert-Stiftung, 2011), Table 7, p. 61.
61. Ibid., Figure 10, p. 74.
62. Kaya, *Islam, Migration and Integration*, p. 5.
63. Ibid., p. xiv.
64. 'En Belgique, le voile d'une députée régionale alimente le débat sur la laïcité', *Le Monde*, 24 June 2009.
65. Adrian Favell, 'Immigration, Migration, and Free Movement in the Making of Europe', in Jeffrey T. Checkel and Peter J. Katzenstein (eds), *European Identity* (Cambridge: Cambridge University Press, 2009), p. 188. See also his *Eurostars and Eurocities: Free Movement and Mobility in an Integrating Europe* (Oxford: Blackwell, 2008).
66. A major international survey has been initiated on the descendants of immigrants from Turkey, ex-Yugoslavia and Morocco living in fifteen European cities located in eight countries. Called The Integration of the European Second Generation (TIES), research findings can be found at http://www.tiesproject.eu/component/option,com_frontpage/Itemid,1/lang,en/
67. This typology is adapted from one proposed by Bernhard Peters, 'Collective Identity, Cultural Difference and the Developmental Trajectories of Immigrant Groups', in Rosemarie Sackmann, Bernhard Peters and Thomas Faist (eds), *Identity and Integration: Migrants in Western Europe* (Aldershot: Ashgate, 2003), pp. 30–1.
68. Christina Boswell and Oana Ciobanu, 'Culture, Utility or Social Systems? Explaining the Cross-national Ties of Emigrants from Borşa, Romania', *Ethnic and Racial Studies* 32 (2009), pp. 1346–64. See also her *The Political Uses of Expert Knowledge: Immigration Policy and Social Research* (Cambridge: Cambridge University Press, 2009)

and *European Migration Policies in Flux: Changing Patterns of Inclusion and Exclusion* (Oxford: Blackwell, 2003), also Christina Boswell and Andrew Geddes, *Migration and Mobility in the European Union* (Basingstoke: Palgrave Macmillan, 2010).

69. Boswell and Ciobanu, 'Culture, Utility or Social Systems?'.

70. Douglas S. Massey, Graeme Hugo, Joaquin Arango, Ali Kouaouci and Adela Pellegrino, *Worlds in Motion: Understanding International Migration at the End of the Millennium* (Oxford: Clarendon Press, 1998), p. 43.

71. Eva G. T. Green, 'Guarding the Gates of Europe: A Typological Analysis of Immigration Attitudes across 21 Countries', *International Journal of Psychology* 42 (2007), p. 366.

72. Ibid., p. 367.

73. These were: (1) good educational qualifications, (2) ability to speak a country's official language, (3) possession of work skills needed in a country, (4) a commitment to the way of life in the country, (5) expulsion if immigrants commit a serious crime, (6) expulsion if immigrants commit *any* crime and (7) expulsion if immigrants are long-term unemployed.

74. Green, 'Guarding the Gates of Europe', p. 372. The 'subtle racists–bigots–egalitarians' typology is taken from Thomas F. Pettigrew and Roel W. Meertens, 'Subtle and Blatant Prejudice in Western Europe', *European Journal of Social Psychology* 25 (1995), pp. 57–75.

75. Green, 'Guarding the Gates of Europe', p. 367.

76. Ibid., Fig. 1, p. 374.

77. Ibid., p. 376.

78. John Sides and Jack Citrin, 'European Opinion about Immigration: The Role of Identities, Interests and Information', *British Journal of Political Science* 37 (2007), pp. 477–504. The European data were taken from the 2002 and 2004 ESS. See also the analysis of these data provided by Dale L. Smith, Sabri Ciftci and Josipa Larson, 'The Determinants of Anti-immigrant Attitudes in Europe: The Impact of Existing Immigrant Populations and National Political Parties', unpublished paper presented at the World International Studies Conference, Ljubljana, Slovenia, 23–26 July 2008.

79. Jack Citrin and John Sides, 'Immigration and the Imagined Community in Europe and the United States', *Political Studies* 56 (2008), p. 39.

80. Gary P. Freeman, 'Winners and Losers: Politics and the Costs and Benefits of Migration', in Anthony. M. Messina (ed.), *West European Immigration and Integration Policy in the New Century* (Westport, CT: Praeger, 2002), pp. 77–8.

81. Citrin and Sides, 'Immigration and the Imagined Community in Europe and the United States', p. 46.

82. Ibid., p. 51.

83. Jens Hainmueller and Michael Hiscox, 'Educated Preferences: Explaining Attitudes toward Immigration in Europe', unpublished paper presented at the annual meeting of the American Political Science Association, Chicago, 2 September 2004. This was based on 2003 ESS data.

84. Marcel Coenders, Mérove Gijsberts and Peer Scheepers, 'Resistance to the Presence of Immigrants and Refugees in 22 Countries', in Mérove Gijsberts, Louk Hagendoorn and Peer Scheepers (eds), *Nationalism and Exclusion of Migrants: Cross-national Comparisons* (Aldershot: Ashgate, 2004), pp. 118–20.

85. Randall Hansen, 'The Free Economy and the Jacobin State, or How Europe Can Cope with the Coming Immigration Wave', in Carol Swain (ed.), *Debating Immigration* (Cambridge: Cambridge University Press, 2007), pp. 223–36; Ruud Koopmans, Paul Statham, Marco Giugni and Florence Passy, *Contested Citizenship: Immigration and Cultural Diversity in Europe* (Minneapolis: University of Minnesota Press, 2007).

86. Citrin and Sides, 'Immigration and the Imagined Community in Europe and the United States', p. 53.

87. Sean Richey, 'The Impact of Anti-assimilationist Beliefs on Attitudes towards Immigration', *International Studies Quarterly* 54 (2010), p. 209.

88. David C. Earnest, 'Neither Citizen nor Stranger: Why States Enfranchise Resident Aliens', *World Politics* 58 (2006), p. 268.

89. I have reviewed these findings in my *Europe Old and New: Transnationalism, Belonging, Xenophobia* (Lanham, MD: Rowman and Littlefield, 2008), Chapter 5.

90. Citrin and Sides, 'Immigration and the Imagined Community in Europe and the United States', p. 37.

91. Enric Martínez-Herrera and Djaouida Moualhi, 'Predispositions to Discriminatory Immigration Policies in Western Europe: An Exploration of Political Causes', *Portuguese Journal of Social Science* 5 (2007), pp. 218–19.

92. Ibid.

93. Ibid., p. 219.

94. Ibid., p. 220.

95. Ibid., pp. 221–2.

96. Centre for the Study of Political Change, *European Elites Survey: Key Findings 2007*, (Siena: Centre for the Study of Political Change, 2007), pp. 12, 15, 18; also *Transatlantic Trends 2008: Key Findings 2008*, Transatlantic Trends website, pp. 19-21, http://trends.gmfus.org/doc/2008_english_key.pdf, accessed 10 February 2012.

97. Lahav, *Immigration and Politics in the New Europe*, p. 224. For a comprehensive comparative study see Rainer Bauböck, Eva Ersbøll, Kees Groenendijk and Harald Waldrauch (eds), *Acquisition and Loss of Nationality: Policies and Trends in 15 European Countries*, 2 vols (Amsterdam: Amsterdam University Press, 2006). Data and additional analyses are available at http://www.imiscoe.org/index.php?option=com_content&view=category&layout=blog&id=26&Itemid=31, accessed 26 January 2012.

98. Ronald Inglehart and Christian Welzel, *Modernisation, Cultural Change, and Democracy: The Human Development Sequence* (Cambridge: Cambridge University Press, 2005).

99. Ole Waever, 'Identity, Integration and Security: Solving the Sovereignty Puzzle in EU Studies', *Journal of International Affairs* 48 (1995), p. 430.

100. Wayne Cornelius and James E. Hollifield, 'Introduction: The Ambivalent Quest for Immigration Control', in Wayne Cornelius, Takeyuki Tsuda, Philip L. Martin and James E. Hollifield (eds), *Controlling Immigration: A Global Perspective* (Stanford, CA: Stanford University Press, 1994), pp. 3–42.

101. John E. Roemer, Woojin Lee and Karine Van der Straeten, *Racism, Xenophobia, and Distribution: Multi-issue Politics in Advanced Democracies* (Cambridge, MA: Harvard University Press, 2007).

102. 'Annual Report on ECRI's Activities Covering the Period from 1 January to 31 December 2005'.
103. For a formal model of xenophobic-based political competition between parties, see Roemer et al., *Racism, Xenophobia, and Distribution*.
104. Kenneth Benoit and Michael Laver, *Party Policy in Modern Democracies* (Abingdon: Routledge, 2006). Their website is at www.politics.tcd.ie/ppmd/, accessed 26 January 2012.
105. Cas Mudde, *Racist Extremism in Central and Eastern Europe* (London: Routledge, 2005). See also his *Populist Radical Right Parties in Europe* (Cambridge: Cambridge University Press, 2007).
106. John Hooper and Kate Connolly, 'Berlusconi breaks ranks over Islam', *The Guardian*, 27 September 2001.
107. 'Calderoli: "Una Francia fatta di negri e islamici"', *Il Giornale*, 11 July 2006.
108. 'International Muslim concern at minaret vote', Swissinfo website, 29 November 2009, at http://www.swissinfo.ch/eng/Specials/Islam_and_Switzerland/Minaret_vote/International_Muslim_concern_at_minaret_vote.html?cid=7793858, accessed 26 January 2012.
109. Pippa Norris, *Radical Right: Voters and Parties in the Electoral Market* (Cambridge: Cambridge University Press, 2005), p. 182.
110. 'Swing low, swing right', *The Economist*, 11 June 2009.
111. Anthony M. Messina, *The Logics and Politics of Post-WWII Migration to Western Europe* (Cambridge: Cambridge University Press, 2007), p. 89.
112. Ibid., pp. 95–96.

CHAPTER FOUR

Islamophobia's deep structures and shallow stereotypes

If Europe, like other parts of the world, harbours irrational fears about strangers, a special place among them is set aside for Muslims. Islamophobia is a longstanding phenomenon even if the term has been coined only recently. Like many religious hatreds, it can be traced back a long way.

Within Christianity early church fathers such as John Chrysostom (c. 347–407) gave sermons that attacked Jews and pagans. Islam was assailed already in the lifetime of the Prophet Muhammad (570–632) by rival groups such as the residents of Mecca. But starting with the Arab conquest of Palestine in the seventh century, control over the Holy Land pitted Christianity and Islam directly against each other. The rivalry culminated in the two-century-long series of Christian Crusades, from 1095 to 1291, against Muslim forces. In the campaign Jews and Eastern Orthodox believers were introduced as targets as well.[1]

'BASE AND BASTARD TURKS'

Turks occupy a special place among today's Islamic communities in Europe. They are the largest of all Muslim groups. They constitute a majority of Muslims living in Germany, Austria and Greece. They represent around 40 per cent of Muslims living in the Netherlands and Belgium. And they are inseparable from the diverse populations living in the Balkans.

It is significant, then, that one of the earliest and most offensive of all anti-Muslim invectives originating in Europe named the Turks as Christendom's great enemy. This was found in the address delivered by Pope Urban II at Clermont-Ferrand in 1095 launching the First Crusade. Arguably the most insightful version of the speech is that published about fifteen years later in *Historiae Hierosolymitanae libri IV* and written by Baldric, poet and Bishop of Dol-en-Bretagne:

You have heard what we cannot recount without deep sorrow how, with great hurt and dire sufferings our Christian brothers, members in Christ, are scourged, oppressed and injured in Jerusalem, in Antioch and the other cities of the East . . . Holy men do not possess those cities; nay, base and bastard Turks hold sway over our brothers.

So Urban exhorted: 'Under Jesus Christ, our Leader, may you struggle for your Jerusalem, in Christian battleline . . . that you may assail and drive out the Turks, more execrable than the Jebusites.[2]

The Pope's real message was that *Muslims* had taken hold of Christianity's holy cities. As the Turks lived near these places and were converting to the faith that Arab tribes had introduced in the region, 'bastard Turks' came into use as a generic term for Muslims. Today we are careful to classify Turks as a non-Arab part of the Islamic world but, ironically, nine centuries after Urban's speech they are again sometimes viewed as a proxy for the whole of that world. Opposition to Turkey's bid to join the EU has stressed its fundamental alterity to Europe.

If we focus on Islamic expansion into south-eastern Europe rather than the Holy Land, Turks indeed constituted a Muslim vanguard and Urban II's condemnation was, in retrospect, farsighted. Fear of the Turk rose as Ottoman armies took Mohács (Hungary), Belgrade and other territories in the Balkan peninsula in the early 1500s, around the time Henry VIII's court was unleashing dual attacks on the Papacy and the Turks. In 1518 Martin Luther concluded that the Turk was the scourge of God sent to punish Christians. Christendom should suffer the consequences, Luther advocated, so as to atone for its sins. But as Ottoman armies laid siege to Vienna in 1529, then abandoned it, Luther came to agree with Erasmus's treatise (written just before the Diet of Augsburg in 1530) which fused Christian repentance with the exhortation to fight the Turks. Erasmus had contended:

How many defeats have the Christian peoples suffered at the hands of this race of barbarians, whose very origin is obscure? What atrocities have they not committed against us? For how many cities, how many islands, how many provinces have they snatched away from the domain of Christ? . . . Now there can be no doubt that the Turks have won an immense empire less by their own merits than by our sins.[3]

The absence of central authority on the Balkan peninsula made the struggle against the Turks difficult. It led to an indecisive outcome compared to the anti-Islamic crusade on the Iberian peninsula. For the Slavs living in the Balkans in the sixteenth century

Ottoman military successes abroad and conversions to Islam in their midst maintained the anti-Turkish obsession at high levels, kindled by the fear of extinction, and by the urge to repress the uncertainty about which faith may be truer to God's truth. At this time the indigenous converts to Islam became identified with the Turks, and rejected alongside them . . . They had 'turned Turk,' and would accordingly be resisted and banished at the time of the Christian liberation from Islam [in the next century]. The anti-Turkish obsession thus became anti-Islamic, or anti-Muslim.[4]

The logic was that Muslims belonged to Turkey and Turkey to Asia. It followed that Slavs who converted to Islam had become Asian (Box 4.1). Even today, as Étienne Balibar has put it, the European consensus regards 'Islam as the reincarnation of an old figure: the "interior enemy"'.[5]

Box 4.1 Fear of the Muslims within

Slav Muslims were ostracised due to the entwinement of religious denomination and ethnicity in the region, which transformed them from indigenous Slavs to ethnic aliens or quasi-Turks in the eyes of their Christian neighbours. This perception was reinforced by the Slav Muslim association with Islamic Ottoman theocracy, perceived as oppressive, exploitative, discriminatory, and thus intolerable. Christian struggles for liberation from Turkish rule therefore justified their eradication, as sorts of ethnoreligious quislings, and this attitude survives into our days.

Source: Slobodan Drakulic, 'Anti-Turkish Obsession and Muslim Slavs in the Balkans', paper presented at the Canadian Sociological Association meeting, Vancouver, 5 June 2008, p. 1.

Anti-Ottomanism became an early defining feature of pan-Slavism. The 'anti-Turkish obsession', therefore, 'targeted all Muslims of the region: Turks, Albanians, Greeks, Slavs or Romanians converted to Islam, demanding their expulsion to where Islam and Muslims supposedly belong – in Asia'.[6] Croatian poets captured the fear of the Turk in their works. Around 1500 Marko Marulić wrote *Molitva suprotiva Turkom* ('Prayer against the Turks'). Considered the most patriotic poem of the Croatian Renaissance, it was less a prayer than an appeal to European statesmen for help. Over a century later the principal subject matter for Croatian writers remained much the same: Ivan Gundulić completed his virulently anti-Turk poem *Osman* in 1626. From these narratives it became clear that Turkophobia had evolved into Orientalism, and Orientalism into Islamophobia.

In contrast to the Balkan peninsula, on the Iberian peninsula military force proved decisive in ending Islamic rule and subjugating Muslim communities. The Spanish *Reconquista* in 1492 – the year that Columbus arrived in the Americas – recaptured al-Andalus, the territories conquered by the Umayyad dynasty early in the eighth century. Expelled Arabs and Jews were depicted as peoples with the wrong religion, the indigenous peoples on the new continent as people without religion. Ramón Grosfoguel and Eric Mielants therefore signalled that

> these 'internal' and 'external' conquests of territories and people not only created an international division of labour of core and periphery, but also constituted the internal and external imagined boundaries of Europe related to the global racial/ethnic hierarchy of the world system, privileging populations of European origin over the rest. Jews and Arabs became the subaltern internal 'Others' within Europe, while indigenous people became the external 'Others' of Europe.[7]

A consequence was, for these authors, that Islamophobia had taken its place as a form of racism in world-historical perspective. An alternative interpretation, however, identified Christians as the wrongdoers:

> According to the modern indictment of Christian misdeeds, Christian expansion and intolerance culminated in the destruction of Moorish Spain in 1492. Over the following century, Muslims were subjected to increasing severity, facing forcible conversion and eventually – between 1609 and 1614 – expulsion of the remaining crypto-Muslims.[8]

Contending narratives on the *Reconquista* have, therefore, fuelled the clash-of-religious-civilisations thesis.

Over the next two centuries, persisting European anxiety about Orientalism, and the Turk in particular, found expression in numerous literary and theatrical works. The backdrop to Shakespeare's *Othello* was conflict with the Turks. Molière's *Le Bourgeois Gentilhomme*, presented on the Paris stage in 1670, dealt with *les turqueries*, the fascination at that time with all things Ottoman. Mozart's opera *Die Entführung aus dem Serail*, which he started composing in 1781, fed European stereotypes of Orientalism, in particular of Turkish despotism and sexual libertinage. A 2006 German production of the same composer's *Idomeneo* (which had premiered in Vienna in 1781) had to be cancelled due to the depiction of Muhammad's beheading in the finale. But Germany's cultural legacy also held out promise for European–Islamic relations. Goethe's collection of lyrical poems, *West-östlicher Diwan* ('West–East Divan'), published in 1819, had sensitively explored encounters between the West and the Orient. In 2008 an editor of a leading Turkish newspaper suggested making the collection compulsory reading in schools.[9]

From the time of Molière, East and West were becoming more and more interconnected. The first Muslim society in Europe was formed in 1738 in Potsdam (Prussia). It was made up mostly of Muslims expelled from Turkey who had been recruited as a praetorian guard for Frederick the Great. To be sure, Arabic literature had not largely ignored the West: the term 'West' was only to appear in the nineteenth century. The emergence of a colonising

Europe was spurred by Napoleon Bonaparte's expedition to Egypt in 1798, which was cut short by fierce local resistance. It was significant that the French general wrapped himself in an Islamic cloak during this misadventure. Thus, in a July 1798 leaflet, he appealed:

> Egyptians, you have been told that I have come to suppress your religion . . . That is a blatant lie . . . I worship God Sublime and respect His Prophet and the Holy Qur'an . . . Tell your imams that the French are true Muslims. The proof and evidence for that is that they reached the Great Rome and destroyed the Chair of the Pope who was always urging the Christians to fight Islam.[10]

Besides France, the Arabs' Other was constituted by additional colonial powers of European Christianity: Britain, Germany, Spain, Portugal, Italy, Belgium and the Netherlands.

This account raises the question whether a deep cause – the clash of Western and Islamic civilisations – has led to path dependence that, today, still pits Europeans and Muslims against each other. For Imam Abduljalil Sajid, a member of the Runnymede Trust's Commission on British Muslims and Islamophobia, which published its seminal report in 1997, it has indeed.

> Hostility towards Islam and Muslims has been a feature of European societies since the eighth century of the Common Era. It has taken different forms, however, at different times and has fulfilled a variety of functions. For example, the hostility in Spain in the fifteenth century was not the same as the hostility that had been expressed and mobilised in the Crusades. Nor was the hostility during the time of the Ottoman Empire or that which was prevalent throughout the age of empires and colonialism. It may be more apt to speak of 'Islamophobias' rather than of a single phenomenon. Each version of Islamophobia has its own features as well as similarities with, and borrowings from, other versions.[11]

Christopher Caldwell understood Islamophobia as a labile term that 'encompasses misconduct toward Muslims, racism, fear of Muslim radicalism, and political opposition to certain Islamist political tendencies'.[12] His approach implied that it sometimes had a justifiable and righteous basis. Its elasticity also is reflected in the ambivalence, fascination and *ressentiment*, defined as a mix of admiration, envy and repulsion, that mark the West's view of Islam – at least as much as fear and hostility probably do. 'Today's Islamophobia originates more out of a *relationship of ambivalence* to the Muslim fact than from a biological or even cultural racism.' There is a 'fascination with Islam' that encompasses a resentful admiration for Arabic Muslim civilisation.[13] 'Islamophobia' is, therefore, a loose, at times misleading, term that seeks to capture the relationship of ambivalence between Europeans and Muslims.

Explaining Islamophobia

In 2005 the British Muslim filmmaker Kenan Malik reflected on how 'Islamophobia' had become a buzzword that was being applied to stigmatise numerous targets – some, counterintuitively, themselves Muslim:

> Ten years ago, no one had heard of Islamophobia. Now everyone from Muslim leaders to anti-racist activists to government ministers wants to convince us that Britain is in the grip of a major backlash against Islam. But does Islamophobia exist? The trouble with the idea is that it confuses hatred of, and discrimination against, Muslims on the one hand with criticism of Islam on the other. The charge of 'Islamophobia' is all too often used not to highlight racism but to silence critics of Islam, or even Muslims fighting for reform of their communities.[14]

Islamophobia has become not just a description of anti-Muslim prejudice, then, but also a prescription for what can or cannot be said about Islam. This is a significant addition to the understanding of the impact of Islamophobia.

The term has been used to cast a wide net. Two specialists on France, Jonathan Laurence and Justin Vaisse, noted the 'infernal couples' in Western thinking that 'connect Islam to all of the problems of our era: Islam and immigration, Islam and conflicts in the Middle East, Islam and terrorism, Islam and the social exclusion in the *banlieues*, Islam and the "clash of civilisations"'.[15] Another French scholar raised the vital question: 'What makes Muslims the ultimate "others?"' Valérie Amiraux suggested that public receptivity to the clash-of-civilisations thesis was based on an acceptance of 'the assumption that Islam as a denomination and Muslims as believers constitute the ultimate cultural "other" that will never be able to cope with democratic and liberal values'.[16] The supposed historical incompatibility of European and Islamic values is, therefore, central to the rise of Islamophobia (see Box 4.2).

Box 4.2 Islam in the European Space

No single question is more likely to test the capacity of European nations to address the issue of multiple 'belongings', exclusive or incompatible 'loyalties', the growing uncertainty of boundaries between 'insiders' and 'outsiders' (or, rather, the increasing number of 'citizens' who are neither simply inside nor simply outside), than the status and the importance of Islam within the European space.

Source: Étienne Balibar, 'Postface', in Christophe Bertossi (ed.), *European Antidiscrimination and the Politics of Citizenship: Britain and France* (Basingstoke: Palgrave Macmillan, 2007), p. 239.

Sometimes it is just the opposite phenomenon – today's news coverage rather than a millennium of history – that accounts for Islamophobic imagery. French journalist Thomas Deltombe concluded that the media, in particular television, had been disseminating negative images of Muslims in the country for thirty years.[17] Television news was driven by the need to capture large audiences but also by an ideological propensity to stigmatise Others. The phantasm the media created is Islamophobia. Elisabeth Eide, a Norwegian media specialist, emphasised how symbolic elites are key to the discursive reproduction of racism and Islamophobia by which ethnic prejudices are spread. She identified six patronising discourses about minorities, such as Muslims, prevalent in European receiving societies: (1) the image of migrants as a 'colourful community'; (2) 'queen bee' stories about overachieving minority members; (3) satisfaction that such a community was becoming normalised into a receiving society; (4) attention to 'superintegrated heroes' such as sports stars; (5) Muslims as a problem for 'us' and (6) 'us' as a problem for them.[18] Denmark's cartoon crisis furnished just a single striking episode of the media's role in smearing Islam's image.

Whether it entails ascribing to the historical determinism thesis alleging the incompatibility of Islam and the West, or alternatively citing superficial stereotypes of Muslims shared by Europeans today, prejudice against Muslims has 'passed the dinner-table test' and become *salonfähig* – acceptable in polite circles in Europe's most multicultural societies like Britain and Germany.[19] Some of the most outspoken attacks on Islam have been launched by politicians in the Low Countries, traditionally regarded as hospitable societies. The late Dutch politician Pim Fortuyn polemicised that 'there is a tension between the values of modern society and the principles of Islam'. Next door, the Vlaams Blok proclaimed that 'Islam is now the No. 1 enemy not only of Europe, but of the entire free world'.[20]

Many experts on international relations and the Muslim world have securitised the Christian–Muslim divide. That is, as discussed in Chapter 1, the divide has been converted into a question of international and national security.[21] It is not just the direct confrontations between Western and Muslim worlds that are invoked as reasons to be security conscious; the purportedly greater war proneness of Muslim countries is identified as a potential source of international instability.

Here are data from a longitudinal study of civil wars. Of the 191 states in the United Nations in 2003, just twenty-five (13 per cent) defined Islam as the state religion, and only twenty-seven more (14 per cent) had an Islamic orientation, that is, gave preferential treatment to Islam over other religions. Yet if approximately one-quarter of states could be described as Muslim, of forty-two *religious* civil wars fought between 1940 and 2000 incumbent governments and rebels identifying with Islam were involved in thirty-four of them (81 per cent). In civil wars of all kinds, Islamic forces were involved in one-quarter. Given that civil wars tend to be more frequent and longer, entail greater non-combatant deaths, and are less often resolved through negotiations, participation of Islamic groups in them is viewed as even more threatening.

The author of this study offered three explanations for Islam's appearance in so many conflicts. One was the standard historical perspective on the benign effect of secularism in the West: the post-Westphalia system after 1648 ushered in an era of the sovereignty of secular princes which limited religious wars. A second reason was a simple geographical fact: the co-location of Islam's holy sites with some of the world's largest oil reserves, thereby dragging Muslim countries into international competition over energy. Finally, a structural explanation distinctive to Islam was advanced: the Muslim principle of jihad or struggle.[22]

If Muslim countries have been cast as more war prone and less politically stable, this can serve as the pretext for the West to raise the importance of national security. The purported threat of the Muslim community inside the country is added to this security calculus, even though it does not logically follow from any external security threat that the Islamic world may pose. Elspeth Guild, a leading expert on European immigration law, stressed that 'there is a tension between internal security and external security'. The structures established to deal with each are typically mutually exclusive. Thus,

> the institutions engaged in security within the state are multiple – for instance social affairs and health ministries concern themselves with limiting the risk of pandemics killing many people, the police and criminal justice departments occupy themselves with the question of crime: what it is, who commits it and how they should be punished . . . External security, on the other hand, is more limited. In its classical form it is concerned with the physical integrity of the state – ensuring that the state is not overrun by some other state.[23]

Differences in the security architectures designed to meet internal and external threats are reason enough to avoid the pitfall of conflating the outside Islamic world with the Muslim community at home. Arguably a more significant issue for domestic security agencies to address is gauging the impact of bolstering national security by, among other policies, profiling Muslim groups and individuals. Such profiling may produce a backlash and inadvertently create new threats where none existed before. The process reads like this: 'The securitisation of immigration may support the radicalisation of minority groups who feel alienated and are actually suffering from discrimination. The roots of insecurity are not only abroad but also in our backyard.'[24] By this logic, the inability to provide equal opportunities for all can be transformed into an internal security threat. Because of today's high visibility of violence involving Muslims, it is this group that is at the forefront of security concerns.

Islamophobic discourse therefore combines an anti-terrorism thrust with anti-immigration and anti-minority agendas. As one writer observed, in the mid-1990s 'migrants became Muslims, and Europe's right wing found its target'.[25] To be sure, hostility towards Islam would likely persist even if Muslim immigration was stopped and Muslim communities deported. Security concerns can serve as a pretext for articulating deeply seated religious, cultural and ideological fears.[26] Thus in his short study of the subject, Matti Bunzl noted that the concept of Islamophobia

> rarely engages religious questions in a meaningful way. Nor does it turn on the issue of race, although it, too, could be seen as a possible valence. What does stand at the heart of Islamophobic discourse is the question of civilisation, the notion that Islam engenders a world view that is fundamentally incompatible with and inferior to Western culture.[27]

But I would counter that superficial stereotypes of Muslims play their part in constructing Islamophobic frames.

Within Europe the purported civilisational incompatibility is said to account for various forms of discrimination against Muslims. The European Union Monitoring Centre for Racism and Xenophobia (EUMC) referenced internationally accepted standards on combating racism to condemn Islamophobic acts in EU states. It recognised that Muslim communities are subject to prejudice 'through negative general attitudes but also to varying degrees through discriminatory acts and through violence and harassment'.[28] The EUMC formulated a chicken-and-egg question about the rise of Islamophobia: 'Do higher rates of discrimination lead to a feeling of isolation and lack of integration, or does a lack of integration make migrants more vulnerable to discrimination?'[29] These questions set the agenda for the case studies of France and Germany presented in Chapters 5 and 6.

For a number of years the Islamic Human Rights Commission (IHRC), based in Britain, organised a consciousness-raising mock awards ceremony to honour its 'Islamophobe of the Year'. Tongue-in-cheek 'winners' included Israeli prime minister Ariel Sharon in 2003, BNP leader Nick Griffin in 2004, British prime minister Tony Blair in 2005 and US Secretary of State Condoleezza Rice in 2006. The attacks on Palestinians, British Muslims and Iraq may have made these choices self-explanatory. But the IHRC's main purpose is more serious – 'to gather information about, and to publicise, atrocities, oppression, discrimination and other abuses of divinely granted rights'.[30] In an online poll conducted in 2010, it found that 80 per cent of respondents believed that Islamophobia was on the rise.

RELIGIOUS UNDERPINNINGS OF ANTI-ISLAMIC IDEAS

Religion is one of the common denominators inviting comparisons of Islamophobia and anti-Semitism. But two British-based academics contend that race is also a shared feature, clearer in the history of anti-Semitic race-specific legislation than the less self-evident racial framing of Muslims.[31] In France, the historian Pierre-André Taguieff's pioneering work on the similarities of and differences between these two pathologies has had significant influence in shaping research.[32] Vincent Geisser differed from Taguieff in highlighting less troubled popular attitudes about Islam coming under attack compared to more punitive ones when Judaism was criticised. While public criticism of Jews is closely monitored, he contended, that directed at Muslims meets with a more *laissez-faire* response.[33]

Bunzl weighed in as well, underscoring differences in the claims that xenophobes advanced:

> Whereas anti-Semites questioned Jews' fitness for inclusion in the national community, Islamophobes are not particularly worried whether Muslims can be good Germans, Italians, or Danes. Rather, they question whether Muslims can be good Europeans. Islamophobia, in other words, functions less in the interest of national purification than as a means of fortifying Europe.[34]

But it is the difference between a posited European secularism and Islamic practices that has received most attention in analyses of Islamophobia. For many Europeans, some mix of religious agnosticism, secularism and scepticism defines the very essence of Europeanness. Compartmentalising the private character of religious beliefs means these are excluded from public space. Proponents of secularism latch on to the Foucauldian fear that principles, like religious ones, can be transformed into practice. This was to be avoided at all costs.

In sixteen of thirty-seven European states examined by one researcher, Islam is today the second largest religious community. Thirteen European countries still do not officially recognise Islam as a religion.[35] The divergence of approaches to recognising a religion between Europe and Islamic countries is striking. Two researchers studying Muslim attitudes towards the European state found that 'church–state matters that west European states seemed to have settled long ago and that appeared to be politically peripheral were suddenly thrust to the centre of political and policy debate by Muslim efforts'.[36] They drew attention to the ironic character of Muslims raising questions about the separation of the secular from the sacred at a time when secularism had become entrenched across western Europe.

For their part, many of Europe's secular advocates are persuaded that the practice of Islam involves putting religion at the centre of a Muslim's daily life. Islam is not a religion like any other, their logic goes, but the foundation of a civilisation and culture whose precepts and values present a problem for other nations. In particular, Islam is viewed as dictating the conduct of an individual's life and goes further to negate the distinction between private and public spheres. Consequently its success, whether measured in terms of observance, members or converts, poses a threat to Western societies structured around secularism.[37]

Islamophobia is a backlash to the expanded presence of Muslim communities across Europe. The public symbols of Islamism have become more visible, from the headscarf to the burqa, from minarets to Arabic signage. Not surprisingly, these mostly religious symbols have been targeted in legal initiatives seeking to ban or limit their visibility. But outlawing customary practices is notoriously hard to do. In Britain the Office of National Statistics reported that Jack would soon be replaced by Mohammed as the most common boys' name in the country. The high fertility rate of foreign-born Muslim women was largely behind this development: the office noted that the birth rate of women born in Pakistan but living in the UK was three times higher than that of British-born women.[38]

Muslim customary practices have been used to explain not only larger family size but also poverty levels and poor educational achievement scores. The British journalist Yasmin Alibhai-Brown argued provocatively that 'it is not Islamophobia that makes parents take 14-year-old bright girls out of school to marry illiterate men'. But anti-Muslim popular attitudes are regularly identified as the source for Muslim students' failures. For Alibhai-Brown, then, Islamophobia has become 'a convenient label, a figleaf . . . and all too often Islamophobia is used to blackmail society'.[39] A conclusion of this kind from a founding member of British Muslims for Secular Democracy triggers the counterargument that Muslims assimilated into European culture can themselves become virulently Islamophobic.

The status of Islam in Muslim-majority states is typically fixed and not a product of negotiation. Islam usually serves as the state religion and where it does not, it may still be inseparable from the institutions of the state. Nominally secular Muslim countries such as Turkey, Syria and Iraq are anchored in Islamic values, if moderated by state authorities. What is novel for Muslim communities in Europe, then, is 'a release from the "iron grip" of authoritarian Muslim states on Islamic tradition'.[40] Islam in Europe has been undergoing a process of secularisation, it has been argued. 'The secularisation of Islam is witnessed in the emergence of Islamic institutions adapted to the dominant model of church–state relations in the countries in question.'[41] Not all observers, whether secular, Christian or Muslim, agree that this process has actually occurred.

Some Muslim intellectuals in Europe, the most notable of these being the philosopher Tariq Ramadan, have called for the Europeanisation of Islam rather than its secularisation. Ramadan did not dismiss the significance of the clash-of-civilisations thesis:

> If the clash is not a reality, the ingredients that could lead to it are very present in current mentalities: on both sides, the lack of knowledge of the other (and of self), the acceptance of simplistic and absolute caricatures and final judgments, not to mention conflicting political and geostrategic interests.[42]

For Ramadan it followed that the best opportunity to engage in conciliatory dialogue and advance a transformative agenda was found within European societies, not between them and the Islamic world. His Euro-Islamic ideas may not help us understand why Islamophobia has taken root among different sections of European society, but they do represent a thoughtful response to how Muslims can better integrate while still retaining their religious beliefs.

It was Bassam Tibi, a German Islamic reformer at the University of Göttingen, who coined the term 'Euro-Islam' in the early 1990s. For him it embraced 'the idea of Europe based on values of secular democracy, individual human rights, pluralism, civil society and the enlightenment culture of tolerance . . . consonant with cultural modernity'.[43] But the contrary view appears to have made headway in recent years: Muslim communities in Europe have increasingly become defined – and some of the more radical imams define themselves – on the basis of their religion and its symbols. Neither the 'idea of Europe' nor the cultural specificities of their countries of origin help frame their identities. Whether Muslim communities have adopted Euro-Islamic values in order to cement their presence and increase their influence in European societies may be determined by how they organise their community lives. Their choice can, in turn, suggest whether receiving societies will find fuel for anti-Muslim sentiments or not.

MUSLIM COMMUNITY ORGANISATIONS AND ISLAMOPHOBIA

Muslim communities in Europe are diverse and not all owe their origins to late twentieth-century migration from non-European countries. Centuries-old Muslim national communities exist throughout the Balkans and on the Iberian peninsula. Moreover some Muslims have migrated from one European country to another: one-third of the Muslims living in Austria originate in Bosnia and Kosovo while one-quarter of those in Italy are Albanian. How 'Muslim' many of these groups from other European states are is an important question. Some do not represent a visible minority, for example, many Turks across Europe. The result is that different Muslim communities have faced different functional imperatives and engaged in contrasting forms of self-organisation in Europe.

Internal differences within Muslim communities living in particular European states are compounded by external differences between receiving societies. 'Each wealthy country today has its own Muslim immigrants, its own distinct history of dealing with them, and its own way of integrating them.'[44] Germany draws a large proportion of its immigrants from Turkey, a country where for the past century Islamic practice has been circumscribed. Britain grants considerable religious autonomy to its more observant Pakistani immigrants while being sure to monitor their mosque activities. By contrast, France's 'Muslim immigrants are drawn from countries in which there is considerable Islamic fundamentalism while it maintains its high threshold of assimilation'.[45]

The fear of fundamentalism, therefore, has little to do with how integration is promoted by receiving societies; European states do not consider most immigrants, however religious or political they may be, as carriers of fundamentalist ideas. Many of those fleeing civil strife in Algeria for France, or war in Afghanistan for England, are doing so precisely to escape fundamentalist terror. To be sure, some anti-Muslim movements in Europe construe such immigrants as threats. Thus, a specialist on French Islamophobia concluded that 'the increasing visibility of Islam in Europe is not interpreted as the expression of the will of newcomers to find their place as citizens in a Europe undergoing change, but rather as tangible proof of Islamic fundamentalism which propagates itself in European societies'.[46] Islam becomes constructed as the exact reverse of European democracy.

More precisely, it is the radical Islamist movement operating in European countries that has been presented as Western democracy's rival and served as the trigger for the securitisation of immigration. What radical Islam encompasses is debatable and one analyst constructed a simple pyramid of the groups making up this movement: (1) jihadists, who are prepared to use terror to attack infidel European societies, (2) opponents of Western values and proponents of Islamic ones, such as Hizb-ut-Tahrir (Party of Liberation), which the British and German authorities attempted to ban, and (3) the political Islam embraced by the Egyptian-based Muslim Brotherhood, the Pakistani Jamaat-e-Islami, and the Turkish Milli Görüş (National View).[47]

As one writer underscored, 'jihadist networks span Europe from Poland to Portugal, thanks to the spread of radical Islam among the descendants of guest workers once recruited to shore up Europe's postwar economic miracle'.[48] Jihadists can be outsiders – students and asylum seekers who, paradoxically, have fled crackdowns on Islamists in Muslim-majority countries to seek refuge in liberal Europe. Jihadists are also increasingly insiders – alienated second- and third-generation offspring of Muslim immigrants. They also have included some recent European converts to Islam.

The Muslim Brotherhood is regularly identified as the ideological inspiration for the emergence of other radical Islamic groups now found in Europe. An iconoclastic assessment of the activities of these groups highlighted their Janus-faced character:

> These organisations represent themselves as mainstream, even as they continue to embrace the Brotherhood's radical views and maintain links to terrorists. With moderate rhetoric and well-spoken German, Dutch, and French, they have gained acceptance among European governments and media alike. Politicians across the political spectrum rush to engage them whenever an issue involving Muslims arises or, more parochially, when they seek the vote of the burgeoning Muslim community.[49]

While publicly calling for interfaith dialogue and integration, then, it is argued that the mosques controlled by such groups denounce European values and the societies built on them: 'Europeans, eager to create a dialogue with their increasingly disaffected Muslim minority, overlook this duplicity.'[50] Obviously European Islamophobes do not subscribe to this idea of engaging in dialogue with groups they brand as incorrigibly anti-Western.

Most international and national Islamic organisations promote the Muslim faith without embracing radical religious ideas or insurrectionary political methods. With fifty-seven member states comprising 1.5 billion Muslims, the global Organisation of Islamic Cooperation (OIC, whose name was changed in 2011 from Organisation of the Islamic Conference) is the second largest international governmental organisation in the world after the United Nations. Formed in 1969, the OIC charter endorses the principles of the Charter of the United Nations. At the same time, it adds other objectives including:

- To preserve and promote the lofty Islamic values of peace, compassion, tolerance, equality, justice and human dignity; to contribute to international peace and security, understanding and dialogue among civilisations, cultures and religions and promote and encourage friendly relations and good neighbourliness, mutual respect and cooperation;
- to promote human rights and fundamental freedoms, good governance, rule of law, democracy and accountability in member states in accordance with their constitutional and legal systems;
- to foster noble Islamic values concerning moderation, tolerance, respect for diversity, preservation of Islamic symbols and common heritage and to defend the universality of the Islamic religion.[51]

These charter principles share little with the agenda of radical Islam. They do not provide grist to the mill for European Islamophobes, whose construction of Islam is as a faith fundamentally in conflict with Western values. To be sure, the presence of European states in the OIC is limited: Albania is the only full OIC member state lying in Europe while Turkey, which lies mostly on the Asian continent, is also a full member. Bosnia and Russia enjoy observer status. Islamophobes would point to all four countries as European outliers. One of the IOC's recent initiatives has been to compile an Islamophobia Observatory, which documents global efforts to combat the phenomenon.[52]

Another transnational institution for Muslim groups is the Federation of Islamic Organisations in Europe. Its specific mission is to promote the interests of Muslims living in Europe. In addition, the London-based Islamic Human Rights Commission was set up in 1997, after the Runnymede report, as an independent, non-profit, campaign, research and advocacy organisation. It submits reports to governments and international organisations, monitors media coverage of Muslim affairs, produces research papers, and takes on discrimination cases.[53] In European countries with sizeable Muslim minorities, Islamic umbrella groups have been created, sometimes with the support of the parent state. The most notable of these include the Muslim Council of Britain, the Union des Organisations Islamiques de France (UOIF) and the Islamische Gemeinschaft Deutschland (Islamic Society of Germany). All have rival organisations contesting their right to represent all Muslim communities.

If it appears that these transnational and national Islamic organisations pursue moderate policies, there is nevertheless a contrived, sometimes self-contradictory character to them. Any form of central organisation is largely antithetical to Islam. The natural form of organisation of Muslims is as mosque communities. Whether it is the OIC or the UOIF, such institutions are susceptible to the criticism that they are inconsistent with the Islamic concept of a community of believers, or *ummah*. It is precisely in opposition to such 'Westernised' organisations that Muslim fundamentalist groups function. Yet these same institutions are commonly regarded by Islamophobic forces in receiving societies as articulating Muslim values. Their legitimacy has therefore not been fully established.

Imagining the Muslim Other

An innovative theoretical examination of Muslim communities in Europe was carried out by Heiko Henkel, an anthropologist at the University of Copenhagen. He contended that friction between Muslim groups and host societies is partly the result of Muslims not being incorporated into Europe's grand historical compromises. Citing the example of Germany, Henkel suggested that reconciling the grand ideologies and value systems of nationalism, liberalism, socialism and Christianity excluded the unique historical experience of Muslims.

For Henkel, this inner-European consensus was explicitly formulated to contrast with that experience. In order for Muslim groups to be included in a renegotiated compromise, Europe would have to rewrite its secularist historical narrative. As we have noted, in a case like Germany

> strongly normative claims of Muslim organisations easily become a double provocation. For one, they are claims of a social project that (in different ways) rivals those 'traditional' German projects that have dominated German society over the past century. At the same time, the projects of Muslim revival movements challenge (or seem to challenge) the new common denominator of these projects . . . constitutional patriotism.[54]

The impact of political Islam on European Muslims was not determined, therefore, by the success of its ideological proselytising. Olivier Roy, a leading French expert on Islam, argued some time back that political Islam had failed both as a third force in world politics and as an expression of Muslims' own anti-colonial project.[55] Henkel added that European ideological pathways have had an impact as well in alienating and failing Muslims.

Material conditions may shape European Muslims' politics more than Islamic or European narratives. The objective socio-economic experiences of Muslims in large measure determine how susceptible they may be to radical ideas. Across much of western Europe, and particularly since the onset of the economic crisis in 2008, Muslims have registered higher rates of unemployment, lower levels of educational achievement, and significantly lower incomes than their cohorts of British, Dutch, French or German descent. Young Muslims are affected more acutely than most other groups.

Deteriorating or stagnating material conditions have led political leaders representing both the state and Muslim groups to lament the failure of integration. They argue that parallel societies have evolved, with Muslims as the underclass. Even where migrants have secured citizenship and nominally equal rights within the receiving society, the failure to insert them into the socio-economic opportunity structure has made naturalisation hollow. These represent hothouse conditions for extremist ideologies. Even second- or third-generation Muslim youth 'feel disenfranchised in a society that does not fully accept them; they appear to turn to Islam as a badge of cultural identity, and are then radicalised by extremist Muslim clerics'.[56] The waning of traditional family values makes young Muslims susceptible to new influences (see Box 4.3) The spread of Islamophobia is accelerated by a vicious circle that begins with immiserisation and exclusion of Muslims, followed by periodic public protest, rioting, random violence and some extremist mobilisation. The circle is closed by a seething anti-Islamic backlash.

Box 4.3 Marriage and radicalisation of Muslims

Paradoxically, even marriage can be an agent of radicalisation: whereas the first generation of migrants' children pleased their parents by marrying cousins imported from Pakistan or Bangladesh (thereby swelling immigrant numbers), their children's insistence on marrying Muslim partners of their choice is leading to the creation of a Muslim identity that transcends the older patterns of 'encapsulated' settlement based on differences of region, culture, language, and *biradiri* (extended family networks).

Source: Malise Ruthven, 'The Big Muslim Problem!' *New York Review of Books*, 17 December 2009, p. 64.

One analyst described the loop in these terms:

Violent behaviour by young Muslims in the 1990s has buttressed societal misperceptions of Islam as a monolithic religion practiced by foreign extremists rather than citizens of modern states. Large-scale riots indicate that the penchant for violence evident among members of the second and third generations is considerably more widespread than that attributable to isolated acts of terrorism.[57]

Put differently, the fears of European publics are heightened by dramatic acts of Islamic terrorism, but they are nevertheless stoked by banal acts of random violence attributed regularly to young Muslims.

FREEDOM OF EXPRESSION AND ISLAMOPHOBIA

Anti-religious hate speech, including in most countries blasphemy, is illegal in Europe. Explicit limitations on free speech when they express anti-Semitism are standard across much of Europe. Anti-Muslim hate speech is, by contrast, not explicitly prohibited in Europe even though it can be prosecuted as incitement to group hatred. Thus the 1990 Gayssot law in France made it illegal to discriminate against someone on the basis of belonging to an ethnic group, nation, race or religion. It also made questioning the existence or scope of crimes against humanity, which included the Holocaust, a criminal offence. In a similar way a German law enacted in 1998 banned the incitement of hatred against a section of the population. It too encompassed Holocaust denial. Laws of this kind in other European states have been used to prosecute instances of hate speech directed at Muslims.

Some European states limit the exercise of religious freedom. In the recent past the effects of such restrictions seem disproportionately to have been borne by Muslims. For example, France, Belgium, a few regions in Germany, and a number of other European countries have placed restrictions on and, in some instances, banned the wearing of headscarves, veils and the burqa in public spaces. Prohibiting the display of religious symbols in public offices is justified as a way of keeping the public sphere secular or, at least, religiously neutral.[58] But when a legal judgment is handed down against the display of a Christian symbol, such as crucifixes hanging in public school classrooms in Italy, as occurred in a 2009 ruling of the European Court of Human Rights, it caused outrage across that country's political spectrum. European leaders and publics tend to have a more liberal understanding of what freedom of speech and expression signifies when Judeo-Christian rather than Islamic symbols are involved.

Debate over the legal status of anti-Islamic expression came to a head in the wake of the 2005 Danish cartoon crisis. Officially the European Convention of Human Rights protects the right to freedom of expression. But its Article 10(2) recognises that its exercise may be limited by justifications 'necessary in a democratic society', such as the need to protect order or security, and even reputation and other values. Throughout Europe, legislation exists that puts limits on the exercise of free speech, notably, denying the Holocaust (Austria, Germany and France). Denmark's anti-hate legislation penalises expressions that threaten, deride or degrade persons on the grounds of their race, colour, national or ethnic origin, belief or sexual orientation.

The principles of freedom of speech and expression generally permit popular stereotyping, profiling and even scapegoating (if it does not involve degradation) of particular groups, like Muslims, to take place. At what point these expressions become Islamophobic is difficult to establish. But they can at a minimum fuel Islamophobic attitudes. One insidious caricature is the Muslim migrant as parasite: one damning fact may be enough to confirm and propagate such a stereotype, like this example from Denmark: while 5 per cent of the Danish population is Muslim, 40 per cent of social assistance funding has been allocated to members of this community. From this fact it is a short step to lampooning Islam in cartoons.

Essentialising Islam as a censorious religion denying its members individual freedoms figures in the discourse of many non-Muslim intellectuals. This stereotype has also been perpetuated in the impressions many citizens have of Islam. But Muslims who have apostatised have been instrumental, too, in furthering this image of Islam. Months after the Danish cartoon crisis exploded in 2005, twelve prominent Muslim and non-Muslim intellectuals published a manifesto.[59] The signatories included Salman Rushdie, Ayaan Hirsi Ali, the French philosopher Bernard-Henri Lévy and Taslima Nasreen, a Bangladeshi writer in exile. The manifesto took aim at Islam while advocating a form of secular fundamentalism to replace it (see Box 4.4).

Box 4.4 Anti-Islamist or Islamophobic manifesto?

- After having overcome fascism, Nazism and Stalinism, the world now faces a new totalitarian global threat: Islamism. We, writers, journalists, intellectuals, call for resistance to religious totalitarianism and for the promotion of freedom, equal opportunity and secular values for all.
- We reject 'cultural relativism', which consists in accepting that men and women of Muslim culture should be deprived of the right to equality, freedom and secular values in the name of respect for cultures and traditions. We refuse to renounce our critical spirit out of fear of being accused of 'Islamophobia', an unfortunate concept which confuses criticism of Islam as a religion with stigmatisation of its believers.
- We appeal to democrats and free spirits of all countries that our century should be one of Enlightenment, not of obscurantism.

Source: 'Confronting Islamist Totalitarianism', *Middle East Quarterly* 13:3 (2006), pp. 82–3.

Muslim communities organised into influential lobby groups are another popular caricature. Walter Laqueur wrote that 'Turks in Belgium and Arabs in Britain have acquired influence out of proportion to the size of the ethnic group to which they belong'.[60] But this observation has a modest reach compared to Bat Ye'or's thesis of the emergence of 'Eurabia' – an Arab-controlled Europe (critiqued in Chapter 7). Whether such a political entity has emerged across the continent, in individual European countries, or even in specific cities, has been treated both seriously and satirically.[61] This type of conspiracy theory is not new. A century ago documents forged in Paris made their way to Russia where they became known as 'The Protocols of the Elders of Zion'. Published in Russia in 1903, they were used by anti-Semites as evidence supporting the idea of a Jewish plot to control the world. Freedom of the press can be abused, then, without it finding condemnation in a court of law.

SURVEY RESEARCH ON ANTI-MUSLIM ATTITUDES

Studying Western and Muslim values and attitudes has developed into a major research undertaking since 2001. Attention has been directed primarily at value differences and value shifts in Western and Muslim 'worlds'. Are the two irreconcilably different or is convergence taking place? Has worldwide anti-Americanism, triggered by the Bush administration's war on terror, deepened the rift between two civilisations? Do European citizens display a distinct approach to the normative divide?[62]

Much research has been carried out examining the values and attitudes of Muslim minorities in Western societies. The European Social Survey, Eurobarometer (set up by the European Commission) and the Fundamental Rights Agency have regularly investigated these attitudes, as have national surveys carried out in individual EU states.[63] Political scientists have gone beyond social surveys to measure the political participation of immigrants, including Muslim groups, in their receiving societies. The Dutch political scientist Jaap Dronkers and his teams of researchers have been particularly productive in examining such research questions.[64]

In one of these studies, Dronkers and his co-authors made an important, somewhat counterintuitive, finding that sheds light on Muslim political participation: 'the country of origin is much more effective in explaining the differences in the electoral participation of immigrants than the characteristics of the country of destination'. Using different databases, the study revealed that immigrants from Islamic and/or Arab countries had a lower propensity to vote. When tested together, the effect of Islamic origin country remained significant but the effect of Arab origin country did not. Conversely, immigrants from countries of origin where the dominant religion was Protestant or Roman Catholic had a higher propensity to vote.[65]

Even accepting that this distinction largely overlaps with that between non-Western and Western immigrants, such a finding shatters the conventional wisdom that if Muslims do not vote regularly in European countries where they have obtained voting rights, it has more to do with the characteristics of the country of destination and not of origin. The case for the purported political marginalisation of Muslims in the West is, therefore, off the mark if the effects of origin country – Huntingtonians would claim civilisation – are ignored.

When we concentrate on social attitudes with possible Islamophobic orientations, three general sources of data are available. The first is third-party research on levels of discrimination and racism. The other two are attitudinal data that look at the prevailing perceptions and attitudes of either the perpetrator-subject or the victim-target. We begin with third-party reports which monitor anti-Muslim attitudes.

Monitoring anti-Muslim bias

In its detailed 2009 report on ethnic profiling in the EU, the Open Society Institute (OSI) condemned this practice as discriminatory, illegal and unethical:

Ethnic profiling, although widespread, constitutes discrimination and thus breaches basic human rights norms. By relying on ethnic, racial, or religious stereotypes, ethnic profiling breaches one of the most fundamental principles of law: that each person must be treated as an individual, not as a member of a group.[66]

The many different types, methods and targets of profiling, as well as the EU countries in which they took place, were documented in this report. Law enforcement actions ranged from more benign forms, involving police monitoring, surveillance and stop-and-search, to coercive methods entailing raids, arrests and beatings. In its executive summary, the report took care to highlight the special place occupied by profiling of Muslims:

> Since the 9/11 attacks in the United States, 32 per cent of British Muslims report being subjected to discrimination at airports. Police carrying machine guns have conducted identity checks on 11-year-olds at German mosques. Moroccan immigrants have been called *moro de mierda* ('Arab shit') by Spanish police. The personal data of 8.3 million people were searched in a massive German data mining exercise which targeted – among other characteristics – people who were Muslim, and which did not identify a single terrorist.[67]

The OSI released a second report in 2009 focusing on Muslims living in eleven European cities. Its findings were based on more than 2,000 one-on-one interviews with Muslim residents as well as on sixty focus groups and it therefore represents the second kind of attitudinal data illuminating Islamophobic tendencies – the victims' perspective. The OSI report offered generally positive news about how Muslims interacted, participated, integrated and felt they belonged in these European urban communities. But it flagged religious discrimination against Muslims as a continuing, even growing, problem, and it seemed to be unconnected with immigration. Thus,

> European-born Muslims, particularly women, were more likely to perceive higher levels of religious discrimination than Muslims born abroad. European-born Muslim men identify the police as a key source of unfair treatment and discrimination. For Muslims, the persistence of discrimination and prejudice affects their sense of national belonging'. When we take into account the fact that Muslim respondents identified respect for religion as a more important national value than did non-Muslims, the phenomenon of religious discrimination has more profound implications.[68]

Also in 2009, results were published of the first EU-wide survey of immigrant and ethnic minority groups' experiences of discrimination and victimisation in everyday life. Pointing to the lack of reliable, comparable data on minorities in the EU, the EU Minorities and Discrimination Survey (EU-MIDIS) detailed experiences of discriminatory treatment, racist crime victimisation and diverse forms of harassment reported by minorities.

A mean (average) discrimination rate was established for the seven aggregate groups surveyed which had claimed that they had been discriminated against in the preceding twelve months. The minority group in the EU reporting the greatest incidence of experienced discrimination was Roma respondents: 47 per cent, with the highest rate recorded in the Czech Republic. Sub-Saharan Africans came next: 41 per cent, with Ireland being the place where this group of respondents felt most discrimination. Racism inevitably came into play in discriminatory practices against them. North Africans, overwhelmingly Muslim, ranked third: 36 per cent, with Italy rated as the most discriminatory receiving society. Intuitively, then, it appeared that public perception of a gypsy lifestyle trumped racial and religious categories as the basis for discrimination. To be sure, race may also contribute to discriminatory practices targeting Roma. It is also conceivable that Roma were quicker to feel and/or report that they were targets of discrimination than other groups.

Minorities composed of central and eastern Europeans (the vast majority of whom are Slav) living in other EU states (such as Poles in Germany) were tied with Turkish minorities at a 23 per cent felt-discrimination rate. Other predominantly Slav groups – for example, Russian minorities in the Baltic states, and ex-Yugoslav nationalities like Serbs in Sweden – brought up the bottom of the list, at 14 and 12 per cent respectively.[69] These data suggest that manifestations of Islamophobia – against north Africans and Turks – are less common than the racism directed at Roma and black Africans. But they are still more widespread than discrimination experienced by eastern European Slav minorities.

Muslims' experience of victimisation

The EU-MIDIS survey provided additional light on Islamophobia by focusing on the responses of self-identifying Muslims. For 89 per cent of them, religion played a very or fairly important role in their lives.[70] One in three Muslim respondents interviewed in the fourteen EU states where Muslim minorities were surveyed claimed to have experienced discrimination over the previous twelve months. Muslims between sixteen and twenty-four years of age reported a higher degree of discrimination while, somewhat unexpectedly, Muslims wearing traditional or religious clothing reported no more discrimination than the general sample. Having EU citizenship or residing in an EU state for a longer period of time was positively linked with lower levels of felt discrimination.

Categories of race and religion were not always treated as distinct in this research. One in ten Muslims surveyed claimed to have been the victim of a personal 'racially motivated' crime (assault, serious harassment) at least once in the past year. Of these respondents, 72 per cent attributed the crime to a member of the majority population. One in four Muslims had been stopped by the police the preceding year; 40 per cent believed this was attributable to their minority or immigrant status. There was, therefore, 'a growing perception among Muslim leaders and communities that they are being stopped, questioned, and searched not on the basis of evidence and reasonable suspicion but on the basis of "looking Muslim"'.[71] Perpetrator profiling seemed to play a large part in the general pattern of discrimination.

Can this profiling be broken down by specific categories? Some evidence is provided by respondents' own identification of the grounds on which they were discriminated against. All respondents cited their ethnic/immigrant origin, religion/beliefs, or a combination of the two as the cause. The design of the survey was therefore unable to pinpoint the single most important reason that Muslims felt they were discriminated against.

Discrimination against Muslim minorities was also examined in terms of respondents' ethnic origin and their European country of residence. Of all possible combinations, Muslims from both north and sub-Saharan Africa living in Malta complained most (64 per cent) about discrimination (see Table 4.1). This result tells us little given the small sample size for Malta. When we select by large sample numbers, then Muslims of north African origin residing in Italy experienced the highest levels of discrimination, and repeat discrimination, in almost every area identified.[72] North African Muslims living in Spain and Belgium also experienced higher-than-average discrimination.

By contrast, only 26 per cent of this cohort living in France reported experiencing discrimination. Its sub-Saharan co-religionists polled a near-identical percentage (25 per cent). Discrimination reportedly experienced by Muslim groups of different ethnic origins was also uniform, if at higher levels, in the Netherlands and Denmark. In these countries, then, being Islam regardless of one's racial or ethnic background was subjectively viewed as the basis for being discriminated against.

When the focus is put on Turkish minorities across Europe, it was in Denmark that they felt most discriminated against. They felt markedly less so in Germany, the Netherlands[73] and Belgium, and rarely in Austria and Bulgaria. But the news was not good for Turks in another arena. Looking at groups with the highest rates of experienced discrimination when looking for work and at work (setting aside the untypical case of Malta), we find the worst conditions obtaining for Muslims of north African origin in Italy, followed by Turks in Germany and Denmark. In employment matters, Turkish minorities might have become incidental targets in more general European opposition to Turkey's membership of the EU. The campaign slogan of the right-wing Austrian Freedom Party had once been 'Turkey into the EU? Not

Table 4.1 Discrimination rate by ethnic origin and country (over the past twelve months in nine different areas)

Host country	Muslim minority	Discrimination rate (%)
Malta	African	64
Italy	North African	55
Finland	Sub-Saharan African	47
Denmark	Sub-Saharan African	46
Denmark	Turkish	42
Spain	North African	40
Belgium	North African	33
Sweden	Sub-Saharan African	33
Germany	Turkish	31
Netherlands	North African	30
Netherlands	Turkish	29
France	North African	26
France	Sub-Saharan African	25
Belgium	Turkish	20
Slovenia	Ex-Yugoslav	15
Luxembourg	Ex-Yugoslav	12
Sweden	Iraqi	10
Austria	Turkish	10
Bulgaria	Turkish	9
EU average		30

Data in Focus Report 2: Muslims (European Union Agency for Fundamental Rights, 2009), Fig. 3, at http://fra.europa.eu/fraWebsite/eu-midis/eumidis_muslims_en.htm

with me!'[74] The presence of Turks in the European workplace was becoming a battleground for debates on Turkey's membership, just as the spectre of the job-stealing Polish plumber had been in the arguments about earlier EU enlargement.

Among its other findings, the EU-MIDIS survey provided evidence on differing levels and types of discrimination in the most liberal and most xenophobic EU states. As might be expected from earlier empirical findings that we reported, Sweden's discriminatory practices appeared minor compared to most European states. But they varied considerably from one Muslim community to another. Thus 33 per cent of Muslim sub-Saharan Africans claimed to have experienced discrimination, but only 10 per cent of Iraqis did. By contrast, Italy scored poorly on the experienced discrimination scale, again consistent with earlier findings. Repeat discrimination was particularly endemic: north Africans reported they had suffered an average of

20 incidents in the past twelve months, double the number for the next worst case (sub-Saharan Muslims in Finland, with ten cases per year). The next five highest rates of repeat discrimination also involved black Africans in western European countries. Turks in Germany ranked eighth overall (an average of six reported incidents of discrimination over the previous twelve months).

If responses by self-identifying Muslims can help describe the specific characteristics of Islamophobia in Europe, our conclusion has to be that it is complex, nationally differentiated, and not subject to easy generalisations about the role played by race, ethnicity, religion or lifestyle.

THE ETHNIC MAJORITIES' VIEWS

At the centre of the empirical examination of bias against Muslims are the attitudes of ethnic majorities towards Muslim minorities. This is the third type of data illuminating Islamophobic orientations. One important question in attitudinal surveys concerns the issue of Muslims' loyalty to their receiving societies. Response patterns have reflected an apparent clash of perceptions between majorities and minorities. In a 2009 Gallup poll, approximately one-half of British (49 per cent) and German (45 per cent) respondents claimed that Muslims in their countries were not loyal (an additional one in six respondents said they did not know or refused to answer). French respondents were markedly less suspicious about their Muslim communities: just over one-third (35 per cent) did not think they were loyal (one in five said they did not know or refused to answer). In none of these three countries, however, did the survey results offer a ringing endorsement of trust in Muslim communities.

By contrast, strong majorities of Muslim respondents in Britain (82 per cent), France (80 per cent) and Germany (71 per cent) claimed that Muslims were indeed loyal to their respective countries of residence.[75] Disaggregating by Muslim communities in capital cities, 74 per cent of Muslim respondents in London, 73 per cent in Paris and 72 per cent in Berlin thought that Muslims were loyal to these countries.[76]

A clash of perceptions was also reflected in respondents' contrasting impressions of the value of intercultural encounters. In a survey reported in 2008, majorities in all European countries examined viewed greater interaction between the West and the Muslim world as a threat. The highest figure was 79 per cent in Denmark (where the 2005 cartoon crisis polarised views), followed by around two-thirds in the Netherlands, Italy and Spain, and 59 per cent in Belgium. Three out of five Dutch respondents considered Islam to be incompatible with modern European life. Close to two-thirds of respondents in Germany, Italy and Spain claimed that Islam was not compatible with democracy. By contrast, nearly three out of four Muslims surveyed in Europe said they supported democracy.[77] Not surprisingly, the single most-cited suggestion by Muslims on how the West could improve relations was: 'Show greater respect for Islam and stop regarding Muslims as inferior.'[78]

These survey data indicate that significant sections of European society are suspicious of and even hostile to their Muslim communities. It is no surprise, then, that radical right-wing parties have tapped this constituency to bolster their standing in national and European politics. On an individual level, whether candid or cryptic, anti-Islamic cultural narratives have brought a number of European artists and writers fame. Two Dutch film makers, Theo van Gogh and Geert Wilders, capitalised on anti-Muslim views in their films, which turned both into major public figures. English writers such as Martin Amis and Christopher Hitchens have drawn negative portraits of Islamic culture in their fiction and essays respectively. In France, the novelist Michel Houellebecq skilfully exploited Islamophobia to become a best-selling author and celebrity. During the last years of her life the notable Italian journalist Oriana Fallaci launched scathing attacks on Islamic culture and practices in her books.[79]

Most of these creative artists would dispute that they are Islamophobes but at a minimum their polemical works have added fuel to the fire which targets Muslims. What the triumph of Islamophobia would look like has also been depicted in a literary work. A novel by the Catholic writer Jacques Neirynck, *Le Siège de Bruxelles*, describes a Belgium that has been taken over by the radical right. Concentration camps have been set up for those Muslims and Jews who have not already been expelled. The siege of the Muslim ghetto in Brussels results in a bombardment that eerily resembles that of the Bosnian capital, Sarajevo, in the mid-1990s.[80]

In his equally vivid reportage titled *The Last Days of Europe*, Walter Laqueur suggested that it was the naïveté of European governments in accommodating large numbers of Muslim immigrants that was ultimately responsible for a populist Islamophobic backlash:

> The host governments were quite unaware of the social, cultural, and political consequences of welcoming people whose customs and values were so different from their own – immigrants who thought their values were superior and would want eventually, as their numbers grew stronger, to impose these values on the host countries. Nor did the Europeans foresee that these ambitions on the part of the immigrants would generate opposition, strengthen radical xenophobic parties, and add greatly to domestic tensions.[81]

This polemical account addresses the purportedly malign Islamophobic consequences of liberal immigration policies in the larger states of Europe. The next two chapters examine the alleged domestic tensions in France and Germany that have been produced by Laqueur's 'ambitious immigrants'.

NOTES

1. For an original account, see Christopher Tyerman, *God's War: A New History of the Crusades* (Cambridge, MA: Belknap Press, 2006).
2. From August C. Krey, *The First Crusade: The Accounts of Eyewitnesses and Participants* (Princeton, NJ: Princeton University Press, 1921), pp. 33–7. The Jebusites were a tribe which lived around Jerusalem (then called Jebus) before it was conquered by King David about 1000 BC.
3. Desiderius Erasmus, 'On the War against the Turk/*De bello turcico*', in Erika Rummel (ed.), *The Erasmus Reader* (Toronto: University of Toronto Press, 1990), pp. 315–16.
4. Slobodan Drakulic, 'Anti-Turkish Obsession and Muslim Slavs in the Balkans', paper presented at the Canadian Sociological Association meeting, Vancouver, 5 June 2008, p. 12.
5. Étienne Balibar, 'Postface', in Christophe Bertossi (ed.), *European Anti-discrimination and the Politics of Citizenship: Britain and France* (Basingstoke: Palgrave Macmillan, 2007), p. 239.
6. Drakulic, 'Anti-Turkish Obsession and Muslim Slavs in the Balkans'. The term 'anti-Turkish obsession' was coined by Slobodan Prosperov Novak, *Zlatno doba: Marulić, Držić, Gundulića* (Zagreb: Hrvatska Sveučilišna Naklada, 2002), p. 35.
7. Ramón Grosfoguel and Eric Mielants, 'The Long-durée Entanglement between Islamophobia and Racism in the Modern/Colonial Capitalist/Patriarchal World-system: An Introduction', *Human Architecture: A Journal of the Sociology of Self-Knowledge* 5:1 (2006), p. 2.
8. Philip Jenkins, *God's Continent: Christianity, Islam, and Europe's Religious Crisis* (New York: Oxford University Press, 2007), p. 104.
9. Kerem Caliskan, European editor of *Hürriyet*, quoted in 'The Ludwigshafen aftermath: "Merkel discriminates against the Turks"', Spiegel Online International website, 8 February 2008, http://www.spiegel.de/international/germany/0,1518,534030,00.html, accessed 2 February 2012.
10. Ahmed Bouhsane, 'The Other in the Arab Culture', unpublished paper presented at 'Africa's Intellectual Caravans: Bilad as Soudan and al-Maghaarib' conference, Vassar College, Poughkeepsie, NY, 7–9 November 2002.
11. 'Islamophobia: A Definition', Islamophobia Watch website, http://www.islamo phobia-watch.com/islamophobia-a-definition/, accessed 2 February 2012.
12. Christopher Caldwell, *Reflections on the Revolution in Europe: Immigration, Islam, and the West* (New York: Doubleday, 2009), p. 169.
13. Vincent Geissner, 'L'Islamophobie en France au regard du débat européen', in Rémy Leveau and Khadija Mohsen-Finan (eds), *Musulmans de France et d'Europe* (Paris: CNRS, 2005), p. 60.
14. Kenan Malik, 'Islamophobia myth', *Prospect*, February 2005.
15. Jonathan Laurence and Justin Vaisse, *Integrating Islam: Political and Religious Challenges in Contemporary France* (Washington, DC: Brookings Institution Press, 2006), p. x.
16. Valérie Amiraux, 'Religious Discrimination: Muslims Claiming Equality in the EU', in Christophe Bertossi (ed.), *European Anti-discrimination and the Politics of Citizenship: Britain and France* (Basingstoke: Palgrave Macmillan, 2007), p. 147.
17. Thomas Deltombe, *L'Islam imaginaire: la construction médiatique de l'Islamophobie en France, 1975–2005* (Paris: La Découverte, 2005).

18. Elisabeth Eide, 'Suspect Foreigners? Media and Migration', paper presented at the Conference on Integration and Immigrants' Participation, University of Iceland, Reykjavik, 14 November 2011. See also her 'The Long Distance Runner and Discourses on Europe's Others: Ethnic Minority Representation in the Feature Story', paper presented at the 15th Nordic Conference on Media and Communication Research, Reykjavik, August 2001.

19. 'Baroness Warsi says Muslim prejudice seen as normal', BBC News website, 20 January 2011, http://www.bbc.co.uk/news/uk-politics-12235237, accessed 2 February 2012.

20. Matti Bunzl, Anti-Semitism and Islamophobia: Hatreds Old and New in Europe (Chicago: Prickly Paradigm Press, 2007), pp. 38, 40.

21. An excellent example is Juan Cole, Engaging the Muslim World, rev. ed. (New York: Palgrave Macmillan, 2010).

22. Monica Duffy Toft, 'Getting Religion? The Puzzling Case of Islam and Civil War', International Security 31:4 (2007), pp. 115–16, 107.

23. Elspeth Guild, Security and Migration in the 21st Century (Cambridge: Polity, 2009), p. 7.

24. Ariane Chebel d'Appollonia and Simon Reich, 'Immigration: Tensions, Dilemmas, and Unresolved Questions', in Ariane Chebel d'Appollonia and Simon Reich (eds), Immigration, Integration, and Security: America and Europe in Comparative Perspective (Pittsburgh, PA: University of Pittsburgh Press, 2008), p. 337.

25. Bunzl, Anti-Semitism and Islamophobia, p. 37.

26. Amiraux, 'Religious Discrimination', p. 149. See also Vincent Geisser, 'L'Islamophobie en France au regard du débat européen', in Rémy Leveau and Khadija Mohsen-Finan (eds), Musulmans de France et d'Europe (Paris: CNRS, 2005).

27. Bunzl, Anti-Semitism and Islamophobia, p. 13.

28. European Union Monitoring Centre for Racism and Xenophobia, Muslims in the European Union: Discrimination and Islamophobia (Vienna: EUMC, 2006), p. 14.

29. Ibid., p. 33. A major ongoing project funded under the EU's Seventh Framework Program and based at the University of Amsterdam is titled 'Finding a Place for Islam in Europe: Cultural Interactions between Muslim Immigrants and Receiving Societies' (EURISLAM).

30. 'Aims and Objectives', Islamic Human Rights Commission website, http://ihrc.org.uk/about-ihrc/aims-a-objectives, accessed 2 February 2012.

31. Nasar Meer and Tehseen Noorani, 'A Sociological Comparison of Anti-Semitism and Anti-Muslim Sentiment in Britain', Sociological Review 56 (2008), p. 195.

32. Pierre-André Taguieff, La Nouvelle Judéophobie (Paris: Mille et Une Nuits, 2002).

33. Vincent Geisser, La Nouvelle Islamophobie (Paris: La Découverte, 2003).

34. Bunzl, Anti-Semitism and Islamophobia, p. 13.

35. Timothy M. Savage, 'Europe and Islam: Crescent Waxing, Cultures Clashing', Washington Quarterly, Summer 2004, p. 26. See also Christina Schori Liang, 'Europe for the Europeans: The Foreign and Security Policy of the Populist Radical Right', in Christina Schori Liang (ed.), Europe for the Europeans: The Foreign and Security Policy of the Populist Radical Right (Aldershot: Ashgate, 2007), p. 23.

36. Joel S. Fetzer and J. Christopher Soper, Muslims and the State in Great Britain, France, and Germany (Cambridge: Cambridge University Press, 2005), p. 157.

37. On religion and related topics, see the informative European case studies published in

Journal of Muslim Minority Affairs 28:1 (2008), 'Special Issue: Islam in Europe', edited by Wade Jacoby and Hakan Yavuz.

38. 'Mohammed top of baby name table', *Muslim Weekly*, 14–20 December 2007.
39. Quoted in Kenan Malik, 'Islamophobia myth'.
40. Jocelyne Cesari and Seán McLoughlin (eds), *European Muslims and the Secular State* (Aldershot: Ashgate, 2005), p. 4.
41. Ibid., p. 2.
42. Tariq Ramadan, *Western Muslims and the Future of Islam* (Oxford: Oxford University Press, 2005), p. 226.
43. Bassam Tibi, *Political Islam, World Politics and Europe: Democratic Peace and Euro-Islam versus Global Jihad* (London: Routledge, 2008), p. 192.
44. Robert O. Paxton, 'Can you really become French?', *New York Review of Books*, 9 April 2009, pp. 55–6.
45. Ibid.
46. Sami Zemni, 'Islamophobie: Clé de lecture de l'exclusion sociale et politique des musulmans en Occident', in Ural Manço (ed.), *Reconnaissance et discrimination: présence de l'Islam en Europe occidentale et en Amérique du Nord* (Paris: L'Harmattan, 2004), pp. 325–6.
47. Lorenzo Vidino, 'The Tripartite Threat of Radical Islam to Europe', *inFocus Quarterly*, Winter 2007.
48. Robert S. Leiken, 'Europe's Angry Muslims', *Foreign Affairs*, July–August 2005.
49. Lorenzo Vidino, 'The Muslim Brotherhood's Conquest of Europe', *Middle East Quarterly* 12:1 (2005), pp. 1–11.
50. Ibid.
51 Charter of the Organisation of the Islamic Conference, at http://www.oic-oci.org/is11/english/Charter-en.pdf, accessed 2 February 2012. This is a partial list of objectives and is not given in the order in which they appear in the charter.
52. 'Islamophobia Observatory', Organisation of Islamic Cooperation website, http://www.oic-oci.org/page_detail.asp?p_id=182, accessed 2 February 2012.
53. The respective websites are http://www.ihrc.org.uk and http://www.fioe.org/
54. Heiko Henkel, 'Turkish Islam in Germany: A Problematic Tradition or the Fifth Project of Constitutional Patriotism?', *Journal of Muslim Minority Affairs* 28 (2008), p. 121.
55. Olivier Roy, *The Failure of Political Islam* (Cambridge, MA: Harvard University Press, 1994).
56. Congressional Research Service, *Islamist Extremism in Europe* (Washington, DC: Congressional Research Service, 2006), p. 3.
57. Robert J. Pauly, Jr., *Islam in Europe: Integration or Marginalization?* (Aldershot: Ashgate, 2004), p. 174.
58. Ruti Teitel, 'No Laughing Matter: The Controversial Danish Cartoons Depicting the Prophet Mohammed, and Their Broader Meaning for Europe's Public Square', FindLaw website, 15 February 2006, at http://writ.news.findlaw.com/scripts/printer_friendly.pl?page=/commentary/20060215_teitel.html, accessed 5 February 2012.
59. It originally appeared on the French website Proche-Orient.info. It was then published in the Danish *Jyllands-Posten*, which had carried the controversial cartoons.
60. Walter Laqueur, *The Last Days of Europe: Epitaph for an Old Continent* (New York: Thomas Dunne, 2007), p. 209.

61. Bat Ye'or, *Eurabia: The Euro-Arab Axis* (Madison, NJ : Fairleigh Dickinson University Press, 2005). A popular book on this topic is Melanie Phillips, *Londonistan* (New York: Encounter, 2006).

62. The most ambitious research on these issues has been carried out by the Washington-based non-profit Pew Charitable Trust. See 'The Great Divide: How Westerners and Muslims View Each Other', Pew Research Center website, 22 June 2006, http://pewglobal.org/reports/display.php?ReportID=253, accessed 5 February 2012.

63. For example, Ipsos MORI in Britain, TNS Sofres in France and ALLBUS in Germany.

64. For a current list of Dronkers' research papers on immigrants, see http://www.eui.eu/Personal/Dronkers/nonDutchpapers.htm

65. Stéfanie André, Jaap Dronkers and Ariana Need, 'To Vote Or Not To Vote? Electoral Participation Of Immigrants From Different Countries Of Origin in 24 European Countries Of Destination', paper presented at the ECSR conference 'Changing Societies in the Context of the European Union Enlargement', Sciences Po-CNRS, Paris, 11–12 December 2009, p. 13.

66. Open Society Justice Initiative, *Ethnic Profiling in the European Union: Pervasive, Ineffective, and Discriminatory* (New York: Open Society Institute, 2009), p. 9.

67. Ibid., p. 7.

68. At Home in Europe Project, *Muslims in Europe: A Report on 11 EU Cities* (New York & Budapest: Open Society Institute / London: Open Society Foundation, 2009), pp. 22–3.

69. EU-MIDIS conducted face-to-face interviews with 23,500 people from selected immigrant and ethnic minority groups in all twenty-seven EU member states. In addition, 5,000 people from the majority population were interviewed. The report was commissioned by the EU Agency for Fundamental Rights. See *EU-MIDIS at a Glance: Introduction to the FRA's EU-wide Discrimination Survey* (European Union Agency for Fundamental Rights, 2009), http://fra.europa.eu/fraWebsite/attachments/EU-MIDIS_GLANCE_EN.pdf, accessed 5 February 2012.

70. *Data in Focus Report 2: Muslims* (European Union Agency for Fundamental Rights, 2009), http://fra.europa.eu/fraWebsite/eu-midis/eumidis_muslims_en.htm, accessed 5 February 2012.

71. EU Accession Monitoring Program, *Monitoring Minority Protection in EU Member States* (New York: Open Society Institute, 2004), p. 53. See also Open Society Justice Initiative, *Ethnic Profiling in the European Union*.

72. These were: (1) when looking for work, (2) at work, (3) when looking for a house or an apartment to rent or buy, (4) by healthcare personnel, (5) by social services personnel, (6) by school personnel, (7) at a café, restaurant or bar, (8) when entering or in a shop and (9) when trying to open a bank account or get a loan.

73. For a comprehensive analysis of Turkish civil associations in the Netherlands and the social capital they have accumulated, see Talip Küçükcan, 'Bridging the European Union and Turkey: The Turkish Diaspora in Europe', *Insight Turkey*, October–December 2007, pp. 85–99.

74. Bunzl, *Anti-Semitism and Islamophobia*, p. 33.

75. *The Gallup Coexist Index 2009: A Global Study of Interfaith Relations*, (Washington, DC: Gallup, 2009), Fig. 15. An unexciting 2009 documentary film describes how the worldwide Gallup survey of Muslim opinion was made; see Rob Gardner (dir.), *Inside Islam: What a Billion Muslims Really Think* (Unity Productions Foundation), http:

//www.snagfilms.com/films/title/inside_islam_what_a_billion_muslims_really_think, accessed 5 February 2012.

76. *Islam and the West: Annual Report on the State of Dialogue – January 2008* (Geneva: World Economic Forum, 2008), pp. 42–3. This was also reported in Chebel d'Appollonia and Reich, *Immigration, Integration, and Security*, p. 282.

77. *Islam and the West*, pp. 25, 42–3.

78. Ibid., pp. 22–3.

79. For analysis of Houellebecq and Fallaci, see my *Europe Old and New: Transnationalism, Belonging, Xenophobia* (Lanham, MD: Rowman and Littlefield, 2009), ch. 8.

80. Jacques Neirynck, *Le Siège de Bruxelles* (Paris: Desclée de Brouwer, 1996). Another novel set in France dealing with a right-wing political backlash is Clément Weill Raynal's *Le Songe du guerrier* (Paris: Albin Michel, 2006).

81. Laqueur, *The Last Days of Europe*, p. 79.

CHAPTER FIVE

France: from assimilation to affirmative action?

Xenophobia has been succinctly defined as 'the fear of difference embodied in persons or groups'.[1] The term entered the vernacular in France in 1901 with the publication of Anatole France's *Monsieur Bergeret à Paris*, a volume in his contemporary history series that examined the anti-Semitic aspect of the Dreyfus affair.[2] But it was not until the end of the twentieth century that the systematic study of xenophobia and racism in France took off. Two pioneers were Pierre-André Taguieff, who focused on differences between xenophobia and racism – itself subdivided into the racism of exclusion and that of extermination[3] – and Michel Wieviorka, who carried out empirical studies of comparative xenophobia.[4] Much subsequent research has taken its cues from these conceptualisations.

IMMIGRATION GROWTH, INTEGRATION OUTCOMES

Scholarly interest in xenophobia has been sparked by France's long immigration history and even more so by its recent character.[5] Muslim immigration alone comprises a major field of inquiry. Believed to number at least five million, the country's Muslim population is the largest in Europe. Muslims far outnumber the combined total of Protestants (800,000) and Jews (500,000) in the country. It is also estimated that about 40 per cent are not French citizens. Some demographers have claimed that since 1967 the Muslim community in France has grown from 90,000 to more than six million.[6] One main cause of the Muslim influx was the Algerian war of independence: when Algeria obtained statehood in 1962, the 60,000 or so Algerians who had fought with the French were granted asylum in France. It is calculated that the descendants of this first group of Algerian refugees number around 500,000 today.[7] But that accounts for only about one-tenth of the overall Muslim population.

A straightforward explanation for the rapid growth of the immigrant population was the need to rebuild French industry, a policy priority set by Gaullist governments in the 1960s. France supplemented its labour force by drawing heavily on its colonies in north Africa. By the early 1970s, this guest worker population numbered around one million.[8]

A further cause was the French government's adoption of a liberal family reunification policy (*regroupement familial*). One study reported that 'family reunification from all countries grew from 55,000 a year in the late 1960s to 81,000 in 1973, before decreasing over time to about 25,000 in 2004'.[9] As in other major receiving societies like Britain and Germany, the pursuit of such a programme produced a demographic shift from a predominantly male Muslim population in France to nuclear and then extended Muslim family structures.

It also provoked a backlash in France. As William Safran astutely pointed out,

> many French citizens who welcome immigrants in their midst do not necessarily welcome their families or communities, a phenomenon that may suggest that economic considerations (e.g. obtaining social benefits) compete with matters of principle, that is, with the Jacobin notion of an ethnoculturally undifferentiated structure of society.[10]

Put differently, public perceptions of freeriding by families of migrants weaken citizens' enthusiasm for the egalitarian, colour-blind republic that France holds itself up to be. Such economic resentment has little to do with citizens' disdain for the ethnoreligious background of migrants, though Muslim identity is likely to intensify the 'freeriding' resentment.

The French state initially regarded new Muslim arrivals as temporary – a naïve view given the disastrous political and economic conditions obtaining throughout north Africa, from where most migrants came. Like Britain and Germany, it did not initially develop a comprehensive and coherent integration policy. Evidence suggested that at first north Africans registered both upward socio-economic mobility and high rates of intermarriage. For example, in 1990 an estimated 30 per cent of men and 40 per cent of women had married a spouse of a different nationality. The rate of exogamy increased the longer migrants lived in France. There did not seem reason for concern about Muslim integration into French society, especially given most north Africans' proficiency in French.

Another reassuring indicator feeding the impression of seamless integration came from later survey results. The percentage of respondents agreeing that there were too many immigrants in France fell from 35 per cent in 1988 to 25 per cent in 2006. Three-quarters believed that immigration was a source of enrichment for the country, and 77 per cent asserted that Muslim practices should be respected. A 2005 survey found that about half of people of north

African and Turkish origin agreed that 'in France, everybody can succeed whatever the colour of his/her skin'. They took a far more optimistic view than the French sample, in which only 43 per cent believed in the reality of colour-blind success. Both north African and Turkish respondents (88 per cent) and the general population (94 per cent) overwhelmingly agreed about the virtues of secularisation as 'the only way for people with different beliefs to live together'.[11] These findings seemed too good to be true.

A different study indicated that 'increasing tolerance vis-à-vis immigrants but ambivalence vis-à-vis immigration was displayed by an expanding majority of French'.[12] These respondents, too, underscored the importance of cultural enrichment but flagged the need to set limits on how many migrants should be allowed into the country.

Such generally positive appraisals of migrant inclusion in French society is at odds with events that shook France subsequently, such as riots involving marginalised youth from the outlying areas of big French cities where much of the state-subsidised basic housing is found. A generational divide may also explain why earlier immigration waves proved less problematic. In an important finding recorded by Catherine Wihtol de Wenden, the tendency for smooth migrant integration weakens as receiving societies experience successive immigration waves. Earlier generations of immigrants were not particularly concerned with securing official residence status or achieving cultural and linguistic integration. They prioritised economic mobility, though they also wanted recognition of being first-class citizens in their new societies. More recently, the very idea of integration has become contested, both by the French state and society and by some of the new arrivals themselves.

Wihtol de Wenden drew attention to the socio-economic and political pecking orders that migrants confront. With France as prototype, she developed a hierarchy of European rights that ranged from the fullest to the most precarious. The top-down pyramid looks this way: (1) nationals of a country, therefore in the case of France *français-français*, (2) residents of other European countries, (3) European non-residents, (4) non-European residents, (5) non-Europeans with temporary residence permits, (6) asylum seekers, (7) unexpellable undocumented migrants and (8) expellable undocumented migrants. This nuanced hierarchy has served as an unofficial framework for formulating an increasingly more selective French immigration policy, the so-called *immigration choisie*.

But formulating such policy is not the same as applying it. In late 2011 President Sarkozy's interior minister expressed his agreement with the view of Front National president Marine Le Pen that the country still accepted too many legal immigrants each year. The annual total of 200,000 was 'the equivalent of a city like Rennes, twice the size of Perpignan'. Even while asserting that 'France is not a xenophobic country' and will remain open to immigrants, the minister emphasised that newcomers need 'to be integrated, accept our laws, and adopt our way of life'.[13] He singled out fraud in marriages, family reunification and social assistance claims by those returning to live in countries of origin as areas where immigration policy had to be tightened up. The rhetorical pressure on immigration flows was being ramped up as France's 2012 elections approached.

POLICY SHIFT TOWARDS SELECTIVITY

Patrick Weil, one of France's leading specialists on immigration, claims that the republican model shaping migration policy dates from 1938, when Philippe Serre was appointed state under-secretary responsible for immigration and foreigners. His policies differentiated broadly between useful and harmful immigration on the basis of socio-occupational class. It was a colour-blind approach that nevertheless reflected a selective immigration policy.[14]

By contrast, the longstanding policy of governments in the Fifth Republic, up to 2007, can be termed *immigration subie*, that is, the state's resigned acceptance of uncontrolled immigration. Its converse, *immigration choisie*, the selective approach devised by Serre, only returned to favour when Nicolas Sarkozy moved into the Élysée Palace in 2007. There are a number of variants of this selective approach, ranging from a closed-door policy altogether to one singling out skill sets useful for the country's economy. The radical option of zero immigration, which appeared both politically incorrect and unviable, had been proposed in 1993 by interior minister Charles Pasqua. He was a leading figure in the centre-right movement which in 2002 served as the bedrock for the Union pour un Mouvement Populaire (UMP) founded by Jacques Chirac and utilised by Sarkozy as an organisational base.

Sarkozy himself had served as interior minister in a UMP-led government in 2005. He advocated a policy of selective immigration which was to be based on quotas. This policy informed the CESEDA (Entry and Residence in France and Asylum Rights Code) law of 24 July 2006 which created new types of temporary residence permits (*cartes de séjour*). Three categories were established: 'skills and talents', 'employees on assignment' and 'interns'. For professional classes, this was a beneficial reform, but it also had an exclusionary dimension for migrants not falling into these categories.

Another law enacted in 2007 by a UMP government tightening up immigration flows proposed voluntary DNA testing for family reunification applicants so that they could verify their blood ties. This law triggered angry demonstrations in Paris. But an additional blow to the sanctity of the family reunification principle was new French legislation assigning priority to 'needed labour' applicants over family members. This law was a blueprint for the introduction of the EU blue card in 2007, designed for use by highly qualified workers and students. The crowning achievement of French immigration reform was, as described in Chapter 2, President Sarkozy's success in prodding the EU to adopt the 2008 Pact on Immigration and Asylum.

The whittling away of opportunities for immigrant admission in France has reflected a growing sentiment that immigration numbers and integration problems were responsible for growing tensions within French society. The 2008 global economic crisis strengthened the case for more rigorous state oversight of immigration and integration processes.

IS THERE A 'FRENCH ISLAMOPHOBIA?'

In 2008 vandals defaced the graves in northern France of Muslim war veterans with painted swastikas and anti-Islamic slogans. The vandalism took place at France's largest military cemetery near Arras, where tens of thousands of soldiers were killed in World War I. It was timed to coincide with the Eid al-Adha commemoration, when Muslims visit the graves of loved ones. The 2008 desecration marked the third attack on the Muslim sector of the cemetery and it was swiftly condemned by President Sarkozy as 'the expression of a repugnant racism directed against the Muslim community of France'.[15]

Many other examples of repugnant racism can be cited, of course, but on a daily basis many Muslims in France feel marginalised and excluded. The police agency that monitors radical groups in France, the Renseignements Généraux, released a report in 2004 stating that a considerable number of 'sensitive neighbourhoods' with majority Muslim populations were exhibiting symptoms of 'community isolation' from national, social and political life. Astonishingly, the Muslim population of these neighbourhoods added up to 1.8 million.[16] Fouad Ajami, a specialist on Arab politics, described French Muslims as 'shut up in these ghettos, secluded and kept apart from French society'.[17] Riva Kastoryano, a leading French specialist on immigration and integration issues, went further to argue that France is beyond the stage of postcolonialism, and that internal colonisation has taken its place.[18]

A fundamental contradiction lies at the core of French Islamophobia. Its framing of Muslims combines a number of variable categories.

> Even though the vast majority of children originating in African, Maghrebi and Turkish immigration are today French nationals, taxonomies continue to designate them as 'young Arab Muslims' – a process of stigmatisation that simultaneously combines an ethnic referential (Arab) with a religious one (Muslim).[19]

Referring to their youth demeans them further.

In 2005 urban riots exploded in various parts of France after two Muslim youths in Paris, who were being pursued by the police, were accidentally electrocuted while fleeing. The violence by young people in the *banlieues* was viewed as an expression of 'deep-rooted problems, such as racial discrimination, unemployment, and exclusion from "Frenchness" – despite the fact that they are predominantly French citizens'.[20] French political leaders were made aware of 'Europe's Muslim Street' – possibly 'a more powerful political force than the fabled Arab street'.[21]

Given that city outskirts have become the arena of social contestation between unempowered young Muslims and the French state, it may be more accurate to refer to a 'municipal Islamophobia' that has spread across France.[22] That was one of the concerns expressed in 2005 by the Mouvement de l'Immigration et des Banlieues (Movement of Immigration and the Suburbs). The point of the riots was to send a message: 'Enough with unpunished police crimes, enough with police profiling, enough with crappy schools, enough with planned unemployment, enough with run-down housing, enough with prisons, enough with humiliations.'[23] Close to 5,000 Muslims were arrested in the 2005 civil disorder.[24]

One possible indicator of anti-Muslim bias is the composition of a country's prison population. A study published in 2006 found that more than half of all those incarcerated in France were Muslims even though they represented less than 10 per cent of the total population.[25] At stake in this pattern of incarceration is not just the judicial bias against Muslims. Many Islamic youth first become exposed to radical Islamist ideas while in prison.

Can a culture be blamed for engendering criminality? French sociologist Hugues Lagrange created a public furore in 2010 with the publication of his data-driven book *Le Déni des cultures* ('The Denial of Cultures').[26] His contention was that cultures did matter in explaining statistical variation in rates of delinquency (loosely understood as 'encounters with the law') in France. Distancing himself from socio-economic explanations of social delinquency, he focused on culture – and by extension ethnoreligious and racial attributes – as the major explanatory factor. Blacks, and in particular those of Sahelian African background (a belt south of the Sahara extending from Senegal on the Atlantic Ocean to Eritrea on the Red Sea), were overrepresented in delinquency statistics.

Lagrange offered an eclectic explanation for this propensity to crime among Sahelian youth: it was the pervasiveness of polygamy, the subordination of women (above all in their role as mothers) and the authoritarianism of fathers, which distinguished this group. By contrast, the lower delinquency rates for students of Maghrebi background could also be explained by cultural features: their families' deeper rootedness in French society and, as a consequence, their upward mobility into the middle class. He did not identify their Muslim background as a factor in lower delinquency rates.

The author's conclusions provoked a wideranging debate and raised many methodological questions: for example, why he had not factored into his analysis the significantly higher rates of being stopped by the police that blacks (six times higher than for whites) and Arabs (eight times higher) had? Lagrange did accept that the receiving society was in part to blame: itself the victim of a moral and ideological backlash, French society had extended lukewarm, even hostile receptions to African immigrants, thereby marginalising and ghettoising them.

As in many other European nations, anti-Muslim biases in France can be traced back centuries. A leading nineteenth-century thinker on nationalism and nation building, Ernest Renan, gave a lecture at the Sorbonne in 1883 in which he stated: 'Any person with a bit of education about current affairs clearly discerns the actual inferiority of Muslim countries, the decadence in states ruled by Islam, the intellectual nullity of races which behold exclusively their culture and education to this religion.'[27] Renan is today cited as an authority on the making of a nation but such bias raises doubts about his credibility.

Over the last two decades, some of France's leading intellectual figures have articulated subtle, cryptic prejudices about Islam. They frequently involve unfavourable comparisons between European and Islamic philosophies. Jacques Derrida suggested that 'democracies to come' which would embrace Western liberal values might not be strong enough to counter the threat of 'rogues', of which Islam could be one.[28] Similarly Julia Kristeva argued that the West had to re-evaluate itself in its struggle with the Other even as she maintained that Western secular values are preferable to Islamic ones.[29] In turn, Étienne Balibar lent support to the headscarf ban in the name of the republican ideal of unity.[30] None of these views is explicitly Islamophobic in the way that Renan's was. But by engaging in Eurocentric critiques of modernity that belittle development in the Islamic world, these intellectuals, along with others such as Michel Foucault and Jean Baudrillard, are left open to the charge that they invoke an Islamic/Arab Orient reflecting an updated variation of Orientalism.[31]

France does not recognise the existence of minorities on its territory. It does not offer political representation to religious, racial or ethnic communities. While this position is justified in the name of colour-blind equality and unity, it simultaneously occludes remedial policies which could address existing inequalities and societal fragmentation. Affirmative action – *discrimination positive* – cannot exist where there is no recognition of diverse groups. Not a single *député* (member) of north African origin or of Muslim heritage was elected to the 577-seat National Assembly in 2007. To be sure, President Sarkozy appointed a number of ministers of Maghrebi background to his first cabinet. Politicians of Berber background have occupied important positions in rival political parties.[32] But such representation of minorities was provided at the pleasure of the political elite rather than as a result of institutional processes. The absence of Muslim representation may not necessarily be an indicator of the strength of Islamophobia, but the failure to redress this imbalance does seem to reflect a fear of Muslims.

FRENCH MUSLIM DIVERSITY

Muslims in France constitute a diverse set of communities. Although by law no official statistics can be compiled on the subject, of an estimated population of five million, those of Arab descent make up somewhere between 50 and 70 per cent of Muslim residents.[33] Of the remainder, close to one million are Berbers of Algerian or Moroccan descent. About half a million people originate from each of Tunisia, Turkey and the former French colonies (in west Africa and islands in the Indian Ocean). Small groups of Asians, French converts to Islam and undocumented asylum seekers also are included in this residual category.[34] Thus in terms both of its own demographic make-up and its geopolitical location, France lies in a pivotal location for European interaction with the Muslim world.

The two million Muslims of Algerian origin hold a special place in French consciousness but they too can be divided into separate communities. Arab and Berber *harkis* (volunteers) served the French colonial administration until Algeria's independence. French residents of Algeria who converted to Islam form a separate group. Then there are Arab labour migrants recruited to France in the decade following decolonialisation. Significantly, in 1973 the Algerian government unilaterally banned out-migration of its citizens to France and, in turn, a year later France formally ended labour in-migration since it was no longer needed. But Algerians rarely migrated to any other place in Europe: as late as 1990, 97 per cent of Algerian emigrants lived in France. This pattern changed with the domestic conflict that wracked Algeria from the 1990s on. It produced a new wave of war refugees exhibiting a new pattern of settlement. Over 100,000 claimed asylum in Europe but less than 20 per cent of them did so in France.[35]

In 1989, President François Mitterrand announced that the country had reached what he termed the 'threshold number' for immigrants. Any additional increase would test what he referred to as the 'tolerance threshold' (*seuil de tolérance*). At the same time, the Mitterrand presidency proposed a degree of unofficial positive bias towards Muslims that could raise their sense of empowerment. It was a time when French society, usually acclaiming itself as an organic whole, underwent a kind of 'internal balkanisation'.[36]

Evidence of diversity was reflected in a 2005 national survey of religious identities. About 80 per cent of respondents (which would add up to about thirty-five million people) identified Catholicism as their 'religion of origin' or 'religion of membership'. About 5 per cent (slightly over two million) identified Islam as such a religion. Close to 2 per cent (estimated at just less than one million) identified themselves as Protestant. About the same number identified some other faith including Judaism; there are close to 600,000 Jews in France. The remaining 11 per cent (five million) stated they did not belong to any denomination.[37] Internal balkanisation may exaggerate the diversity of French religious identities, therefore.

The self-identification of Muslim residents in France has changed over time, too. The first generation of the 1960s and 1970s was largely secular oriented and focused on improving its material well-being. Typical, perhaps, of their cautious approach to a newly opened receiving society were the Turks in France, who featured in an ethnographic study carried out by Riva Kastoryano. She described how tentative their steps towards integrating into the receiving society were.

> Conscious of the provisional nature of their presence in a host society, Turkish migrants keep interactions with global society to a minimum and adaptation remains purely 'instrumental'. As a result, the migrant makes spontaneous recourse to the antecedent social organisation – the collective life of the village or the interrelations of *hemşeri* [townspeople].[38]

Given the critical mass and diasporic culture that Turkish migrants constitute today in European receiving societies, it seems improbable that the lifestyles they led in the country of origin still exert much influence on lifestyles selected for managing the emigration experience.

The next generation – daughters and sons of immigrants – was to become more civic minded and self-confident. Many joined the *Beur* movement, made up of descendants of Maghrebi immigrants, which in the 1980s mobilised across France in response to racism, discrimination and the initial electoral successes of the Front National. Its politicisation took place within the framework of French structures. It demonstrated that, as Alec Hargreaves highlighted, 'like it or not every *Beur* has a foot in two cultures, and this is a situation with which he or she must learn to live'.[39]

By contrast, the third generation of Muslims has been susceptible to re-Islamicisation. This has been described as

> the process whereby French youth of African, Turkish, or Middle Eastern origin turn to Islam in their search for identity – and often, but not always, to a form of abstract and globalised Islam rather than the "family Islam" of their parents.[40]

If we sum up the identity shifts characterising Muslim migrants and their descendants, we arrive at a curious progression: the identity of north African residents has shifted from Algerian to *Beur* to Muslim.

These are not mutually exclusive categories, of course. In particular, religious and ethnic identities often overlap, particularly in popular consciousness. But French academic specialists on migrant communities have elaborated on the fusion of religion and ethnicity. Rachel Bloul advanced the innovative thesis of an ethnicisation of religion in France. When applied to Muslims it signifies that Islam is now treated as *ethnic* identity, regardless of where they originate. Such 'deterritorialised Islam' poses a dilemma for the French state, which insists on the assimilation of other ethnic groups into French society.[41] When Islam comes to be viewed as a deterritorialised global community that has pretences to a universalism rivalling that of the French Republic, the assimilationist imperative loses its rationale. Kastoryano has even pointed to the emergence of 'Islamo-France' – an abstract normative community rather than a territorial one.[42] Even as they laid stress on the organic existence of an Islamic community rather than its internal diversity, such conceptualisations reflect a rapidly shifting, often contradictory and confounding, set of identities attributed to French Muslims.

Radical stereotypes

Part of the French public regards Muslim migrants and their descendants as synonymous with the country's underclass. The stereotype of the unemployed young Muslim whose rage is expressed on the French street has become an enduring image capturing French fears just like that of the Polish plumber taking French jobs was shortly after EU eastern enlargement. Migrant impressions of France, whether as a utopian or a dystopian receiving society, were also often founded on superficial stereotypes. The writer Tahar Ben Jelloun was forced to conclude, then, that 'the dialogue between immigration and France has become a collision of ignorances'.[43]

Much scholarly analysis has been conducted by French and international researchers on immigration and integration. Few dissent from the view that Muslim youth suffer most from discrimination and exclusion. As Michèle Lamont evocatively summarised, 'it has been argued that in France, racism does not pit the French against immigrants, but pits unemployed youth (French and foreign) against everyone else'. But interviews she conducted with French workers confirmed a 'racism directed not only at second generation children of immigrants from the Maghreb, but at all North African immigrants, because "Muslims are Muslims"'.[44] Age may be important in filtering French perceptions of Muslims when riots, invariably associated with young people, break out. Otherwise, if Lamont's research is indicative of more general trends, banal Islamophobia targets the average Muslim regardless of age.

To be sure, a core group of radical youth of Maghrebi background living in city outskirts does exist. Typically they are not recent emigrants but youth who have French nationality and have been re-Islamicised by fundamentalist movements. Some have had links with the Groupe Islamique Armé (GIA) in Algeria.[45] The threats made against France by this Islamist group, as well as by Al Qaeda in the Islamic Maghreb, heighten Maghrebi phobia. The new security *Realpolitik* tags many young Muslims as forming part of an international Islamist movement even if their only political activity has been to take part in a demonstration against police brutality. Vincent Geisser, a specialist on Islam at the Centre National de la Recherche Scientifique, described a process by which 'experts of fear' create an 'imaginary Islam' which is then represented in security discourse as a national threat.[46] Popular xenophobia can become directed, then, at French nationals of Muslim background who are viewed as constituting, illogically, both an internal and external danger.[47]

Critical in the making of French Islamophobia is subjecting Muslim attitudes and behaviour to processes of homogenisation, essentialisation and communitarianisation. Muslims are portrayed as thinking and acting as one, usually in radically transgressive ways. This makes them susceptible to blame for different pathologies. As Geisser observed, even the discovery of a new wave of religiously driven Judeophobia in France pays little attention to the victims – Jews – and much more to its agents – supposedly Muslim youth. In this manner, for Geisser, the ethnic French majority excuses itself from assuming any responsibility for the new anti-Semitism.[48]

The immediate sources of French anxiety about radical Islam can be traced to events that took place in the last decades of the twentieth century. The 1979 Iranian Revolution, inspired by Ayatollah Khomeini, who had been living in exile in France with the consent of its political authorities, signalled the emergence of a more 'radical and potentially violent strain of Islam'.[49] France was on the front line of the Islamist revival. Before the spectacular terrorist attacks in the West early in the new century, France had endured sporadic terrorism for two decades. In 1983 a bomb exploded prematurely near a synagogue in Marseilles, raising fears about the possible start of a terrorist campaign. The then interior minister, Gaston Defferre, who was also mayor of Marseilles, warned that Muslim fanatics might be able to gain supporters in France. His reason was that 'Arabs' had been refusing to integrate into French society.[50]

The series of terrorist attacks launched in 1995, mainly targeting the Paris public transport system, had an external source – the GIA, based in Algeria. This group intended to transpose that country's civil war between government and Islamist forces to the colonial metropole. This terrorism was not the work of discontented Muslims living in France, though the French government acknowledged that the socio-economic conditions of Muslims living in the country could provide fertile ground for copycat terrorist acts. It therefore began to undertake greater efforts at integrating the Muslim population so as to prevent its radicalisation.[51]

Key to thwarting radicalisation was the economic integration of French Muslims. As one diagnosis put it, they did not 'feel like citizens because they can't be integrated the way people are so often integrated into a society: through jobs'.[52] Job discrimination had become commonplace, as a number of studies showed. The French anti-racism organisation SOS Racisme examined the hiring practices of French employers and found that applicants with non-European first names were one and a half times less likely to be employed in many high-skilled industries than those with European first names.[53] Another study, by the Observatoire des Discriminations, a think-tank that investigates workplace discrimination, reported that 'of two French job applicants with identical credentials, the one whose name sounded Moroccan was six times less likely to get an interview than the one whose names sounded Franco-French'.[54]

It took some time for the French government to realise the scope of job discrimination against Muslims and come up with remedies. Purely economic policy innovations, such as job creation programmes, were missing the mark as Muslims still faced largely the same discriminatory labour practices. In 2005 a government agency to combat workforce discrimination (Autorité de Lutte contre les Discriminations et pour l'Égalité) was finally established. But its record in finding solutions to complaints lodged by French Muslims was underwhelming.[55] A paradigmatic shift was needed to address the specific concerns articulated by minority communities.

In theory, giving the leaders of ethnic and religious communities responsibilities for their communities' welfare represents an infringement of the republican principle; it should be the unitary colour-blind secular French state, after all, that serves as the embodiment of all French communities. But as a recent study of Muslim integration in France observed, 'the parameters of French policies toward the country's minorities have changed drastically in the past decades, from a classically republican and "colour-blind" approach to something more nuanced'.[56] As a result, from the 1980s on a number of national Islamic organisations were established with the support of France's political authorities. While holding to the principles of republicanism, the French state informally endorsed a paradigm shift allowing for the incorporation of organisations representing minorities into the policy formulation process. If this change has not directly been linked to the adoption of a new security policy, it does represent state recognition of the centrality of French Muslims to the national interest.

FRANCISING ISLAM

The institutionalisation of Islam in France was the product of sixteen years of dialogue between officials from the interior ministry and Muslim community leaders. The initiative was first launched in 1988 but it was a consultative process instituted in 1999 under interior minister Jean-Pierre Chevênement that identified negotiating partners – 'good Muslim representatives' – for the French state. The hope was for 'the birth of a tolerant, moderate, and "modern" Islam in France and Europe'.[57]

The main result of the consultations was the creation in 2002 of the Conseil Français du Culte Musulman (CFCM, or French Council for the Muslim Faith). Set up while Nicolas Sarkozy was interior minister, it reflected some of his personal views on minorities. As a student he had opposed the liberal left and instead joined a right-wing student organisation when the May 1968 student protests broke out and led to President de Gaulle's eventual resignation. No sooner had the CFCM been created than the so-called *loi Sarkozy* was enacted in 2003, which made it possible for France to deport 25,000 irregular immigrants per year and to restrict asylum options for them in France.[58] Following the 2005 riots, a second *loi Sarkozy* increased by 50 per cent the number of illegal immigrants that could be deported.[59] French authorities were switching from a policy of 'generosity' to one of 'firmness'.[60]

How was it, then, that Sarkozy approved the creation of a national Muslim association? He explained the rationale behind the CFCM's founding: 'What we should be afraid of is Islam gone astray, garage Islam, basement Islam, underground Islam. It is not the Islam of the mosques, open to the light of day.'[61] For Sarkozy, an *Islam de France* was preferable to an *Islam en France*.[62] Academic John Bowen believed it was absurd to speak of Islam in one country.[63] Nevertheless the practical way of domesticating Islam – creating a Western Islam – began by channelling Muslims into a single organisation. Sarkozy's ambitions for the CFCM were grandiose: to help create 'a transparent, open, modern, and liberal Islam compatible with the laws of the Republic'.[64]

The CFCM had a number of unstated purposes. These included to etatise and francise Islam and to 'cast religious practice in a national framework that acknowledges the primacy of the secular state'.[65] In some respects, then, the French state was politicising Islam so as to regulate its expression. This *Islam de France* was part of an assimilationist strategy: the CFCM was to articulate a single Muslim view. In addition, the security regime could take advantage of the organisation's existence to detect, repress and prosecute 'refractory' Muslims.[66]

The person chosen to lead the CFCM was Algerian-born physician Dalil Boubakeur, rector of the Grande Mosquée de Paris. Predictably, he came under criticism from various groups. Some Muslim leaders accused him of being too secular and too intimate with French authorities. In turn the French right suspected him of fundamentalist ideas, pointing to his support for the fatwa issued against Salman Rushdie in 1979. Boubakeur served as

CFCM president from 2003 to 2008. He was succeeded by the Moroccan-born mathematics professor Mohammad Moussaoui, who had just applied for French citizenship, that year.

Many of the council's first leaders had few connections to France's Muslim community. They were drawn from religious elites from Algeria connected to France only through the Paris mosque. These Algerian religious 'exiles' were accused of espousing a backward variant of Islam at odds with Euro-Islamic ideas.[67] The representative nature of the council came under question from French Muslims as much as its Muslim identity was attacked by secular French.

The CFCM comprises more than 200 Islamic groups and has nearly 100,000 members. Its ethnic diversity is apparent: one important constituent group is the Moroccan-dominated Fédération Nationale des Musulmans de France. Another is a Turkish association, the Comité de Coordination des Musulmans Turcs de France. The council also includes student organisations, such as the Étudiants Musulmans de France, and a self-styled humanitarian organisation, the Comité de Bienfaisance et de Secours aux Palestiniens (Committee for Palestinian Charity and Aid), which the US Treasury Department has accused of being a fundraiser for Hamas. The training of future imams for France is not directly controlled by the council; the European Institute for Human Sciences plays the key instructional role here.[68]

The CFCM is not the only national Muslim organisation that claims to represent French Muslim interests. An older association less influenced by the French state is the Union des Organisations Islamiques de France (UOIF). Founded in 1983, it has been assailed for its alleged ties to the Muslim Brotherhood. A PBS Frontline report concluded that 'although it denies any formal link, the UOIF draws its inspiration from Egypt's banned Muslim Brotherhood'.[69] It also receives a quarter of its annual budget from Saudi Arabia, the United Arab Emirates, Kuwait and other foreign donors. The UOIF denies links to radical Islamic groups and insists it holds moderate views.[70] But its leaders uphold the difference between Islamic and non-Islamic communities, leading a Wall Street Journal article to allege that 'inside UOIF mosques, the talk isn't of integration, but of how to protect oneself from harmful French society'.[71]

French officials recognise the calculated risk in dealing with the UIOF. On the one hand, they recognise that it is the best organised of all Muslim associations and 'has the most reach in France's troubled ethnic neighbourhoods'.[72] The policy of containing of Islamist views through engagement is reason enough to keep the UOIF inside the political process rather than outside it. On the other hand, the UIOF may be a lightning rod around which radical Muslim forces assemble.

Two interrelated purposes of these Muslim national associations are to promote the interests of Muslims in France, and to combat Islamophobia. But the UOIF and, to a lesser degree, the CFCM have in their own right generated blowback against Islam. Well-organised Muslim communities, even when they seek to advance a reform agenda, are seen by Islamophobes as evidence of Europe's Islamicisation.

CONTEMPORARY ANTI-MUSLIM ATTITUDES

Various kinds of evidence are offered as to why sections of French society are hostile towards Islam. One study developed a threefold typology of such hostility. Most people expressing antipathy to Muslims function as traditional *ethnocentrists*. Often socially disadvantaged themselves, they reject all alien cultures and groups and are generally intolerant of foreigners. A second, smaller, group embraces *Catholicism* and its values. Islam is accordingly discounted on purely religious grounds. The third group, also small, is located on the *political left*. Though it displays little ethnocentrism and is concerned about discrimination, it rejects Islamic practices when they appear in the public sphere. The anti-Islamic left is willing to accept only the private practice of Islam.[73]

Let us review the empirical evidence indicating anti-Muslim attitudinal trends since 2000. It has been argued that following 9/11, uninformed views about the Muslim world have come to displace those of experts. This has been reflected in the reconfiguring of who the experts on Islam are. According to Vincent Geisser, the securitisation of immigration, especially as it involves migrants from Muslim countries, has led to the dislodgement of area specialists, such as on the Middle East, by 'new experts on fear'. Instead of examining international relations through the lens of realism or liberal internationalism, the new experts are obsessed with security. The result has been that the security obsession, 'far from repudiating popular passions, assuages them'.[74]

The Commission National Consultative des Droits de l'Homme (National Consultative Commission for Human Rights, CNCDH), set up by the French legislature in 1990, has issued annual reports shedding light on the changing force of racism, anti-Semitism and Islamophobia. Its 2001 report first signalled how Muslims as targets had become a more encompassing category: 'If Maghrebi immigrants and their descendants have been particular targets up to now, violence has expanded to include Arab Muslim communities.'[75] The positive news from the 2004 CNCDH poll was that 74 per cent of French respondents asserted that immigration is a source of enrichment, and that 77 per cent believed that Muslim practices should be respected. Only 15 per cent of the French population claimed 'there is a hierarchy between races', though somewhat more (24 per cent) thought that 'some races are less capable than others'.[76]

The 2008 CNCDH annual report, in turn, noted that incidents of racist and xenophobic threats and violence had declined from their peak in 2004. It blamed 42 per cent of all racist violence on extremist right-wing movements.[77] Those of Maghrebi origin were the primary targets of racist violence – 68 per cent of the total – as well as of racist threats (60 per cent). About one-third of violence and threats against Maghrebis had a specifically Islamophobic character, targeting mosques, memorials and believers.[78] The 2010 report confirmed that Maghrebis remained the main victims of racism, with the greater Paris region being the most hostile to them. The CNDCH poll noted that 84 per cent of respondents identified racism as an expanding phenomenon, confirmed by figures on the number of racist acts, which were up on previous years.[79] In its 2011 study, the twentieth such annual report, the CNDCH discovered an increase in most indicators of anti-immigrant and racist attitudes. Containing data for 2010, it underlined the fact that 56 per cent of respondents agreed that there were too many immigrants in France – a 9-point increase on the previous year. Fifty-nine per cent believed that integration of foreigners was functioning very badly. Fewer violent incidents of racism, Islamophobia, and anti-Semitism were recorded in 2010, leading to the intriguing CNDCH conclusion that most citizens rejected violence but not necessarily racist attitudes.[80]

Like all communities, Muslims can themselves be perpetrators of discriminatory activities. While more than half of all anti-Semitic violence in 2007 was attributable to people and groups with poorly defined motives, about one-third originated in the Muslim Arab milieu. Right-wing fanatics accounted for 10 per cent of such violence.[81] In 2009, after the Israeli attack on Gaza, Prime Minister François Fillon acknowledged that the number of anti-Semitic acts in France was growing. He gave no indication that Muslims were behind the increase and instead focused on the harsher punishment that would be meted out to those convicted of such acts.[82]

It should not be surprising to learn that, in turn, some observers allege there was Jewish inspiration for increased anti-Islamic rhetoric. The French journalist Thomas Deltombe asserted that 'in France, Islamophobic discourse owes much to views circulated by pro-Israeli think-tanks and popularised by "experts" such as philosopher and TV presenter Alain Finkielkraut'.[83] Deltombe found hope in the establishment of new interreligious and interracial groups to counter this trend.

Survey results indicate that racist attitudes in France remain a problem. The 2008 CNCDH report noted that 46 per cent of respondents in the national survey recognised that north Africans and Muslims were victims of racism, compared to 27 per cent for immigrants in general and 26 per cent for Africans/blacks.[84] These proportions had held steady since a 2002 survey, though Africans/blacks were now identified more frequently as victims.

While 82 per cent agreed that the insult 'dirty black' should be condemned by the courts, the proportion fell steadily for 'dirty Jew' (78 per cent) and 'dirty Arab' (69 per cent).[85] Moreover, while 90 per cent considered refusing to give a job to a qualified black as a serious matter, the number declined to 83 per cent for someone of Maghreb origin. In addition, 67 per cent said 'it was a serious matter' to oppose a son or daughter's marriage to a black compared to just 58 per cent for someone of Maghrebi background.[86] The survey did not measure popular reactions to use of the term 'dirty gypsy'. Sarkozy's controversial deportation of several hundred Roma in 2011 back to the Balkans, justified in terms of their alleged criminal activity, was generally well received in France as much as it was strongly condemned outside the country. It could well be that antipathy among French towards Roma communities was on a par with Islamophobia.

Islam's status has remained low in the religious hierarchy constructed by French respondents. It evoked something positive in only 28 per cent of the national sample, compared to 38 per cent for Protestantism, 39 per cent for Judaism, 50 per cent for Catholicism and 71 per cent for laïcité.[87] France's anti-Huguenot and anti-Semitic historical episodes may be reflected in the significant gap found between the less frequent 'positive' views of Protestantism and Judaism compared to Catholicism and secularism. If only about one-quarter of respondents saw something positive in Islam, just under half of respondents asserted that Muslims formed a community apart; nevertheless this figure was twice as high as for blacks. Maghrebis were thought to form a community apart by 43 per cent of the sample.[88] Only 69 per cent agreed that French Muslims are French like everyone else, indicating a failing in the republican model of assimilation.[89]

Some Muslims can be found in the ranks of Islamophobes. Several Muslim leaders in France have run afoul of mainstream Muslim opinion on issues ranging from support for a headscarf and burqa ban to endorsement of the wars in Afghanistan and Iraq. One of these was Farid Smahi, an advisor to the former Front National leader, Jean-Marie Le Pen, whose anti-immigrant rhetoric made no distinction between Muslims and non-Muslims. Another was UMP activist Rachid Kaci, an ardent supporter of laïcité and of immigrant assimilation, who was appointed an advisor to President Sarkozy.[90]

A systematic study of French Islamophobia must include the discourse and policy initiatives of the country's leaders. Sarkozy's campaign speeches during the 2007 presidential election were interjected with cryptic Islamophobic remarks. He warned that 'if there are people in France who are not comfortable, they should feel free to leave a country which they do not love'.[91] He succeeded in capturing much of the xenophobic vote that would otherwise have gone to the Front national.

Once president, Sarkozy fought vigorously for the EU's adoption of the European Pact on Immigration and Asylum (discussed in Chapter 2). In promoting selective immigration, the pact raised fears that EU states were closing the door on disadvantaged migrants from poorer countries.[92] For Sarkozy, however, whatever problems such allegations might raise were more than compensated for by his conviction that racism and xenophobia were weaker in countries where a selective immigration regime exists.[93] In 2008 he accordingly established a new Ministry of Immigration, Integration, National Identity and Co-Development, charged with responsibility for implementing the pact. French public opinion was supportive: 72 per cent approved of this institution.[94]

Generally regarded as the most energetic of Fifth Republic presidents, Sarkozy also wanted to prove himself to be a man of ideas. Complementing his reform of immigration policy was the launch of a national debate on French identity in 2009. The President hoped that it would lead to a consensus on what it meant to be French, but instead it became a platform to express fears of and hostility towards immigrants and, specifically, Muslims. The law banning public wearing of the burqa coincided with this debate. Sarkozy's party fared poorly in the 2010 regional elections and one of the reasons identified was the way the national identity debate had backfired. It was discreetly shelved in spring of that year.

Some Muslims were blindsided by the opening up of public discussion about what it meant to be French. Their criticism of the French President pointed to his more considerate treatment of the Jewish community. They cited his 2008 proposal that every ten-year-old French school pupil be entrusted with the memory of one of the 11,000 French child victims of the Holocaust. Sarkozy dropped the proposal after a French education ministry committee recommended that pupils learn more about the fate of French Jewish children who were victims of the Holocaust rather than their 'adopting' the identity of an individual victim.[95]

In 2010 President Sarkozy returned to the theme of France's misguided immigration and integration policies in a speech given in Grenoble to law enforcement officers. He observed that the country had experienced 'fifty years of insufficiently regulated immigration that had produced a failure of integration'. In his view the values of French culture had not been transmitted effectively either to new arrivals or to those of second- and third-generation immigrant background who 'feel less French than their parents or grandparents'. Among Sarkozy's proposed solutions were gaining mastery over in-migration, stripping delinquents of their French citizenship, and reconsidering what rights should be accorded to people living illegally in the country.[96] Some observers saw the Grenoble speech as the start of his 2012 re-election campaign, where votes of right-wing supporters would be pivotal.

In 2011 Sarkozy's ruling UMP convened a debate on Islam. It put forward a 26-point secularism charter that would forbid citizens from invoking religious beliefs and practices in order to disobey rules governing public spaces. President Sarkozy emphasised the need for public policy to deal with overt displays of Islamic faith, such as the wearing of veils and recitation of prayers on streets, which he suggested weakened secular identity. Muslim groups objected to the proposed restrictions on their religious freedoms.[97] Sarkozy's Grenoble speech together with the UMP charter on secularism suggest that policies anti-Muslim in design are regarded as the surest way to maximise electoral support. Indeed, in March 2012 while campaigning against Socialist candidate François Hollande, Sarkozy inveighed against 'too many foreigners on our territory'.

DISTINCTIVE BUT NOT UNUSUAL ISLAMOPHOBIA?

The defining characteristic of French Islamophobia is religion as much as racism. For Vincent Geisser, 'Islamophobia is not simply a transposition of racism that is anti-Arab, anti-Maghrebi, and anti-*jeunes de banlieues*, it is also *religiophobia*'.[98] What has occurred in France has been 'a progressive abandonment of traditional anti-immigrant and anti-stranger registers in favour of exclusively Islamophobic registers, as if the hatred of Islam and Muslims becomes the rallying point of ultranationalists'.[99] This conclusion is not in keeping with the research findings we have reviewed in this chapter, where other manifestations of anti-immigrant, anti-foreigner orientations, including anti-Semitism, have not disappeared.

For Geisser, French Islamophobia did exhibit distinctive features.

> If in other European countries attacks on Muslim people and property still largely arise from traditional registers of anti-immigrant xenophobia and the rejection of the stranger, Islamophobia *à la française* is grafted onto a contentious history in which Islam is considered at one and the same time a religion in the process of *francisation* and a national problem.[100]

He singled out the 'racism from above' in France, which contrasted with other EU countries' more populist and security-related Islamophobia that often originated in international events.[101]

Is France unique in developing an Islamophobia combining racist and religious elements? Its southern and northern neighbours have also experienced growing anti-Muslim sentiments. The origins of Maurophobia in Spain are complex and historically rooted.[102] At the same time, a new wave of anti-immigrant sentiment has targeted Moroccans and other Maghrebis, as in

France. Immigration from South America is not without controversy either, including the policy of granting, under certain conditions, Spanish citizenship after only two years' residency. While racialisation of immigrants from Andean regions may occur, it is not as extreme or consequential as that of Maghrebis.

Spain's immigrant population more than doubled between 2002 and 2007, creating significant stress on its infrastructure, housing and transportation, health and education, and other social services. No other European country absorbed 2.5 million migrants in such a short period of time; this represented the second highest absolute net migration in the world after the United States. One factor that accounted for this was its then porous borders (especially the Canary Islands, close to the African continent, which became an entry point to Europe for illegal migrants). Another factor is Spain's geographic position across the Strait of Gibraltar from Morocco, and its sovereignty over two cities (Ceuta and Melilla) located there. This makes Spain a viable country of destination for much of the Maghreb.

Until 2008 Spain's booming economy was primarily based on real estate, which created a demand from the construction sector for low-cost labour. In addition, Spain's extensive underground economy was attractive to migrants. After the 2004 Madrid train bombings, securitisation of immigration became a priority which, when added to the stress points created by massive new in-migration, made the issue of Maurophobia salient again. Spain's unemployment rate, which was as high as 20 per cent by some calculations, led to the return to power in late 2011 of the right-wing Popular Party, sometimes associated with an anti-Muslim orientation. Unlike French leaders, Prime Minister Mariano Rajoy studiously avoided Islamophobic rhetoric in his electoral campaign. But stress points in Spanish society made Muslims vulnerable as scapegoats for economic decline.

Belgium, France's northeastern neighbour, has not had a centralised model or policy for inclusion of migrants – not surprising given that it did not even have a functioning government for nearly two years, from April 2010 until November 2011. The country's flexible and fluid approaches on diversity management reflected its administrative division into two regions plus greater Brussels.[103] In the capital, an exodus of Flemish and French speakers to adjoining districts has left some neighbourhoods with Muslim majorities, with the possibility that the city itself would become majority Muslim by 2030. Muhammad has become the most common name for boys in the capital as well as in Antwerp. In Flanders, Vlaams Belang (Flemish Interest) has become, for Stephen Fisher, 'the most blatantly racist and xenophobic of the extreme-right parties in Western Europe'.[104] Wallonia may not have an equivalent party – its right-wing Front National prioritises the region joining France and does not reflect the party programme of its French namesake. With higher unemployment and significantly lower per capita income, the region has been a less attractive option for migrant settlement than Flanders or Brussels. Immigrants have developed different adjustment strategies as a result (see Box 5.1).

Box 5.1 Cultural trade-offs and psychological angst among young Turks in Belgium: key findings

1. An optimal – or balanced – psychological functioning . . . can be achieved by a higher-order organisation of relatedness (versus separatedness) and autonomy (versus conformity) since integration and differentiation are basic needs for human beings.
2. [Turkish] adolescents who endorse both separatedness and conformity are able to enjoy contact with both cultures, which in turn help them to adapt both socioculturally and psychologically. At the same time, they seem to experience internal adjustment problems . . .
3. Turkish older and younger generation migrants in Belgium favoured conformity and tradition values more and separatedness less strongly than Belgians did.

Source: Derya Güngör, 'The Interplay between Values, Acculturation and Adaptation: A Study on Turkish-Belgian Adolescents', *International Journal of Psychology* 42, pp. 389–90.

It follows that large Muslim minorities like the Turks – who total over 200,000 in Belgium (behind Moroccans, who number at least 350,000) – have had to be flexible in accommodating to contrasting imperatives of integration into Flemish and Walloon societies. Even if Belgium lurched from one governmental crisis to another, legislators nevertheless were able to enact a law banning the burqa from public places, making it the first country in Europe to do so. While it is inaccurate to conclude that Islam has become the common Other for both Flemish and Walloon communities, each of them is vulnerable to radical right-wing politics.

In the context of its northern and southern neighbour as well as of Switzerland, where the xenophobic Swiss People's Party (SVO) has had the support of over 22 per cent of the electorate since 1999, France's republican model of integration has demonstrated stability, consistency and resoluteness. Philippe d'Iribarne, CNRS researcher and specialist on the impact of national cultures, concludes a comparative critical study of diversity management by favouring the French republican ideal, even with its shortcomings, over its rivals:

The French tradition which expects everyone to intermix and achieve solidarity, without regard to their origins, in a public space characterised by an exacting *laïcité* deserves to be defended. For the liberty that it offers is more profound than that promised by the combination of communitarianism and the market.[105]

For d'Iribarne as well as many of Europe's leaders, the competing multicultural model had reached an impasse, a defeat, a failure by 2011. The case study of Germany presented in the following chapter assesses the performance of and prospects for multiculturalism in a country once enthusiastic about its possibilities.

Notes

1. Mabel Berezin, 'Xenophobia and the New Nationalisms', in Gerard Delanty and Krishan Kumar (eds), *The Sage Handbook of Nations and Nationalism* (London: Sage, 2006), p. 273.
2. Translated into English as *Monsieur Bergeret in Paris* (Charleston, SC: BiblioLife, [1921] 2009).
3. Pierre-André Taguieff, *The Force of Prejudice: On Racism and Its Doubles* (Minneapolis: University of Minnesota Press, 2001).
4. Michel Wieviorka (ed.), *La France raciste* (Paris: Seuil, 1992); Michel Wieviorka (ed.), *Racisme et xénophobie en Europe: une comparaison internationale* (Paris: La Découverte, 1994).
5. For an overview, see 'L'Invention de l'immigration', *Agone* 40 (2008).
6. William Safran, *The French Polity*, 7th ed. (New York: Pearson Longman, 2009), p. 38.
7. Congressional Research Service, *Muslims in Europe: Integration in Selected Countries* (Washington, DC: Congressional Research Service, 2005). See also Claude Moniquet, 'The Radicalisation of Muslim Youth in Europe: The Reality and Scale of the Threat', Capitol Hill hearing testimony, House Committee on International Relations: Subcommittee on Europe and Emerging Threats (27 April 2005). I acknowledge research assistance provided for this section by Jared Eisenberg.
8. Stéphanie Giry, 'France and Its Muslims', *Foreign Affairs*, September–October 2006, pp. 87–104.
9. Jonathan Laurence and Justin Vaisse, *Integrating Islam: Political and Religious Challenges in Contemporary France* (Washington, DC: Brookings Institution Press, 2006), p. 17.
10. Safran, *The French Polity*, p. 77.
11. 2005 RAPFI survey conducted by CEVIPOF and reported by Ariane Chebel d'Appollonia, 'Race, Racism and Anti-Discrimination in France', in Sylvain Brouard, Andrew M. Appleton and Amy G. Mazur (eds), *The French Fifth Republic at Fifty: Beyond Stereotypes* (Basingstoke: Palgrave Macmillan, 2009), pp. 275–6.
12. Laurence and Vaisse, *Integrating Islam*, p. 60.
13. 'La France accueille "trop" d'étrangers en situation régulière, selon Guéant', *Le Monde*, 27 November 2011.
14. Patrick Weil, *La France et ses étrangers: l'aventure d'une politique de l'immigration de 1938 à nos jours* (Paris: Calmann-Lévy, 1991), pp. 42–8.
15. 'Vandals hit French Muslim graves', BBC News website, 8 December 2008, http://news.bbc.co.uk/1/hi/world/europe/7771491.stm, accessed 6 February 2012.

16. Laurence and Vaisse, *Integrating Islam*, p. 37.
17. Quoted in Paul Davis and Daniel Krauthammer, 'Continental Clash: As Cultural Tensions Mount, Europe's Aging Population Must Deal with an Influx of Muslims', *Harvard Political Review*, 31:4 (2005), pp. 14–15.
18. Riva Kastoryano, 'Roundtable on Muslim Immigration', International Studies Association annual convention, New York, 15 February 2009.
19. Vincent Geisser, *La Nouvelle Islamophobie* (Paris: La Découverte, 2003), p. 11.
20. Chebel d'Appollonia, 'Race, Racism and Anti-discrimination in France', p. 267. *Banlieue* can mean 'suburb' but it may more accurately refer to the outskirts of French cities where low-income housing blocks are concentrated. For a select bibliography on the riots in France, see http://riotsfrance.ssrc.org/
21. Ömer Taşpınar, 'Europe's Muslim Street', *Foreign Policy*, February–March 2003.
22. See Geisser, *La Nouvelle Islamophobie*, p. 15.
23. Fatima El-Tayeb, '"The Birth of a European Public": Migration, Postnationality, and Race in the Uniting of Europe', *American Quarterly* 60 (2008), p. 663.
24. Samah Jabr, 'The Rebellion of France's Poor: An Act of Anger, Not of Hatred', *Washington Report on Middle East Affairs*, January–February 2006, pp. 34–5.
25. Giry, 'France and Its Muslims', p. 95.
26. Hugues Lagrange, *Le Déni des cultures* (Paris: Seuil, 2010).
27. Ernest Renan, *L'Islam et la science* (Montpellier: L'Archange Minotaure, 2003).
28. For an excellent summary of Derrida's views, see Alex Thomson, 'Derrida's Rogues: Islam and the Futures of Deconstruction', in Madeleine Fagan, Ludovic Glorieux, Indira Hasimbegovic and Marie Suetsugu (eds), *Derrida: Negotiating the Legacy* (Edinburgh: Edinburgh University Press, 2007), pp. 66–79.
29. Julia Kristeva, *Strangers to Ourselves* (New York: Columbia University Press, 1991).
30. See the summary by Joan Wallach Scott, *The Politics of the Veil* (Princeton, NJ: Princeton University Press, 2007), pp. 114ff.
31. Ian Almond, *The New Orientalists: Postmodern Representation of Islam from Foucault to Baudrillard* (London: I. B. Tauris, 2007), p. 2.
32. For example, see Daniel Lav, 'Rachid Kaci and Sophia Chikirou: North African Roots, French Identity, Universal Ideals', Middle East Media Research Institute website, 28 May 2007, http://www.memri.org/report/en/0/0/0/0/0/0/2216.htm, accessed 6 February 2012.
33. It is 50 per cent Arab for Alain Boyer, *L'Islam en France* (Paris: Presses Universitaires de France, 1998). It is 69 per cent Arab for Laurence and Vaisse, *Integrating Islam*, p. 75.
34. Boyer, *L'Islam en France*.
35. Michael Collyer, 'Emigration, Immigration, and Transit in the Maghreb: Externalisation of EU Policy?', in Yahia H. Zoubir and Haizam Amirah-Fernández (eds), *North Africa: Politics, Region and the Limits of Transformation* (London: Routledge, 2008), p. 163.
36. Geisser, *La Nouvelle Islamophobie*, p. 88.
37. Institut National des Enquêtes Démographiques (INED), 'Les Relations familiales et intergénérationnelles'. Cited in '80% des Français se déclarent catholiques', *Le Figaro*, 18 July 2008.
38. Riva Kastoryano, *Etre Turc en France: reflexions sur familles et communauté* (Paris:

L'Harmattan, 1986), p. 39. Her French cases were Terrasson, a small village in the Dordogne, and Paris.

39. Alec G. Hargreaves, *Immigration and Identity in Beur Fiction: Voices from the North African Immigrant Community in France* (Oxford: Berg, 1997), p. 26.

40. Laurence and Vaisse, *Integrating Islam*, pp. 88-90.

41. Rachel Bloul, 'Engendering Muslim Identities: Deterritorialisation and the Ethnicisation Process in France', in Barbara Daly Metcalf (ed.), *Making Muslim Space in North America and Europe* (Berkeley: University of California Press, 1996).

42. Kastoryano, 'Roundtable on Muslim Immigration'.

43. Tahar Ben Jelloun, 'Le minaret est tombé, on a pendu le coiffeur', *Le Monde*, 20 December 2009.

44. Michèle Lamont, 'Immigration and the Salience of Racial Boundaries among French Workers', in Herrick Chapman and Laura L. Frader (eds), *Race in France: Interdisciplinary Perspectives on the Politics of Difference* (New York: Berghahn, 2004), p. 148. See also her seminal book *The Dignity of Working Men: Morality and the Boundaries of Race, Class, and Immigration* (Cambridge, MA: Harvard University Press, 2000).

45. Jocelyne Cesari, 'Islam in France: Social Challenge or Challenge of Secularism?', in Steven Vertovec and Alisdair Rogers (eds), *Muslim European Youth: Reproducing Ethnicity, Religion and Culture* (Aldershot: Ashgate, 1998), pp. 25–38.

46. See Geisser, *La Nouvelle Islamophobie*, p. 56.

47. Pascal Blanchard and Nicolas Bancel, *De l'indigène à l'immigré* (Paris: Gallimard, 1998).

48. Geisser, *La Nouvelle Islamophobie*, p. 91.

49. Congressional Research Service, *Muslims in Europe*, p. 25.

50. See Neil MacMaster, 'Islamophobia in France and the "Algerian Problem"', in Emran Qureshi and Michael A. Sells (eds), *The New Crusades: Constructing the Muslim Enemy* (New York: Columbia University Press, 2003), pp. 289–90.

51. Moniquet, 'The Radicalisation of Muslim Youth in Europe'.

52. Molly Lanzarotta, 'Pepper Culpepper on Changing Demographics in France and Europe', Harvard Kennedy School website, 22 November 2005, http://www.hks.harvard.edu/news-events/publications/insight/democratic/pepper-culpepper, accessed 6 February 2012.

53. Laurence and Vaisse, *Integrating Islam*.

54. Giry, 'France and Its Muslims', p. 94.

55. Ibid., p. 99.

56. Laurence and Vaisse, *Integrating Islam*, quoted by Stéphanie Giry, 'An integrated France?', *Prospect*, February 2007.

57. Ibid.

58. Sally Marthaler, 'Nicolas Sarkozy and the Politics of French Immigration Policy', *Journal of European Public Policy*, 15 (2008), p. 388.

59. Ibid., p. 389.

60. Ibid., p. 390.

61. 'France creates Muslim council', BBC News website, 20 December 2002, http://news.bbc.co.uk/1/hi/world/europe/2593623.stm, accessed 6 February 2012.

62. Alexandre Caeiro, 'Religious Authorities or Political Actors? The Muslim Leaders of the French Representative Body of Islam', in Jocelyne Cesari and Seán

McLoughlin (eds), *European Muslims and the Secular State* (Aldershot: Ashgate, 2005), p. 71.

63. John R. Bowen, *Can Islam Be French? Pluralism and Pragmatism in a Secularist State* (Princeton, NJ: Princeton University Press, 2010).

64. Quoted by *Le Monde*, 8 April 2003.

65. Congressional Research Service, *Muslims in Europe*, p. 28.

66. R. John Matthies, '"Kicking the Anthill"': The Destabilization of the Extremist Base in France,' *Journal of Muslim Minority Affairs* 28 (2008), pp. 139–46.

67. For example, see Latifa Ben Mansour's *Frères musulmans, frères féroces: voyage dans l'enfer du discours islamiste* (Paris: Ramsay, 2002).

68. Glen Feder, 'The Muslim Brotherhood in France', *National Interest*, 21 September 2005.

69. 'Mapping the Threat: France', Frontline: Al-Qaeda's New Front website, 25 January 2005, http://www.pbs.org/wgbh/pages/frontline/shows/front/map/fr.html, accessed 6 February 2012.

70. John Carreyrou and Ian Johnson, 'As Muslims call Europe home, isolation takes root', *Wall Street Journal*, 11 July 2005.

71. Congressional Research Service, *Muslims in Europe*, p. 28.

72. Carreyrou and Johnson, 'As Muslims call Europe home, isolation takes root'.

73. Nonna Mayer, Guy Michelat and Vincent Tiberj, 'Étranger, immigré, musulman: les representations de "l'autre" dans la société française', in Commission Nationale Consultative des Droits de l'Homme, *La Lutte contre le racisme, l'antisémitisme et la xénophobie: année 2007* (Paris: La Documentation Française, 2008), pp. 119, 123.

74. Geisser, *La Nouvelle islamophobie*, p. 69.

75. Commission Nationale Consultative des Droits de l'Homme, *La Lutte contre le racisme et la xénophobie: rapport d'activité 2001* (Paris: La Documentation Française, 2002).

76. Reported by Chebel d'Appollonia, 'Race, Racism and Anti-Discrimination in France', p. 275.

77. Commission Nationale Consultative des Droits de l'Homme, *La Lutte contre le racisme, l'antisémitisme et la xénophobie: année 2007*.

78. Ibid., pp. 35–8.

79. Cordélia Bonal: 'Racisme: "Les Français sont dans l'acceptation tant qu'on ne touche pas à leur petit jardin"', *Libération*, 1 June 2010.

80. 'Racisme: un verrou a sauté dans le discours politique admis ou admissible', *Le Monde*, 12 April 2011.

81. Commission Nationale Consultative des Droits de l'Homme, *La Lutte contre le racisme, l'antisémitisme et la xénophobie: année 2007*, p. 44.

82. 'France raises alert after spate of anti-Semitic attacks over Gaza op', Haaretz.com website, 25 January 2009, http://www.haaretz.com/jewish-world/news/france-raises-alert-after-spate-of-anti-semitic-attacks-over-gaza-op-1.268369, accessed 7 February 2012.

83. Thomas Deltombe, *L'Islam imaginaire: la construction médiatique de l'islamophobie en France, 1975–2005* (Paris: La Découverte, 2005), p. 198. This book served to rebut the arguments found in Guillaume Weill-Raynal, *Une Haine imaginaire: contre-enquête sur le nouvel antisémitisme* (Paris: Armand Colin, 2005). Finkielkraut's views are rejected by most Jewish intellectuals.

84. Commission Nationale Consultative des Droits de L'Homme, *La Lutte contre le racisme, l'antisémitisme et la xénophobie: année 2007*, Annexe, p. 296.
85. Ibid., pp. 316–18.
86. Ibid., pp. 320–1.
87. Ibid., pp. 322–3.
88. Ibid., pp. 302–3.
89. Ibid., p. 311.
90. See Fatiha Kaoues, 'Compte rendu d'une conférence sur l'islamophobie à Sciences-Po', Oumma.com website, 6 January 2004, http://oumma.com/Compte-rendu-d-une-conference-sur, accessed 7 February 2012.
91. Marthaler, 'Nicolas Sarkozy and the Politics of French Immigration Policy', p. 391.
92. Ferda Ataman, 'A plan for more segregation', Spiegel Online International website, 17 October 2008, http://www.spiegel.de/international/europe/0,1518,584741,00. html, accessed 7 February 2012.
93. Sarkozy quoted in *Le Monde*, 28 April 2006.
94. Marthaler, 'Nicolas Sarkozy and the Politics of French Immigration Policy', p. 382.
95. 'President Nicolas Sarkozy calls for a fight against anti-Semitism and Islamophobia in France', Euro-Islam.info website, 3 March 2009, http://www.euro-islam. info/2009/03/03/president-nicolas-sarkozy-calls-for-a-fight-against-anti-semitism-and -islamophobia-in-france/, accessed 7 February 2012.
96. Nicolas Cori, 'Sarkozy dégaine les clichés et cible les immigrés', *Libération*, 31 July 2010.
97. 'France's ruling party proposes 26-point secularism platform', Islam Today website, 6 April 2011, http://en.islamtoday.net/artshow-229-4017.htm, accessed 7 February 2012.
98. Geisser, *La Nouvelle islamophobie*, p. 11.
99. Ibid., p. 12.
100. Ibid., p. 10.
101. Ibid., p. 79.
102. Ricard Zapata-Barrero, 'The Muslim Community and Spanish tradition: Maurophobia as a Fact, and Impartiality as a Desideratum', in Tariq Modood, Anna Triandafyllidou and Ricard Zapata-Barrero (eds), *Multiculturalism, Muslims and Citizenship: A European Approach* (London: Routledge, 2006), pp. 143–61.
103. Hassan Bousetta and Dirk Jacobs, 'Multiculturalism, Citizenship and Islam in Problematic Encounters in Belgium', in Tariq Modood, Anna Triandafyllidou and Ricard Zapata-Barrero (eds), *Multiculturalism, Muslims and Citizenship: A European Approach* (London: Routledge, 2006), pp. 23–36.
104. Abdal-Hakim Murad, 'Muslims and the European Right', paper presented at the Annual World Humanities Lecture, University of Leicester, 3 April 2000.
105. Philippe d'Iribarne, *Les Immigrés de la République: impasses du multiculturalisme* (Paris: Seuil, 2010), p. 121.

CHAPTER SIX

Germany: from multiculturalism to Realpolitik?

In 2008 construction began of a central mosque in Cologne's largely immigrant-populated Ehrenfeld district. Around 330,000 immigrants, the majority Muslim, live in the city, representing about a third of the urban population. Cologne city council gave its approval for building plans for the mosque: Ottoman-style architecture featuring glass walls and a dome, while a bazaar for secular and interfaith use made it an attractive addition to the neighbourhood. But it was the two 180ft-tall minarets that provoked most controversy. Funding issues were less contentious: the Diyanet İşleri Türk İslam Birliği (DITIB, Turkish Islamic Union for Religious Affairs), a branch of the Turkish government's religious affairs office, was the principal investor, followed by donations from 900 Muslim associations in Germany.

The federal authorities were not involved in the planning process. Article 4 of the Basic Law (or German constitution) states that places of worship can be built without needing approval by the federal government. With the construction of this large mosque, Cologne's historic image of 'Cathedral, Catholicism and Carnival' was fundamentally recast.

The mosque project became a catalyst for mobilisation by anti-Muslim forces. Radical right groups convened a meeting in the city to coincide with the start of construction. A so-called 'Anti-Islamisation Conference', which signalled the fear of identity change as well as opposition to the growing visibility of Muslims, drew speakers from across Europe, including from right-wing parties like the Vlaams Blok, the Front National and Austria's FVO. The conference described itself as a 'European, patriotic, populist right-wing movement'. Participants expressed concern that 'mosques are shooting out of the ground like mushrooms, and the muezzin call and headscarves are flooding our streets'. Some of the speakers played the securitisation card, claiming that mosques throughout Europe were being used to conceal weapons, drugs and illegal immigrants.[1] In the case of the Cologne mosque, after an initial surge of opposition, its construction was to progress steadily.

Protests, violence and rhetoric

Since its establishment in 1949 the Federal Republic of Germany has been sensitive to all manifestations of racism, xenophobia, religious bigotry and anti-Semitism. The authorities were confronted with a major crisis when anti-immigrant attacks increased in the 1990s. They were both an ignorant racist skinhead event and a considered backlash against liberal immigration and asylum policies that had allowed many foreigners to settle in the country legally.

The most horrific of the anti-immigrant violence was an arson attack carried out by German youths in Solingen in 1993 which killed five Turkish females. The previous year, in Mölln, a young German right-wing extremist had set off a bomb that killed three Turks. The responses by Germany's leaders became controversial in their own right. Instead of meeting personally with the Mölln survivors, Chancellor Helmut Kohl sent a telegram of condolence to the Turkish president and dispatched Klaus Kinkel, his *foreign* minister, to represent him at the funeral service. Kinkel displayed little more sensitivity than Kohl had. He 'listed down to the decimal point, the amount of taxes and duties paid by the Turkish population of the day. This was intended as an argument against killing them'.[2]

The authorities' response to the Anti-Islamisation Conference of 2008 was, accordingly, blunt. The interior ministry condemned the meeting by arguing that 'such an event organised by populists and extremists in Cologne is damaging to the good co-operation between the city and its Muslim citizens'.[3] At the municipal level, the mayor urged the city's inhabitants to ignore the right-wingers. For its part, the Zentralrat der Muslime in Deutschland (Central Council of Muslims in Germany) called the conference 'an unparalleled abuse of freedom of opinion' that would heighten Islamophobia. Established political elites joined ranks in expressing their disapproval of populist groups targeting a Muslim religious project.

There was a sense of *déjà vu* about the Cologne mosque controversy. Two years earlier city leaders in Berlin had granted permission to the Ahmadiyya Muslim Jamaat Deutschland (German Ahmadiyya Muslim Community), representing an old Muslim community living in the city since 1924, to build a new mosque. Located in Heinersdorf, the eastern part of the city (in the former communist German Democratic Republic) where few Muslims have settled, the two-storey mosque with a forty-foot minaret was to be situated at the end of a run-down street on the site of an abandoned sauerkraut factory.

That did not matter to ethnic German nationalists, who opposed the mosque. One rally included a banner with the slogan 'Democracy yes! Caliphate no!' A local resident expressed shock that 'they want to have a minaret with a muezzin who gives the call to prayer five times a day. Can you imagine? Five times a day over our rooftops.'[4] This anti-Muslim thrust was combined with classic 'not in my back yard' (NIMBY) arguments: the mosque should be built not in Heinersdorf but where 'a lot of Muslims live', for example, Kreuzberg or Wedding. But these two districts of West Berlin were where many Turks had moved in the 1960s under the guest worker programme. The mosque in Heinersdorf was to serve Ahmadis, a mainly Pakistani sect of Islam.

It is ironic that German Islamophobes identify Ahmadis as mainstream Muslims and expect them to live with other Muslim communities. The Ahmadi community in Germany numbers over 30,000 members and has seventeen mosques. Because of their eclectic beliefs – Ahmadis recognise shadow prophets – the Pakistani government declared in 1974 that they were not true Muslims. The following year they were expelled from the Saudi-led Muslim World League. To be sure, some Heinersdorf protesters were well informed and subtle, voicing fears about the emergence of an 'Islamic-Ahmadiyya parallel society, which would have the goal of overturning our liberal-democratic order'.[5] But this argument echoed a more general view of many Germans about all Muslims living in a parallel society.

Is there a deepening religious cleavage in Germany? It has been argued that a German-language address by Pope Benedict XVI (himself a German) at the University of Regensburg in 2006 contributed to rising tensions between Christianity and Islam in Europe. Quoting a Byzantine emperor's statement from 1391 (who foreshadowed the fall of Constantinople to the Ottomans in 1453), the Pope repeated: 'Show me just what Muhammad brought that was new and there you will find things only evil and inhuman, such as his command to spread by the sword the faith he preached.' The Pope was labelled an Islamophobe for citing this remark. Anti-Papist demonstrations soon erupted in many Muslim-majority countries.

In 2006 Pope Benedict visited Istanbul to bolster efforts at reconciliation between the Catholic Church and both Eastern Orthodoxy and Islam. But at a joint appearance, Turkey's chief Islamic cleric, Ali Bardakoğlu, admonished Benedict for his Regensburg speech: 'The so-called conviction that the sword is used to expand Islam in the world and growing Islamophobia hurts all Muslims,' he asserted.[6] The cleric's remarks were intended not just for Pope Benedict but also Germany's large Turkish population.

Compared to German leaders' insensitive response to the killing of refugees in the 1990s, the protests against the Cologne mosque and the impact of the German Pope's quoting an anti-Muslim passage on relations with the Islamic world, Thilo Sarrazin's 2010 book, translated as 'Germany Does Away with Itself', attained a new peak in Islamophobic discourse among the German elite.[7] A longtime member of the board of the Deutsche Bundesbank and a lifelong Social Democrat, Sarrazin's damning assessment of how Muslims had become the country's albatross produced an unprecedented national debate that challenged the postwar consensus on constitutional, as opposed to nationalist, patriotism. Chancellor Angela Merkel's remark that multiculturalism had proven a failure added fuel to the fire. Prominent citizens of Turkish origin published an open letter not only condemning the book but the discussion around it: 'We all feel discredited through the current debate.'

Sarrazin condensed his book to three extremely provocative ideas. First, ethnic Germans are having too few children, Muslim immigrants too many. In eighty years' time Muslims will make up a majority in Germany. Second, intelligence is inherited rather than nurtured. Muslims are less intelligent than ethnic Germans. It follows that the population of Germany is being dumbed down. Third, Germany needs more immigrants but bringing more Muslims into the country will worsen conditions. On the basis of three indicators – levels of success in education and in employment and rate of dependency on welfare – Muslims drag Germany's overall scores down. By contrast, Sarrazin claimed that 'immigrants from non-Islamic countries show no statistical difference to the German population at all. On the other hand, immigrants from Muslim countries pose much greater problems. Their language skills, academic skills and professional skills are much below average.'[8]

Aylin Selçuk, founder of DeuKische Generation, a group promoting the interests of young Turkish-born Germans, rejected what she saw as the author's major assumption. Quoting Sarrazin's statement that 'a large number of Arabs and Turks make no constructive contribution anywhere but the vegetable trade', Selçuk observed: 'Sarrazin's argument rests on one of the most schoolchildish insults around: that Turkish people are stupid.'[9]

GUEST WORKERS AND MIGRATION

Large-scale immigration to postwar Germany was launched when the government of Chancellor Konrad Adenauer signed bilateral agreements with southern European states for the recruitment of *Gastarbeiter* ('guest workers'). In what was regarded as a temporary period of *Wirtschaftswunder* ('economic miracle'), Germany needed to ease its labour shortage. Guest workers, who were expected to return home after their contracts ended, were the answer. The first recruiting agreement was signed with Italy in 1955, followed by Spain and Greece in 1960, Turkey in 1961 and Yugoslavia in 1968. How temporary Germany's labour needs really were came into question in the wake of this string of agreements.

The result of the guest worker programme was that by 1973 the number of foreigners living in Germany had increased to more than four million. The Federal Republic imposed limited regulations on their stay – in contrast to its communist counterpart, the German Democratic Republic. East Germany firmly controlled immigration, and guest workers recruited from socialist states like Vietnam and Mozambique were sent back at the end of their labour contracts or when they were no longer needed.[10]

Since 1973 the number of foreigners in Germany has doubled again, to roughly eight million (out of a total population in unified Germany of eighty-two million). The disintegration of the Soviet bloc and fall of the Berlin Wall in 1989 gave many eastern Europeans, including those of German ancestry, a chance to move overnight to a prosperous western European state rather than patiently await job and wage growth in their home country. After the Turks, Poles were assuming second place as the most sizeable immigrant group. They started arriving in large numbers in the Federal Republic in the Cold War days, including just before and during martial law in Poland, which was imposed in 1981. Then a second major wave occurred after 1989 at the start of the democratic transition. Most recently a new migration cycle began in 2011 when Poles became eligible to find work on the German labour market after a seven-year moratorium following Poland's accession to the EU. Some studies show that Poles are the most integrated immigrant group in Germany.[11] But they also have suffered from a highly negative image among Germans as untrustworthy, uncouth and unsophisticated.

Today every fifth person in Germany has an immigrant background. About four and a half million are Muslim – around 5 per cent of the overall population. Nearly two-thirds of Muslims are Turks.

The steady increase in immigrant numbers was accompanied by more frequent calls for setting limits on migration. Xenophobic violence perpetrated mainly by young racists (most of whom self-identified as skinheads) peaked in the 1990s and brought matters to a head. Chancellor Kohl appealed to Germans to show more tolerance towards newcomers but, simultaneously, he promised a crackdown on abusers of the asylum system. The tolerance he urged asked for a recognition of migrants' autonomy, but it did not demand an inclusionary tolerance enabling majority and minority to share common values.[12]

The German Chancellor's exhortation for citizens to be tolerant so that the state could be harsh towards certain foreigners revealed how the institutional bases of discrimination were anchored in the state. As examples, the very idea of a 'nation-state', the politics of ethnicity, the principle of *jus sanguinis*, state monopoly on the use of violence, and naturalisation laws were state centred. The discourse of state leaders contributed further to the impression that foreigners were inviting violence upon themselves. 'By way of ambiguous discourse, linking social difficulties of diverse scales with a call to defensive behaviour in the face of strangers, the State was carrying out a central function in the process of constructing xenophobia.'[13] The victim was being transformed into the guilty party.[14]

This misguided logic was never more clearly discernible than in the killings of eight Turks and one Greek (the latter probably a case of mistaken identity) carried out between 2000 and 2006 in a number of German cities. Crudely called the 'doner murders' by the media – all but one of the victims had been shopkeepers – they had been thought to involve Turkish gangs' settling of accounts. But in 2011 it came to light that the murder weapon used belonged to three German neo-Nazi extremists who had also murdered a policewoman.

The German state had nothing to do with this misrepresentation of Turks as perpetrators rather than victims. But it has played a pivotal role in determining the overall character of Islam in Germany. As one study put it, Germany's *Islampolitik* has been based on the concept of extraterritorialisation: 'Regarded up to now as a religion of the *outsider*, the question of Islam in Germany has for a long time remained subsidiary to the German state – a simple component of *Ausländerpolitik*.'[15] State policy on foreigners dictated the nature of official treatment of Islam.

Unlike France, Germany set itself the goal of developing a multicultural society even if it was never an enthusiast in the way that Britain or the Netherlands were. This multiculturalism was to bring Muslim and other minority groups into an organic whole. Such a policy was emphasised by leaders even as specifically anti-Turkish sentiment in German society grew. An Islamic scholar in the country insightfully elaborated on the binarity between these two worlds. Today 'one encounters two extremes: the populist, unacceptable Islamophobic view on the one hand, and indiscriminate multiculturalism, based on the cultural-relativist understanding of "anything goes", on the other'.[16] How did the German state seek to mediate the two?

PERMANENT FOREIGNERS?

The Turkish presence in Germany dates back to the time of Frederick the Great in the mid-eighteenth century. But it was after the guest worker programme had been established in the 1960s that Turks were to become the country's largest ethnic minority. From then on they seemed destined to fall between two stools. Instead of assimilation into German society or reinsertion back into the society of origin, there was a 'permanence of an intermediary position situated between German society in which Turks remain *Ausländer* (foreigners), and Turk society to which the *Alamancis* no longer fully belong'.[17]

Turks in Germany have come to be defined, then, as *Ausländische Mitbürger*, or 'fellow citizens'.[18] But as one specialist on German multiculturalism explained, 'for many Turkish residents, post-unification developments resulted in a demotion from co-citizenship to third-class citizenship'. The smooth incorporation of East Germany into the Federal Republic, which was a priority of successive German governments after 1990, made the Turks into bystanders. For the most part they responded by localising their identity rather than extending it to the German state: 'Their identification with Germany is sooner rooted in the local community than in an historical-national territory.'[19]

In many ways the Turkish minority's religious character was shaped from outside. In 1972 the Turkish government established the Diyanet İşleri Türk İslam Birliği (DITIB, Turkish Islamic Union for Religious Affairs). Its main purpose was to address the religious needs of Turks abroad as well as to lobby for Turkish Muslim interests within the EU. A secular-oriented *diyanet* had originally been formed by Kemal Atatürk to manage religious affairs in the post-Ottoman Turkish state – and to keep Islam out of politics.

Other Turkish organisations in Germany, some with the backing of the Ankara government, were stronger advocates of Islamist teaching than the DITIB. The result was that the Turkish community was pulled in different directions.

> While the aim of German policy has been the integration of the Turkish communities, the aim of the Islamist organisations supported by the Turkish government has been diametrically opposed to integration. The Turks in Germany remain Turks even if they have adopted the German nationality.[20]

This became even truer during the 1990s' tide of xenophobic violence when the reaction of many Turks was to place greater emphasis on religion as their identity marker.[21]

Inevitably some research results have led to different conclusions. Ayhan Kaya's empirical findings for Germany as well as for France in 2003 and 2004 indicated that the identity orientations of Euro-Turks emphasised Europe. The most common answer on identification that suited Turkish respondents in both countries was 'first Turkish then European'. Not only that, the majority endorsed the progressive ideal of a political Europe embracing diversity. Addressing Western securitisation framing of Muslim migrants, Kaya offered an original perspective:

> Euro-Turks do not pose a threat to the political and social system of their countries of settlement, but rather have the willingness to incorporate themselves into the system. Research uncovers that orientation to Islam among Euro-Turks may be regarded as a quest for *justice* and *fairness*, originating from their reaction to structural problems like poverty, racism and exclusion.[22]

What was true of the Turkish-German construction of ethnoreligious identity also applied to other Muslim groups in the country. As a different study found,

> for many young Muslims in Germany, the goal became not to assimilate themselves into the secular values of the West, but instead to adopt a true Islamic identity

while living in the West. In many ways, German citizenship and settlement policies were ill prepared to facilitate this goal.[23]

Paradoxically, then, it seemed that life in Germany transformed many Muslim migrants into better Muslims.

This had not been the intention of the German programme for welcoming migrants. In his provocative analysis of the Turkish fact in Germany, Walter Laqueur highlighted how the German state had gone to painstaking efforts to accommodate the Turks.

> In no other country have immigrants been the subject of so many initiatives by so many well-intentioned institutions to promote their integration – social workers, academic researchers, churches eager to enter a dialogue, political parties (such as the Greens and the Liberals) interested in gaining a foothold in these communities.[24]

This is a contentious interpretation of a multifaceted effort to promote social integration.

As if this state-supported hospitality programme was not enough, Laqueur contended that German social workers and migration experts 'showed the Turks how to work the social safety net – that is to say, to get a maximum of financial and other aid from the state and the local authorities with a minimum of contribution to the common good'.[25] Postwar German liberalism, he suggested, required the German state to atone for its wartime crimes, especially against the Jews, by, paradoxically, lavishing a wide array of benefits on its large new Muslim minority.

The supposed unworthiness of the recipients of this new-found German generosity was tagged in another way. Their places of origin were often backward areas of backward countries, thus giving them the least in common with their country of destination. Laqueur put in this way:

> The Turkish (and Kurdish) immigrants were in no way prepared for life in Europe. They came from the least developed parts of Turkey such as Eastern Anatolia, many were illiterate, and they were far more conservative in both their religious beliefs and political orientation than middle-class Turkish society in Istanbul or Ankara.[26]

These differences among Turks may have been lost upon the Germans receiving them, and it is Laqueur's nuanced framing that, paradoxically, reflects the Turkophobic attitude that has emerged in Germany.

INTEGRATING AN UNDERCLASS

A different picture of Turks' integration into German society emerges if we consider the analysis of a Turkish-born German sociologist. Necla Kelek, a representative of the so-called 'Islam-Lite' school that expects Muslims to assimilate into host European societies, observed a trend similar to the one we found in Maghrebi identity shifts in France. 'These people came as Turks, now they are demanding services from the German state as Muslims.'

As a secular European Muslim, Kelek believed that the elevated importance of religion as an identity marker was the consequence of a failure of integration, a dysfunctional event, rather than a revival in the power of Islamic beliefs. She held mosque associations responsible for impeding the integration process by propagating the political values of their countries of origin. In addition, local imams advanced conservative interpretations of Islam that were at odds with Europe's secular norms. Kelek thus lent support to the suspicion that Islam has a hidden agenda in Europe.

Not unexpectedly, Kelek's group received strong backing from conservative political circles in Germany. It also obtained the support of many feminists including Germany's best-known advocate of women's rights, Alice Schwarzer.[27] Kelek's concern about the threat posed by Islamic fundamentalism to Turkish integration differs from Laqueur's view of the threat posed by Turkish backwardness. We consider this issue further in this chapter when examining reciprocal images in German and Turkish perspectives on each other's civilisation.

German integration efforts have not produced results much different from those in France. In 2010 only two members of the 612-seat Bundestag were of Turkish background, and just eight others had other minority origins. After four decades of life in Germany, many Turkish women enjoyed fewer personal freedoms than their counterparts in Turkey did. This is largely due to the influence of religiously conservative Turkish groups whose activities are circumscribed in Turkey itself. Ghettoisation, high youth unemployment and educational failure are among other problems that characterise Turks in Germany.

Until 1999 the most important difficulty longtime Turkish residents faced was becoming naturalised German citizens. No matter how long they had lived in the country, they faced near-insurmountable obstacles to obtaining citizenship. The explanation for this lay in the German state's adherence to the principle of *jus sanguinis*, or blood ties as the basis for citizenship, which overrode *jus soli*, or citizenship through birth on German soil. The 1999 German nationality law (which came into effect the following year) eased citizenship requirements, especially for German-born children of foreigners. The new law thus substantially increased the rate of naturalisation. A detailed study by the Nuremberg-based Federal Office for Migration and Refugees (BAMF) published in 2009 found that 45 per cent of Muslims living in the country now had a German passport.[28] Still, a sizeable number of established Turkish residents had become convinced that they had become 'permanent foreigners'.[29] They were to become the object of interest of fundamentalist groups in Turkey which sought to radicalise their politics.

Not all socially excluded groups turn to radical politics or religious fundamentalism. A more typical response, particularly among young people, is to turn to anomic non-political violence. Accordingly, as young Turks felt more excluded from mainstream German society, many became involved in gang violence. The derogatory term used by some Germans about foreigners, *Barbaren*, became adopted as a name by some Turkish street gangs because it 'connotes power, inclusiveness, and acceptance – perhaps even a sense of invincibility and righteousness'. Identifying as *Barbaren* instilled pride in being the Other of Germans. It also facilitated in-group solidarity, and even group survival.[30]

Is it accurate, then, to describe the Turks in Germany as constituting an underclass? One comparative study of educational levels of the Turkish second generation found differentiated results. 'In terms of higher education, the French educational system appears more effective at guiding Turkish young people towards university than the German system, while the German system is better at incorporating young adults into the labour market.'[31] Turks may therefore underachieve in educational terms but dispose of better employment prospects in Germany.

Those of Turkish origin in Germany exhibit mixed educational achievement records. A 2009 national study of German Muslims found that those born in Germany, especially girls, recorded higher levels of educational achievement than their parents did. But that was small consolation for the fact that Muslims, above all those of Turkish descent, accounted for a disproportionately high level of school drop-outs, the unemployed and people below the poverty line.[32] This finding is consistent with the poor educational performance of Bangladeshi and Pakistani Muslims in Britain when compared to South Asian Hindu and Sikh Indians.[33]

To label Turks an underclass living in a deprived parallel society is simplistic. A more nuanced conclusion is that 'in some countries, a sizeable number of second-generation Turks have fallen behind to the point where they now seriously risk becoming an underclass. In other countries, the Turks seem to be performing well enough, either through education or the apprenticeship system.'[34] Such an observation conveys the alarming message that Germany's Turkish community remains in large measure a group of permanent foreigners.

ORGANISING GERMANY'S TURKS

The institutionalisation of Islam is at odds with the individualisation of Islam:

Institutions need their own clientele to survive; the survival of, say, Islamic institutions depends on the existence of faithful subjects who are ready to remain within the boundaries of the religious community without having the need to incorporate themselves in the mainstream society.[35]

It can result in the reminoritising of minorities.

These considerations have not prevented the establishment of ethnic Turkish organisations in Germany to promote the interests of Turks and protect them from discriminatory practices. Some are religious associations with an ethnic dimension. They tend to be community based; Jytte Klausen, a Danish-born academic who has written extensively on Muslims in Europe, found no references to the Islamic *ummah* in these institutions.[36] Bassam Tibi offered an explanation:

> In Germany religious associations (*Moscheevereine*) are not purely Islamic, but rather Sunni or Shi'ite, Turkish, Bosnian, Arab or Pakistani, or perhaps divided between Ahmadi and Sunni, but almost always divided along ethnic and sectarian lines. Apart from the rhetoric of an overall Islam ethnicised in confrontation with Europe, one very rarely finds comprehensive Islamic mosques or associations.[37]

The first DITIB representative in Germany was appointed by the Turkish government in the early 1980s. This move came at a time when many Turks had already been living in Germany for over a decade and had drifted away from Islam or had begun to organise their religious life independent of Turkey's main Islamic school. The DITIB official was entrusted with overseeing the training of imams and religious teachers in Germany.

The concern of the Ankara government for the spiritual life of Turks in Germany went beyond the threat posed by secularism. It also involved an Islamist movement in Turkey which had become widespread among German-based Turks, Milli Görüş (National Vision), which oversaw more than 300 mosques in the country. This spiritual movement was associated with the former Turkish Prime Minister Necmettin Erbakan. He had been banned from political life for advocating an overtly religious conception of politics and for championing Islamic unity. Turkish political authorities accused Erbakan of fundamentalist leanings, that is, guilt by association with a peculiar kind of fundamentalist movement:

> According to the teaching of the Turkish fundamentalists, the Jews had founded two states – Israel and Turkey – because the founders of modern Turkey, the Young Turks and Kemal Atatürk, had all been *Doenme* by origin, that is to say, Jews who centuries ago had converted to Islam with the intention gradually to subvert, modernise, and secularise it.[38]

Erbakan's adherents in Germany were sceptical of the gains that Kemalism had supposedly produced for Turkey, in this way justifying their choice of emigration.

The secular–Islamic cleavage punctuating Turkish politics was transplanted to the Turkish community in Germany, therefore. This cleavage may have represented one side of the equation for why Turkish integration into German society had run into problems: according to Ünal Bilir, a Turkish academic,

> during the four-decade-long emigration history of the Turkish Diaspora, the integration problem stemmed from mainly two reasons: the continuing national and religious linkages with Turkey hindered the integration with German society; and German policy-makers were unwilling to accept the guest workers as an integral part of German society.[39]

If Bilir was right, then Islamic movements in Turkey were as much to blame for the failure of Turks to integrate into German society as the German authorities or German Turkophobes might be. The two may even have become dialectically linked: the more Turks in Germany appeared to be subscribing to an Islamic fundamentalist movement, the greater the anti-Islamic sentiment among Germans became. Conversely, the more widespread Islamophobia became, the greater the reason for Turks to retreat into the protective shell that Milli Görüş provided.

Which religious organisation was most representative of the Turkish community developed into a salient political issue. For some time German leaders had encountered difficulties accommodating Turkish guest workers because of the absence of a central Muslim organisation in Germany that could serve as the state's partner. For Bilir, 'the already radical Islamic political groups, such as *Milli Görüş*, do not meet the demands of the state, since they do not earn the trust of the German state, even though they always strive for collaboration with the state'.[40]

Another potential partner organisation was the Zentralrat de Muslime in Deutschland (ZMD, or Central Council of Muslims in Germany). Formed in 1994, in some respects it resembled the CFCM in France and brought together about twenty different Turkish associations. But the legal hurdle it faced was getting recognition from a German court that it constituted a peak organisation (*Spitzenverband*), which would entitle it to participation in specialised areas of policy making. A German court had rejected its application on the grounds that rival Turkish associations existed in Germany.

Among these were the Süleymancilar, named after the Turkish religious reformer Süleyman Efendi. His followers had already organised an association in the 1970s called the Verband der Islamischen Kulturzentren (VIKZ, or Association of Islamic Cultural Centres). Identifying themselves as Sunnis, they have stayed out of the orbit of the DITIB while pressing for religious instruction in public schools for Muslim pupils.

Despite internal differences about the role to assign to religion, these Turkish organisations have a common goal: 'to establish Islam as a legally recognised religion in Germany, which would place religious instruction into the German public school curriculum, facilitate mosque building, and provide many other rights in public and private life'.[41] They have carved out autonomy from authorities in Turkey. At the same time, most of these organisations favour introducing dual citizenship for Turks resident in Germany. The emergence of *Türk(iye) Müslümanliği*, a specific 'Turkey-Islam' that creates a symbiosis of Turkishness and religious Islam, has been the product of Turkish organisational activities in Germany.[42]

The most important secular organisation for Turks is the Türkische Gemeinde in Deutschland (Turkish Community in Germany, or TGD). It has emphasised the economic contribution, entrepreneurial initiative, occupational skills, industriousness, and problem-solving abilities that Turkish migrants have brought to the country. For the TGD leadership, their material culture, ranging from use of public space to gastronomy, has enriched Germany. The organisation therefore stays clear of the sensitive religious differences that separate Turks from Germans.

In France, Muslim community and religious leaders have regularly been recruited from a Muslim majority state such as Algeria. This is largely the case in Germany, too. For Klausen, 'the new Muslim elite is not drawn primarily from the native-born descendants of earlier generations of labour migrants. It is largely made up of recent immigrants or refugees whose political engagement predates their arrival in Europe.'[43] But this statement is not entirely accurate. In November 2008, while Barack Obama was winning the US presidency, Cem Özdemir became the first ethnic Turk to be elected co-head of a major German political party, Bündnis 90/die Grünen (Alliance 90/the Greens). In his campaign for the leadership position his supporters adopted the cute slogan 'Yes We Cem'.[44] While generating enthusiasm across ethnic groups, Özdemir's call for a colour-blind Germany and his ambivalence on minority rights and minority integration have put him at odds with Turkish community leaders.

Özdemir's moderate secular politics form part of a broader pattern of Turkish community leaders being disinclined to embrace Islamic fundamentalism. Milli Görüş may be the exception to this since it is perceived as having fundamentalist tendencies. But Klausen's conclusion is insightful and persuasive: 'Muslims who hold public office in the European political system are not religious fundamentalists. They do not insist on a literal reading of the Koran, nor do they aim to create a European Caliphate.' As one such leader explained their relative lack of interest in arguing about Islamic strictures, 'most of us are engineers or businessmen'.[45]

GERMAN TURKOPHOBIA

What have been German citizens' attitudes to the growing Muslim presence in the country? Put differently, as an American academic asked in the mid-1990s, 'is Germany's xenophobia qualitatively different from everybody else's?'[46] The answer Gilbert Geis gave was a qualified yes:

> The German attitude toward foreigners in their midst fuel doubts concerning whether the neo-Nazi movement, with its savage brutality, is but one of a considerable number of such movements throughout the world or whether it reflects a fundamentally distinctive German ethos.[47]

The height of skinhead violence in the country was reached about two decades ago, so the appropriate question today is whether we can detect a specifically German variant of hostility towards Muslims (see Box 6.1).

Box 6.1 One Type of Turk: Elfriede Jelinek's Parody of Viennese

You can't talk about the Turk's private life, for it doesn't exist. He works. And after work, he must be stored somewhere, to be protected against the elements; but no one knows where. Evidently in the streetcar, for which he doesn't buy a ticket. To the non-Turkish world around him he is a cardboard figure, the kind you aim at in a shooting gallery. In case he's needed for work, he is pulled out and set in motion; someone shoots at him, and, whether hit or not, he vanishes at the other side of the gallery, then revolves invisibly (no one sees him, but there's probably nothing worth seeing).

Source: Elfriede Jelinek, *The Piano Teacher* (London: Serpent's Tail, 1989), pp. 134–5.

The backlash against the influx of migrants in Germany peaked when the EU expanded into eastern Europe in 2004. German fears of losing control over their homeland were heightened as tens of millions of Slavs living to the south and east became part of the European integration project. The country's leaky borders, well-paid jobs, generous social services and lax enforcement of asylum and benefits claims were a magnet to outsiders. For their part, many Germans bought into the stereotype of the disreputable foreigner living illegally in Germany. *Ausländerfeindlichkeit*, or animosity towards foreigners, rose, thereby providing hothouse conditions for the emergence of radical right politics.

In Germany, as in most European countries, multiple sources of data on immigrants, including their values and attitudes, are available.[48] The closest

Table 6.1 How significantly do the following groups living in Germany differ in their lifestyles from Germans?

	Little or not at all (%)	Somewhat or very much (%)
Asylum seekers	4	59
Turks	4	45
German speakers from eastern Europe	13	24
Jews	52	11
Italians	42	6

Source: ALLBUS German General Social Survey, 'Cumulated ALLBUS 1980–2006' (Allbus, 2006), Tables V150–V154, pp. 120–4. 'Little or not at all' scores include the first two (1, 2) on the seven-point scale. 'Somewhat or very much' include the last two (6, 7) on the seven-point scale. This question and that in Table 6.2 form part of the ALLBUS topical module 'Attitudes to ethnic groups in Germany' and are replicated every ten years.

that Germany has to a single authoritative national survey is ALLBUS. Since 1990 this public opinion survey has been asking respondents whether they believe the entry of certain groups of immigrants should be unrestricted, limited or stopped completely. Between 1990 and 2006 respondents gradually shifted their views on asylum seekers, who can be treated as a proxy for non-Europeans from faraway countries, from an open-minded to a restrictive orientation. In 2006 73 per cent of respondents (in both Western and Eastern Germany) answered 'immigration should be restricted' for asylum seekers and a further 14 per cent in the West (16 per cent in East Germany) agreed that 'immigration should be stopped completely'. Only 13 per cent in the West, and 11 per cent in the East, still thought asylum seekers should have an unrestricted right to settle in Germany.

In assessing how markedly the lifestyles of certain groups living in Germany differed from the German one, nearly half of ALLBUS respondents claimed that Turks somewhat or very much differed; only asylum seekers ranked more non-German in lifestyles (see Table 6.1). Regarding marriage of an ethnic German with a member of one of these groups, asylum seekers and Turks were neck-and-neck in terms of how unpleasant for a German respondent the prospect of such a marriage was (see Table 6.2). In turn, German respondents were evenly divided over whether Turks should have all the same rights as Germans (29 per cent agreed, 30 per cent disagreed).

These survey results generally reveal German circumspection, and sometimes antipathy, towards the Turkish minority. The inescapable finding is that the average German is far more hostile to groups coming from far away, or which are Muslim, than to groups with cultural affinities such as Italians,

Table 6.2 How pleasant or unpleasant would it be for you if a member of one of the following groups married into your family?

	Very/quite pleasant (%)	Very/quite unpleasant (%)
Asylum seekers	9	43
Turks	12	40
German speakers from eastern Europe	17	20
Jews	19	16
Italians	32	7

Source: ALLBUS German General Social Survey, 'Cumulated ALLBUS 1980–2006' (Allbus, 2006), Tables V160–V164, pp. 128–31. 'Very/quite unpleasant' scores include the first two (1, 2) on the seven-point scale. 'Quite/very pleasant' include the last two (6, 7) on the seven-point scale.

eastern European German speakers and Jews. It is safe to say that Germans are therefore not exceptional or distinctive in the nature of their xenophobia in comparisons with France or other European receiving societies.

BERLIN'S POLICIES, ANKARA'S OBJECTIONS

As in other EU countries, German governments have adopted policies aimed at increasing interaction between majority and minority populations. In 2007 Chancellor Merkel convened an integration summit focusing on ways to improve the life of the country's estimated fifteen million immigrants and offspring. It was also designed to address mounting Islamophobic and anti-Turkish attitudes. The summit agreed on a National Integration Plan, which comprised some 400 specific measures to improve conditions affecting migrants. But the credibility of the summit's decisions was undermined by the boycott staged by several Turkish organisations including the TGD. It was not the summit itself but a new immigration law that was the target of the protest.

In 2005 the German Immigration Act had been passed to tighten up regulations regarding labour immigration, asylum seekers and refugees, as well as integration of immigrants.[49] It was followed by a 2007 law that took aim at family reunification practices from developing countries, including Turkey. The minimum age for foreign spouses allowed into the country was raised to eighteen (still six years younger than the minimum in Denmark). Spouses now also had to demonstrate basic proficiency in German before being admitted. The rationale for these restrictions was to crack down on forced and/or arranged marriages, which were thought to be common practice among many groups from developing countries.[50] Exceptions from these provisions were made for 'spouses of short-term expatriates of certain privileged nationalities and for those holding a university or polytechnic degree'.[51]

Even more discriminatory was the introduction of a so-called 'attitude test' – *Gesinnungstest* – as part of the citizenship application process. It was first implemented in Baden-Württemberg in 2006 and became a national test in 2007 following the passing of the amended Nationality Act. Under this test applicants for citizenship are quizzed on their basic knowledge of the German legal and social order, its way of life, and on German language competency – standard subjects in many countries' citizenship tests. In addition, however, applicants are asked for their views on domestic violence, arranged marriages, religious freedom and terrorism – questions aimed primarily at Muslim immigrants and their descendants. As Ayhan Kaya has persuasively argued, tests of this kind measuring levels of civic integration are discriminatory against Muslims, who are negatively targeted as a group under the guise of liberalism.[52]

The head of the secular-oriented TGD condemned the new procedures as unconstitutional and discriminatory, but Chancellor Merkel retorted that no one could issue an ultimatum to the German federal government, especially over laws passed by the Bundestag. At the integration summit she was confronted by a journalist displaying that day's front page of the Turkish newspaper *Hürriyet*. It had Merkel's photograph inscribed with the words *Düpedüz Irkçılık* – 'pure racism'.[53]

In the aftermath of these conflicts the Turkish Prime Minister, Recep Tayyip Erdoğan, visited Germany. He assured a Turkish audience in Cologne, where the mosque-building protests had taken place in 2008, that the German state and police could be trusted. He also extolled the virtue of multiculturalism, which he defined as a right, not a mere policy. In this way Erdoğan was emphatic that Turkish migrants belonged to both Germany and Turkey (see Box 6.2).

A tragic event during Erdoğan's visit reminded Germans of the darkest moments in their cohabitation with the Turkish minority. A fire in an apartment block in Ludwigshafen killed nine Turkish immigrants, including five children, and injured scores of others. It immediately raised the question whether anti-Turkish extremists were involved. An investigation found that they were not, but the misfortune triggered memories of the attacks on Turks in Mölln and Solingen in 1992 and 1993. Nevertheless some Turkish commentators described Chancellor Merkel's reaction to the Ludwigshafen tragedy as 'frosty'.

The outpouring of sympathy for the Turkish leader while visiting Germany in 2008 vanished, however, when he asserted that Turks in the country had a right to be educated in Turkish-language schools, including secondary ones, and to set up Turkish-speaking institutions. He called for Turks to be accom-

---

Box 6.2 Two types of belonging

Turkish Nobel Prize laureate Orhan Pamuk embodies the distinctive relationship that Turks have with Europe. Twenty-four years after travelling to
Europe the first time, Pamuk applied for a new passport in order to meet
with his Turkish readers in Germany:

> It was during that trip that I came to associate my passport with the sort of
> 'identity crisis' that has afflicted so many others in the years since then – that
> is, the question of how much we belong to the country of our first passport
> and how much we belong to the 'other countries' that it allows us to enter.

Source: Orhan Pamuk, 'My first passport', *New Yorker*, 16 April 2007, p. 57.

---

modated as a parallel society in Germany. Ironically, it was exactly this idea
that raised concerns about Muslim exclusion in France.

Returning to Ankara, Prime Minister Erdoğan warned Germany's leadership not to confuse assimilation with integration of the Turkish minority. In
a speech to the Turkish parliament he inveighed: 'I repeat: assimilation is a
crime against humanity.'[54] Later in 2008, Erdoğan added another contender
for the title of crime against humanity – Islamophobia itself. He explained:
'We expect members of other civilisations to declare Islamophobia a crime
against humanity, especially while we say that anti-Semitism is a crime
against humanity.' The Prime Minister branded the fear of Islam that had
spread in the West as nothing short of paranoia and a pathological state of
mind.[55]

It is not unusual for the leader of a foreign country to play the role of
patron and defender of ethnic kin and diaspora residents in another country.
But for some international-relations analysts, Prime Minister Erdoğan's
advice to the German government on how to treat its Turkish minority had
blurred the line between domestic and international politics. Other analysts
believed Erdoğan had overplayed his hand.

Opposing Turkey's EU bid: how distinctly German?

Germany's relations with Turkey have been muddied not just by controversial speeches from leaders of both countries but also by Turkey's application
to join the EU. From initial tentative backing, Chancellor Merkel raised a
series of obstacles to the application. These ranged from Turkey's unflinch-
ing support for the disputed Northern Cyprus government to the preference

for the EU to consolidate itself as a functional transnational organisation after a period of enlargement. Turkey's future relationship with the EU was redefined as becoming one of 'privileged partnership' in place of membership.

The radical right in Germany, as elsewhere in Europe, has opposed Turkey's accession to the EU on ethnoreligious grounds. One of the more demeaning slogans it coined was that 'Europe is not an Oriental bazaar'.[56] Many Germans are sceptical about further EU expansion because Germany would again become the primary country of destination for new EU citizens, in this case, from Turkey.

For their part, Turks increasingly resort to negative framing of Europe (see Box 6.3). This more EU-sceptic approach is also mirrored in polling data. The percentage of Turks who thought Turkish membership in the EU would be a good thing reached a high point in 2004, when 73 per cent of respondents were in favour. But it dramatically dropped to a low point of 38 per cent in 2010. This was primarily a negative assessment of the lack of progress in EU negotiations: by 2010 only thirteen out of thirty-five EU chapters had been opened for negotiation and just one – on science and research – had been successfully concluded. Enthusiasm for EU membership regained ground subsequently to reach 48 per cent in 2011.[57] How important accession to the EU was for Turks when EU economies were in crisis, Turkey's was performing well, and the choice of individual migration to Germany or elsewhere remained a realistic option represented an important consideration.

Box 6.3 A Turkish cartoon depicts the Western religious Other

Turhan Selcuk, Turkey's leading Kemalist cartoonist, drew the EU as a mother pig nursing numerous baby pigs, while the lone Turkish lamb waited aside, desperately hungry and isolated, suggesting the existence of a strong and irreconcilable biological difference between Europe and Turkey. No matter how badly Turks want to drink from European milk, they cannot have it: not necessarily because Europe does not want to give it, but because it will not be accepted by the Turkish body. Europe as the pig image essentially stems from a religious imagery of difference; it reflects a religiously charged description of folk Europe as a pig, the untouchable of Muslim cultural identity. A pig is dirty (*necis*) and therefore one should stay away.

Source: Hasan Kösebalaban, 'The Permanent "Other"? Turkey and the Question of European Identity', *Mediterranean Quarterly* 18:4 (2007), p. 91.

The question can be posed whether there is anything exceptional about German opposition to Turkey's membership compared to that of its neighbours. France's leaders have long been sceptical of Turkish membership. Former President Valéry Giscard d'Estaing, who drafted the first European constitution that was defeated in referendums, explained that 'Turkey has developed its own history and its own culture, which deserve respect. However, the foundations of Europe's identity, so vital to the cohesion of the EU today, are different. Turkey's accession would change the nature of the European project.'[58] In 2007 President Sarkozy campaigned on a 'rejectionist' platform, arguing that Turkey did not form part of Europe in geographical terms. In office, he supported starting up negotiations with Turkey on several chapters of the *acquis communautaire*, perhaps convinced that the protracted process would dampen Turkish enthusiasm. This calculation seemed to pay dividends, as our review of survey data on support for membership indicated.

The Belgian Islamophobic right has been blunter than Sarkozy: 'The person who opens the door to Turkey moves Europe's borders to Egypt, Syria, Iraq and the Caucasus, and flings open the gates to a new and massive tidal wave of immigration.'[59] Another western neighbour of Germany, the Netherlands, has displayed ambiguity. Dutch public opinion was unenthusiastic about EU membership for Turkey: growing Dutch fears of Islam, in part triggered by a resident Turkish community that is one of the largest in Europe, were a catalyst. Prime Minister Jan Peter Balkenende backed the start of talks on Turkey's application in 2004 and was supported by the majority of the Dutch parliament. But this stance became political capital for the Lijst Pim Fortuyn, a conservative Christian party, and Geert Wilders's explicitly Islamophobic movement. A combination of increasing anti-Muslim sentiment, the killings of prominent anti-Muslim figures provoking popular outrage, and deepening disillusion with the Dutch model of multiculturalism has reflected some of the same trends as in Germany.

Germans' southern neighbours and linguistic kin, the Austrians, have had a more consistent record of confronting Turkey. A Eurobarometer opinion poll conducted in 2005, just before membership talks between the EU and Turkey began, found that Austrian respondents rejected Turkey's membership more decisively than any other EU country: 80 per cent were against and only 10 per cent for.[60] Three-quarters of respondents thought that the cultural differences between Turkey and western Europe were too great. Only one-quarter believed EU membership would increase understanding between Europe and the Muslim world. Aware of their history as the place where Ottoman expansion was stopped, for many Austrians EU enlargement would mean that Turks had attained the right to live and work in their country.

Germany's large eastern neighbour, Poland, has taken a nuanced view of Turkey in Europe. A substantial majority of Poles has supported the idea of

EU enlargement. At the same time, in a 2008 survey, Turks ranked thirtieth out of thirty-five in terms of Poles' favourite nationalities, ahead only of Russians, Arabs, Romanians and Roma.[61] The Polish Prime Minister, Donald Tusk, publicly backed Turkey's EU bid while hosting Erdoğan in 2009, putting himself at loggerheads with German and French leaders – which may have been his intention in the first place.

Comparative survey data suggest that only a handful of EU member states would approve Turkey's application if referendums were held. In both Germany and France, opponents outnumbered supporters by about two to one. It is clear, then, that nothing exceptional marks German scepticism of Turkish EU membership. If Germany plays any role, it may be as opinion leader in western Europe. It is France and the Greek government of divided Cyprus that have created the practical roadblocks to Turkish accession.

This is not to underestimate the influence of popular opposition to Turkey's application in Germany. It had been running high even before Prime Minister Erdoğan made his controversial comments in 2008. His depiction of assimilation as a crime against humanity, the accompanying call for people of Turkish descent not to give up their cultural heritage, and the proposal to establish Turkish-language high schools in Germany led to charges of outside interference in German affairs. In some respects, the Turkish leader was taking on the role that national Muslim councils in France and Britain usually performed.

Erdoğan's visit to Berlin in November 2011, to honour Turkish guest workers on the fiftieth anniversary of their first arriving in Germany, was also filled with controversy. He complained of the German authorities' neglect of the three million Turks trying to integrate into German society. At the same time he warned that Turks should not be required to assimilate into German society. He repeated the call for dual citizenship for Turks, which Germany does not permit. In referring to the 72,000 Turkish employers in Germany, employing 350,000 people, Erdoğan underscored their importance to German enterprise, research and culture: 'The guest workers of yesterday are slowly becoming employers, academics, artists.' The Turkish Prime Minister also ridiculed the law that required a Turkish woman who had married a Turkish resident of Germany to first learn German before emigrating. 'It cannot be that the love of young people is only allowed to exist in German by decree,' Erdoğan inveighed.[62]

The blurring of the boundary between foreign and domestic policy was not limited to Erdoğan's interventions in Germany. On the one hand, politicians in Turkey lashed out at the German government for indirectly protecting Kurdish terrorists. Cemil Çiçek, speaker of the Turkish parliament and a party colleague of Erdoğan's, claimed that 'twice as many PKK [Partiya Karkerên Kurdistan, Kurdistan Workers' Party] members live in Germany as in the Qandil mountains in northern Iraq'.[63] On the other hand, Erwin Huber, leader of Bavaria's conservative Christlich-Soziale Union (Christian Social Union), demanded a review of Turkey's EU accession talks. 'Erdoğan preached Turkish nationalism on German soil,' he charged. 'That is anti-European and confirms our misgivings regarding Turkish EU membership.'[64] In other words, the Turkish state should pay a price for Erdoğan's meddling in German affairs. Chancellor Merkel, too, criticised Erdoğan's views on assimilation. She insisted that anyone possessing German citizenship was a full-fledged citizen of the country regardless of their origin: 'Their loyalty then belongs to the German state.'[65]

TURKEY'S EUROPEAN VALUES

The irony underlying the disagreement between German and Turkish leaders on the rights that Turks in Germany should enjoy and the desirability of Turkey's admission into the EU is that Prime Minister Erdoğan had been a champion of the achievements of European civilisation. For one Turkish analyst, 'Erdoğan has come to embrace Turkey's entry into the EU as an opportunity for a "reconciliation of civilisations"'.[66] The Prime Minister highlighted how

> a country like Turkey, where the cultures of Islam and democracy have merged together, taking part in such an institution as the EU, will bring harmony of civilisations. That is why we think it is the project of the century. We are there as a guarantee of an entente between the civilisations.[67]

The bridging of a civilisational divide was Erdoğan's promise to western Europe:

> Our greatest claim is that of civilisational alliance. We claimed that [if Turkey is rejected] the EU is doomed to stay as a Christian club. Only if Turkey joins the EU, then it will not be remembered as a Christian club, but rather as the address for civilisational alliance.[68]

Therefore, as Turkey expert Hakan Yavuz put it, Erdoğan and his AKP (Adalet ve Kalkınma Partisi, Justice and Development Party), though more Islamic than other Turkish parties, is 'championing the liberal democratic basis of Westernisation that the Kemalist Westernisers often chose to ignore'.[69] Among other advantages – which include its growing diplomatic clout in the Middle East and its attractiveness as a trade partner – Turkey's admission to the EU would help Europe better integrate its Muslim minorities.

Oddly, the secular republican model operating in Turkey does not recognise ethnic and religious minorities – precisely what Erdoğan has been insisting on for Turks in Germany. However, it was his AKP that had adopted a more responsive approach to the grievances expressed by the Kurdish minority.[70]

The EU itself seems uncertain whether it is a civilisational, a geographic, a religious, a rights-based or merely an economic organisation. The incentives for Europe to embrace Turkey are the country's geostrategic importance as a conduit to the wider Turkic world, as well as a secular state model promoted by the EU for other Muslim states to emulate.[71] The Christian-versus-Muslim template injected into the debate may be a red herring (Box 6.4). It exacerbates friction between majority and minority in Germany. But that may be precisely why this red herring is introduced.

Box 6.4 The semantics of ethnic and religious identity

[EU elites should] disentangle the question of Turkey's accession from the fear of Muslim immigration, which would help Turkey's accession prospects. The language of the debate on Turkey's accession should focus on Turks, not Muslims. Many Turks in Germany complain, for instance, that whereas before the September 11 attacks they were referred to as 'Turks' by German opinion makers and media, after September 11, they suddenly became 'Muslims'.

Source: Bahar Güngör, 'Turkey Fears anti-Turkish Campaign before EU-Elections 2009', *Deutsche Welle*, at http://www.bpb.de/files/RJ35NS.pdf, accessed 8 February 2012.

One Turkish analyst advanced a more complex set of reasons why EU foreign policy objectives should prioritise Turkey's accession:

> Turks in Europe have a potentially effective stock of social capital stemming from their population size, economic power, political participation and civil organisations. This social capital can be mobilised to bridge Turkey and the European Union if proper strategies and mechanisms are employed.[72]

EU foreign policy towards Turkey should, then, ideally entail *la politique du dehors avec les raisons du dedans* – an external policy that utilises domestic imperatives – for mutual gain.

The case of the Turkish community in Germany and its hypothetical assets – social capital – and liabilities – shaky integration into the host society – point to the potential for both enrichment and poisoning of national politics through in-migration of citizens from another country. As seen in the case of Turks in Germany, a repeated stimulus–response cycle can turn communities towards each other, but also against one other.

Notes

1. 'Anger at Europe's far right "anti-Islam" conference, Times Online website, 18 September 2008, http://www.timesonline.co.uk/tol/news/world/europe/article4783532.ece

2. Reported in *Die Tageszeitung*, 11 February 2008.

3. 'Confrontation over German mosque', BBC News website, 19 September 2008, http://news.bbc.co.uk/go/pr/fr/-/2/hi/europe/7625906.stm, accessed 7 February 2012.

4. Michael Scott Moore and Jochen-Martin Gutsch, 'The Muslims are Coming!', Spiegel Online International website, 28 December 2006, http://www.spiegel.de/international/0,1518,456751,00.html, accessed 7 February 2012.

5. Ibid.

6. For the broader context, see Robert Carle, 'Pope Benedict XVI Confronts Religious Relativism', *Society* 45 (2008), pp. 549–55.

7. Thilo Sarrazin, *Deutschland schafft sich ab: Wie wir unser Land aufs Spiel setzen* (Munich: Deutsche Verlags-Anstalt, 2010).

8. Michael Slackman, 'With words on Muslims, opening a door long shut', *New York Times*, 13 November 2010, p. A6.

9. Aylin Selçuk, 'Educating Thilo Sarrazin', *The Guardian*, 18 March 2011.

10. Douglas B. Klusmeyer and Demetrios G. Papademetriou, *Immigration Policy in the Federal Republic of Germany: Negotiating Membership and Remaking the Nation* (New York: Berghahn, 2009), pp. 91–3.

11. Kerstin Schulz, 'Jeder fünfte Deutsche ist fremdenfeindlich', Spiegel Online Politik website, 5 November 2010, http://www.spiegel.de/politik/deutschland/0,1518,694325,00.html, accessed 10 February 2012.

12. Bican Sahin and Nezahat Altuntas, 'Between Enlightened Exclusion and Conscientious Inclusion: Tolerating the Muslims in Germany', *Journal of Muslim Minority Affairs* 29 (2009), pp. 27–41.

13. Angelina Peralva, 'Racisme et xénophobie dans l'Allemagne contemporaine', in Michel Wieviorka (ed.), *Racisme et xénophobie en Europe: une comparaison internationale* (Paris: La Découverte, 1994), p. 164.

14. Ibid.

15. Claire de Galembert, 'Allemagne: l'Islam des années 70 à aujourd'hui – entre marginalisation et reconnaissance', in Ural Manço (ed.), *Reconnaissance et discrimination: présence de l'Islam en Europe occidentale et en Amérique du Nord* (Paris: L'Harmattan, 2004), p. 51.

16. Bassam Tibi, *Political Islam, World Politics and Europe: Democratic Peace and Euro-Islam versus Global Jihad* (London: Routledge, 2008), p. 191.

17. De Galembert, 'Allemagne', p. 54.

18. Claire de Galembert, 'Les Boucs émissaires de la réunification allemande', *Autrement*, September 1995, pp. 87–99.

19. Joyce Marie Mushaben, *The Changing Faces of Citizenship: Social Integration and Political Mobilization among Ethnic Minorities in Germany* (New York: Berghahn, 2008), p. 309.

20. Walter Laqueur, *The Last Days of Europe: Epitaph for an Old Continent* (New York: Thomas Dunne, 2007), p. 66.

21. Joel S. Fetzer and J. Christopher Soper, *Muslims and the State in Great Britain, France, and Germany* (Cambridge: Cambridge University Press, 2005), p. 105.

22. Ayhan Kaya, 'European Union, Europeanness, and Euro-Turks: Hyphenated and

Multiple Identities', Eurozine website, 10 April 2005, http://www.eurozine.com/articles/2005-10-04-kaya-en.html, accessed 7 February 2012.

23. Fetzer and Soper, *Muslims and the State in Great Britain, France, and Germany*, p. 105.

24. Laqueur, *The Last Days of Europe*, p. 61.

25. Ibid.

26. Ibid.

27. 'Who's Afraid of Euro-Islam?' *taz* Conference, Berlin, 17–19 April 2009.

28. 'Germany has 1 million more Muslims than previously thought', Spiegel Online International website, 24 June 2009, http://www.spiegel.de/international/germany/0,1518,632290,00.html, accessed 8 February 2012.

29. See Ruth Mandel, *Cosmopolitan Anxieties: Turkish Challenges to Citizenship and Belonging in Germany* (Durham, NC: Duke University Press, 2008).

30. Tara Lewelling, 'Exploring Muslim Diaspora Communities in Europe through a Social Movement Lens', *Strategic Insights* 4:5 (2005).

31. Maurice Crul and Hans Vermeulen, 'Immigration, Education, and the Turkish Second Generation in Five European Nations: A Comparative Study', in Craig A. Parsons and Timothy M. Smeeding (eds), *Immigration and the Transformation of Europe* (Cambridge: Cambridge University Press, 2006), p. 242.

32. 'Germany has 1 million more Muslims than previously thought'.

33 See Tahir Abbas, 'How South Asians Achieve Education: A Comparative Study of Bangladeshis, Indians and Pakistanis in Birmingham Schools and Colleges', PhD thesis, University of Warwick, 2000.

34. Crul and Vermeulen, 'Immigration, Education, and the Turkish Second Generation in Five European Nations', p. 246.

35. Ayhan Kaya, 'Individualisation and Institutionalisation of Islam in Europe in the Age of Securitisation', *Insight Turkey* 12:1 (2010), pp. 59–60.

36. Jytte Klausen, *The Islamic Challenge: Politics and Religion in Western Europe* (Oxford: Oxford University Press, 2005), p. 205.

37. Tibi, *Political Islam, World Politics and Europe*, p. 205.

38. Laqueur, *The Last Days of Europe*, p. 62.

39. Ünal Bilir, '"Turkey-Islam": Recipe for Success or Hindrance to the Integration of the Turkish Diaspora Community in Germany?', *Journal of Muslim Minority Affairs* 24 (2004), p. 275.

40. Ibid.

41. Barbara Freyer Stowasser, 'The Turks in Germany: From Sojourners to Citizens', in Yvonne Yazbeck Haddad (ed.), *Muslims in the West: From Sojourners to Citizens* (Oxford: Oxford University Press, 2002), p. 67.

42. See for example *Journal of Muslim Minority Affairs* 24:2 (2004), a special issue on Turks and Turkey edited by Roberta Micallef and M. Hakan Yavuz.

43. Klausen, *The Islamic Challenge*, p. 47.

44. Eunji Chung, 'Europe's Obama: Please Stand Up', *Harvard International Review* 30:4 (2009).

45. Klausen, *The Islamic Challenge*, p. 47.

46. Gilbert Geis, 'Is Germany's Xenophobia Qualitatively Different from Everybody Else's?', *Crime, Law and Social Change* 24 (1995), pp. 65–75.

47. Ibid., p. 66.

48. See the discussion in Oya S. Abah, 'German Public Opinion on Immigration and

Integration', in Bertelsmann-Stiftung, Migration Policy Institute (eds), *Migration, Public Opinion and Politics: The Transatlantic Council on Migration* (Gütersloh: Bertelsmann-Stiftung, 2009), p. 48. The Institut für Demoskopie Allensbach provides regular survey data on attitudes regarding immigrants.

49. For details of the 2005 law, see Rita Süssmuth and Christal Morehouse, 'The Future of Migration and Integration Policy in Germany', in Bertelsmann-Stiftung, Migration Policy Institute (eds), *Migration, Public Opinion and Politics: The Transatlantic Council on Migration* (Gütersloh: Bertelsmann-Stiftung, 2009), Table 1, pp. 265–6.

50. 'Germany's integration summit clouded by Turkish boycott', *Deutsche Well*, 11 July 2007.

51. Bettina Offer, 'New Changes in German Immigration Law, September 07 2007', International Law Office website, http://www.internationallawoffice.com/newsletters/detail.aspx?g=79dbafbe-c56e-481a-98ad-335f5edd7dad, accessed 8 February 2012.

52. Ayhan Kaya, *Islamophobia as a Form of Governmentality: Unbearable Weightiness of the Politics of Fear* (Malmö: Malmö University, 2011), p. 29.

53. Ciğdem Akyol, 'Germany needs immigrants', *Atlantic Times*, August 2007.

54. 'Erdoğan: assimilation is crime against humanity', EuropeNews website, 13 February 2008, http://europenews.dk/en/node/7132, accessed 8 February 2012.

55. Quoted in Thomas Seibert, 'Enmity with Islam "crime against humanity"', *The National*, 17 September 2008.

56. Christina Schori Liang, '"Nationalism Ensures Peace": The Foreign and Security Policy of the German Populist Radical Right after (Re)unification', in Christina Schori Liang (ed.), *Europe for the Europeans: The Foreign and Security Policy of the Populist Radical Right* (Aldershot: Ashgate, 2007), p. 164.

57. Ersin Kalaycıoğlu, 'Turkey's Views of the European Union in 2011', *On Turkey*, 21 September 2011.

58. Valéry Giscard d'Estaing, 'A better European bridge to Turkey', *Financial Times*, 25 November 2004.

59. *Vlaams Staat, Europese Natie: Europees verkiezingsprogramma* (Brussels: Vlaams Blok, 2004). Quoted by Marc Swyngedouw, Koen Abts and Maarten Van Craen, 'Our Own People First in a Europe of Peoples: The International Policy of the Vlaams Blok', in Christina Schori Liang (ed.), *Europe for the Europeans: The Foreign and Security Policy of the Populist Radical Right* (Aldershot: Ashgate, 2007), p. 92.

60. Standard Eurobarometer 63 (Spring 2005), at http://ec.europa.eu/public_opinion/archives/eb/eb63/eb63_en.htm, accessed 8 February 2012.

61. 'Attitude to Other Nations', *Polish Public Opinion*, December 2008, http://www.cbos.pl/PL/publikacje/public_opinion/2008/12_2008.pdf, accessed 13 February 2012.

62. Anna Reimann, 'Erdoğan Escalates Germany Criticism', Spiegel Online International website, 2 November 2011, http://www.spiegel.de/international/europe/0,1518,795423,00.html

63. Ibid.

64. 'Erdoğan's Visit Leaves German Conservatives Fuming', Spiegel Online International website, 12 February 2008, http://www.spiegel.de/international/germany/0,1518,druck-534724,00.html, accessed 8 February 2012.

65. Quoted ibid.

66. Kösebalaban, 'The Permanent "Other"?', p. 95.

67. Quotes are from Tayyip Erdoğan, interview, *The Independent*, 13 December 2004, reported by Kösebalaban, 'The Permanent "Other"?' p. 95.
68. Ibid.
69. M. Hakan Yavuz, *Secularism and Muslim Democracy in Turkey* (Cambridge: Cambridge University Press, 2009), p. 204.
70. Evangelos Liaras, *Turkey's Party System and the Paucity of Minority Policy Reform* (San Domenico di Fiesole, Italy: Robert Schuman Centre for Advanced Studies, 2009).
71. Yavuz, *Secularism and Muslim Democracy in Turkey*, p. 208.
72. Talip Küçükcan, 'Bridging the European Union and Turkey: The Turkish Diaspora in Europe', *Insight Turkey* 9:4 (2007).

CHAPTER SEVEN

Undoing Islamophobia

THE MAKING OF ANTI-MUSLIM PREJUDICE

A series of empirically supported propositions follow from our diachronic examination of Islamophobia in Europe. Some of these are self-evident or have been part of conventional wisdom for many years, but others represent new perspectives. The propositions can be listed in the following sequence, though it does not presuppose the nature of the interconnectedness – causal or not – between them:

- Anxiety, fear, prejudice, hostility and hatred are psychological responses whose origins lie in infancy and the nurturing process. The contemporary imperative to be prejudiced against prejudice is inconsistent with human nature, constitutes an internal contradiction and is self-defeating. Being unprejudiced is unnatural so developing benign, constructive forms of prejudice channelled at targets that will suffer no harm is what psychology and related fields regard as a realistic resolution of emotional tension.
- Beginning in the 1960s an unprecedented increase in migration, mostly southern European and non-European, to industrialised European countries took place. Muslims made up a significant proportion of these but initially they were not singled out from among other groups coming from poorer countries.
- As the European integration project gathered steam, the liberal values governing immigration policies adopted by the major industrial states were transferred to the emerging supranational level. Subsequently the EU promoted liberal (more accurately, *laissez-faire*) policies not just on immigration but also on the social integration of immigrants that had arrived in member states. There was a linear progression to this liberalism which ran counter to the public's growing opposition to unmanaged immigration.
- It is not possible to identify a tipping point at which anti-immigrant

attitudes crystallised. Enoch Powell's 'Rivers of Blood' speech of 1968 is a possibility but it was directed against in-migration from the British Commonwealth rather than labour migrants and so is untypical. At some point in the 1970s when labour markets had reached an equilibrium point, a liberal normative regime took up the call for continued in-migration, this time on humanitarian grounds. This subtle transition in rationales was nevertheless flagged by political (union activists) and electoral (radical right party leaders) entrepreneurs to mobilise anti-immigrant forces.

- It is not possible to identify a tipping point at which, and a country where, anti-immigrant attitudes were transformed, in part at least, into anti-Muslim attitudes. President Mitterrand's announcement in 1989 that France had reached the threshold number of immigrants beyond which the country's tolerance would become tested may unintentionally have triggered a spike in hostility towards France's largest migrant community – Muslims from the Maghreb countries. It was around this time that a shift in self-identification from migrant to Muslim also took place. The 1997 Runnymede Trust report on Islamophobia in Britain was official confirmation of an ongoing trend in Europe.

- A stimulus–response model emerged as national Muslim organisations were established to promote and protect their adherents. As Islamophobic rhetoric from radical right politicians became shriller, so Muslim communities in European states advanced new rights-based claims. Turkish organisations in Germany were particularly assertive, oftentimes with the backing of the Ankara government. In turn this led to the next stage in an anti-Muslim backlash. The turn to grander mosque building to serve larger Muslim communities, taller minarets, and more commonplace public displays of religious symbols, clothing and worship evoked an even sharper official reaction, leading to referendum decisions banning minarets, laws prohibiting burqas and regulations banning prayer meetings on city streets. The EU's liberal normative regime has come into question.

- The consequences of this cyclical dynamic have been to sideline the advocates of a moderate, mediating Euro-Islam philosophic movement and to empower radical right anti-immigrant and explicitly anti-Muslim parties which were on the electoral fringe before. While few of these parties gain enough parliamentary seats to take part in coalition governments – xenophobic parties in Austria, the Netherlands, Switzerland and for a time Denmark have been the major exceptions – more European countries than ever have elected representatives from such parties in their national parliaments. Anti-Muslim programmes have crossed the firewall to become mainstream, even shaping policies of centrist parties.

- Public attitudes to migrants and Muslim communities have developed into a political cleavage in European receiving societies with sizeable

Muslim minorities; this includes Scandinavian states such as Denmark and Sweden which have enjoyed a reputation for liberalism and tolerance. More recent EU member states in central and eastern Europe have so far not been marked by this cleavage.

* Elite responses to both growing Muslim communities and the backlash against them have involved, at the discursive level, critique of multiculturalism as a diversity management mechanism. In terms of public policy and public administration, the responses have been to whittle away at migrant rights while raising the bar for integration obligations.

These findings have been ordered sequentially, roughly corresponding to a time line extending from the 1960s to the present. Such sequential ordering suggests that a causal chain has structured the emergence of anti-Muslim attitudes in Europe. There are two junctures at which developments took place simultaneously and seemingly interconnectedly: one possibility is the conversion of anti-immigrant into anti-Muslim attitudes, which occurred around the time that Muslim immigrants and their descendants came to assert their Muslim identity; a second may be the rapid-fire stimulus–response cycle of anti-Muslim vitriol and Muslim assertiveness. Even at these two points, a causal linkage is improbable – and impossible to establish: events might have occurred as they did even without the cues, or stimuli, having to be present.

INTRODUCING CONTINGENT FACTORS

If the diachronic analysis of Islamophobia at least suggests a causal sequence, we need to ask whether contingent factors played a key role in the chain of events. Such factors are defined by the uncertainty that they will appear, that is, they can be described as chance events. The extent of contingency in producing a given outcome can be unpacked by engaging in counterfactual analysis, one that runs contrary to the established facts. The purpose of employing counterfactual analysis is as a 'learning device', 'mind-set changer' and 'mind-opening' experimentation, not as an explanatory variable or data point.[1] It gives us licence to pose the 'what if?' and 'what might have been?' questions, allowing us to explore 'possible' or 'alternate' worlds.

Questions that we ask about history's turning points are largely the product of the imagination. Here are examples. Had large numbers of immigrants, among them many Muslims, not come to Europe or been kept away from Europe in the 1970s, would Islamophobia have still developed on the continent anyway, for example, because of a clash of world civilisations? Or was the rise of an anti-Islamic movement contingent on Muslim migrants being present in large numbers? If that was the case, we can introduce another counterfactual (that is, contrary to the fact there were many Muslims): had

Germany expanded the labour recruitment agreements it had signed with Italy, Spain and Greece rather than concluding an additional agreement with Turkey in 1961, German society today would have fewer Turks; anti-Turkish attitudes would consequently be less politically salient in the country.

This diachronic analysis makes no reference to 'Islamic terrorism'. That is because other kinds of terrorism, including one plausibly called 'Christian', occurred during the period we have examined: the clearest example is a 'war on terror' launched by the Bush administration which brought Western militaries into Muslim-majority states. These events would require us to go in a different direction and inquire into Muslims' fear of the West. But what if the 11 September 2001 attacks had not taken place? Would their non-existence have ensured that subsequent terrorist attacks in Bali, London, Madrid, Delhi – even Oslo – would not have been carried out? If so, absent this terrorism as contingent factor, would the spread across much of Europe of hostility to Muslims have taken place? These 'what if?' questions are important for substantiating the controversial thesis, pervading numerous studies of the Islamic world, that Islamophobia is an exaggerated fear of Muslim fundamentalism.

Counterfactual unpacking allows us to challenge the validity of the historical determinism approach, reflected in some of the popular literature on Islamophobia. Its best known thesis holds that a clash of civilisations – or at least culture wars on the continent – between Europeans and Muslims was fated by the long history of antagonism and ideological competition between the two. Explanations for the Christian–Muslim wars in the Balkans in the 1990s often reach for the ancient hatred explanation. In Chapter 4, I described the sixteenth-century antecedents of the subsequent end-of-millennium wars. Deep underlying causes – civilisational differences – are combined with system causes – shifts in the balance of power – as well as with the clash of ideas and characteristics of leaders to establish causation. Process tracing unearths selective evidence that is used to link hypothesised causes with observed outcomes.

It is such deterministic explanations that led Richard Ned Lebow to emphasise the centrality of contingent factors. He was sceptical about the inevitability and irreversibility of particular outcomes that, for many reasons (among which are scholars' psychological need for closure and theory-driven explanations, and an embrace of hindsight bias), are taken for granted by historians. Lebow illustrated what a 'long-shot counterfactual' was by singling out a contingent event in the distant past that might have prevented the Holocaust. Had Mozart lived to sixty-five, many artists would have continued to imitate his genius. They would have developed a post-Classical style that kept Enlightenment ideas alive, thereby occupying the artistic space that Romanticism was to fill. Romanticism gave birth to extraordinary art, poetry and music, but it also engendered the national idea, which subsequently was converted into aggressive forms of nationalism. It was German nationalism that led to Hitler's rise and the perpetration of the Holocaust that followed. Lebow allows that 'counterfactuals might have changed the world, but in ways that become exponentially more difficult to track over time because of the additional branching points that enter the picture'.[2]

An example of a 'close-call counterfactual' was the assassination of Austrian Grand Duke Franz Ferdinand by a Serb terrorist in Sarajevo in 1914. Had the royal carriage not lost its way in the streets or had Franz Ferdinand left Sarajevo after the first attempt to kill him that day had failed, World War I would not have broken out. As Lebow argued, anti-war sentiment in Europe at the time was much stronger than historians, intent on identifying deterministic underlying causes (structural features), system breakdown, clashing ideas and leadership rivalry, have led us to believe.[3] Historians have generally overdetermined the outbreak of the First World War and Lebow's corrective is to assert that a chance event – a Serb assassin in the right place at the right time – made the war inevitable.

Close-call counterfactual analysis can help chart the point at which the rise and spread of Islamophobia in Europe became irreversible. Given that more than ten million Muslims live in 21st-century Europe, could more profound multiculturalism, making fewer demands on immigrants to integrate, have pre-empted the antagonism between majority and Muslim populations? Or was it just the reverse – that a tougher assimilationist policy might have prevented widening social divides and weaker social cohesion? Would less idealistic and moralistic, and more realistic and populist, EU norms on immigrants and integration at an earlier stage in the event sequence have pre-empted the emergence of an ethnoreligious cleavage? What if Muslim national organisations in France, Germany and Britain had been more submissive after 9/11 rather than asserting collective rights?

These are specific thought experiments focused on undoing short-range events that are intrinsically mutable. For Lebow, such 'imagination-driven strategies sensitise us to possible worlds that could have been, but desensitise us to patterns, regularities, and underlying causes'. The hold that discovering regularities and causes has on scholars is, however, enormous. It is the search for such patterns that has shaped much of the contemporary literature on Islamophobia. A theory-driven causally biased approach, centred on irreconcilable differences between the West and Islam, has attracted most attention. There are trade-offs to such an approach: 'Theory-driven strategies confer the benefits of explanatory closure and parsimony but desensitise us to nuance, complexity, contingency, and the possibility our theory is wrong'.[4]

In studies of the supposedly historic mutual antagonism between Europe and Islam, countless imaginative long-shot counterfactuals can be introduced to cast doubt about the validity of the chain of causation. Let us adopt plausible world counterfactuals in reviewing two such deterministic accounts.[5]

THE HISTORICAL DETERMINISM OF DEEP CAUSES

The assertion that Eurabia, a Europe that has been taken over by Muslims, is coming into existence has been advanced by several writers. The Princeton Islamic scholar Bernard Lewis forecast that by the end of the twenty-first century Europe would be a part of the Arabic west, the Maghreb.[6] American writer Bruce Bawer believed that the process was already advanced.[7] Christopher Caldwell, whose *Reflections on the Revolution in Europe: Immigration, Islam and the West* we examine below, suggested (without using the term) that Europeans are acquiescing in its creation. But it is British-based writer Bat Ye'or (Hebrew for 'Daughter of the Nile' – *nom de plume* of Gisèle Littman) who has claimed that Eurabia has been in existence for decades. What were the causes she identified in transforming Europe into Eurabia?

Bat Ye'or's analysis rests on extensive historical documentation and her conclusions should not be lightly dismissed. The study focuses on what followed from the 1973 oil crisis, in which the Organisation of Arab Petroleum-Exporting Countries restricted shipments of oil to Western countries as payback for their complicity in facilitating Israel's territorial gains in the war of that year. The European Community, she argued, made long-term political concessions to the Arab world in order to have the oil embargo lifted. In particular, it established the Euro-Arab Dialogue (EAD), an ongoing forum which, in her view, has promoted a series of joint Euro-Arab initiatives heavily biased towards Arab interests. Combined with increasing penetration of Europe by Muslim migrants, Europe has purportedly lapsed into chronic Judeophobia and anti-Americanism.

The result is the emergence of Eurabia – an entity 'with political, economic, religious, cultural, and media components superimposed on Europe by powerful government lobbies'.[8] For Bat Ye'or, the making of Eurabia was confirmed when the EAD supported 'implanting in Europe a large Muslim population, which would enjoy all the political, cultural, social, and religious rights of the host country' and 'imposing the political, cultural, and religious influences of Arab Islamism on European countries, through an immigrant population that remained politically and culturally attached to its countries of origin'.[9] Documenting decisions of successive EAD meetings beginning with the first one held in Cairo in 1975, the author claimed that each adopted resolutions supporting Arab immigration, labour and employment in Europe.[10]

A milestone in the supposed Muslim takeover of Europe was the decision in 1976 of the French Prime Minister, Jacques Chirac, to permit family reunification for immigrants. Its effect was to transform temporary Arab immigration into permanent settlement. Muslim immigration had led to topsy-turvy politics: Bat Ye'or polemicised that 'since the EU, aware of the opposition of the Arab League, did not plan an integration policy for the millions of Muslim immigrants, the host population was asked to make the effort to harmonise with the immigrant'.[11] The consequence was that Muslim immigrant groups became agents for promoting pro-Arab policy.

Other than Eurabia, Bat Ye'or's overarching concept is *dhimmitude*. It is taken from the Arabic word signifying 'subjugated, non-Muslim individuals or people that accept the restrictive and humiliating subordination to an ascendant Islamic power to avoid enslavement or death'.[12] After the 1973 oil embargo, she contended, Europe became a timid tributary state espousing a culture of hatred towards Christianity and Judaism. In foreign policy this was manifested in the hostility directed at the US and Israel.

Dhimmitude illustrated how European leaders had become servile to the Arab League.

> The Franco-German plan to build a unified Europe linked to the Arab world – and as a rival to America – led to a strategic, economic and political Euro-Arab alliance. For Arab and Muslim states, this new cooperation was intended to weaken Europe's alliance with America and bring Europe into line with the Arab League's policy toward Israel.[13]

A more recent illustration of Europe's bias favouring Muslim states was, for Bat Ye'or, the Euro-Mediterranean dialogue that dates back to 1995. Designed to establish a 'ring of friends' linking sides of the Mediterranean, this Euro-Mediterranean Partnership, also known as the EU's Barcelona process, was transformed into the Mediterranean Union in 2008. Alongside non-EU Balkan majority-Muslim states like Albania and Bosnia & Herzegovina, Israel has become a member of the EU 'Mediterranean Partner' countries. Why Israel would join an international organisation institutionalising 'Europe's bias favouring Muslim states' is an open question.

Dhimmitude has historical roots that, the author suggested, made Europe's transformation into Eurabia inevitable. She linked the history of non-Muslims living under the dominion of Islam to the ideology of jihad, which had been elaborated by Islamic clerics from the eighth century onwards. This ideology

> separates humanity into two hostile blocks – the community of Muslims (*Dar ul-Islam*) and the infidel non-Muslims (*Dar ul-Harb*). According to this ideology, Allah commands the Muslims to conquer the whole world in order to apply Qur'anic laws. Hence, they have to wage a perpetual war against the infidels who refuse to submit. Its principle is based on the inequality between the community of Allah and the infidels. The first is a superior group, whose mission it is to rule the world. The second must submit.[14]

When they submit, infidels are cowered into *dhimmitude*. The constraints imposed on non-Muslims living under Islam encompass the religious, social, political and economic spheres. Bat Ye'or believed that perpetual war against those not submitting to Islam remained an operative paradigm, including in Europe. Accordingly, *dhimmitude* 'cannot be judged from the circumstantial position of any one community, at a given time and in a given place. *Dhimmitude* must be appraised according to its laws and customs, irrespectively [*sic*] of circumstances and political contingencies'.[15]

The author contradicts herself. She recognised a contingent cause behind the emergence of Eurabia as well as of European *dhimmitude* – the 1973 oil embargo, which was, in turn, a consequent of the war between Egypt and Israel earlier that year. If Egyptian President Anwar El Sadat had not launched his risky surprise attack in October of that year, leading to US backing of Israel and the subsequent Arab world's oil embargo aimed at the US and its Western allies, Europe would not have had to make the alleged concessions to Arab interests that forced it into servitude. Put starkly, Eurabia would not have come to exist. Yet Bat Ye'or also invoked the distant origins of *dhimmitude* to suggest path dependence for non-Muslim societies: their resistance to perpetual jihad was bound to weaken, and the imposition of an oil embargo was not required for the outcome, *dhimmitude*, to occur.

The theory of a Manichean world provides comforting explanatory closure and, after 9/11, an exclamation point for chronicling an apparently irreversible causal chain of religious conflict. But lack of attention to complexity and to contingent one-off events, as well as an unstated assumption of linear development, permits any number of long-shot counterfactuals positing alternative worlds to undermine its validity. A minimal rewrite of history using a long-shot counterfactual is enough to undermine the theory's explanatory power. Here is one illustration.

Suppose that the army of the Ummayad Caliphate and not the Franks had won the Battle of Poitiers in 732. The Islamic incursion into what is today France would have succeeded and Eurabia would have come into existence twelve centuries earlier than Bat Ye'or claims it did. But interjecting a second-order consequent could undo this outcome. Stakes would have been raised in the competition between rival Muslim kingdoms in northern Spain for control of Islamic-occupied territories. An Ummayad victory could have exacerbated existing squabbling, possibly hastening the Christian *Reconquista* of Al-Andalus by 500 years. If this chain of events had occurred, not only would there have been no Eurabia, there would have been little historical experience of *dhimmitude*. Bat Ye'or's posited process of Islamicisation of Europe would have been reversed a mere twenty years after it had begun. The relevance of anti-Islamic orientations in Europe would be a moot issue today.

STRUCTURAL FEATURES AND CONTINGENT EVENTS

Not all approaches to the West's relations with the Islamic world make extensive use of *la longue durée*. Emphasis on the here and now – the structure of the international system, the migration processes characteristic of it, the existence of global inequalities and global opportunities – inform some studies exploring the sources of Islamophobia in contemporary society. Christopher Caldwell's *Reflections on the Revolution in Europe* is a well-researched journalistic account which shares many of Bat Ye'or's normative positions while largely steering clear of historical determinism.

That is not entirely true. Caldwell's fundamental assumption is of the existence of a civilisational divide.

> In theory, any profoundly different culture could prove difficult to assimilate into European life. In practice, it is Islam that is posing the most acute problems. For 1,400 years, the Islamic and the Christian worlds have opposed one another, violently at times. We are living through one of those times.[16]

If there is a constant marking this opposition, it lies, for Caldwell, in the jihad culture of Islam, not of intransigent Western bellicosity. 'As of this writing, Muslim countries or groups are either at war or in a hostile truce with every civilisation that Islam abuts, from Nigeria to Xinjiang.'[17]

Islam has proved a failure in more ways than just its war proneness. Thus,

> if we consider the penury, servitude, violence, and mediocrity of Muslim societies worldwide ... how do we explain it? Either there is a major problem with Islam that must be addressed by Muslims themselves, or a wide variety of non-Muslim cultures has, by incredible coincidence, developed exactly the same unfair malevolence toward Islam.[18]

Using a logical device, Caldwell requires 'Muslims themselves' to join with the West in condemning Muslim penury and mediocrity.

What is the result when this underlying cause of difference between the West and Islam is projected onto contemporary European societies? Early in his book Caldwell asks whether Europe can still be Europe with so many different people living in it and he answers that it cannot. He is concerned that the West has advanced too far too fast. Why? Islam may be backward but for bin Laden and others like him 'the Middle Ages is their selling point'.[19]

The path-dependent nature of conflict between Western and Islamic worlds is underscored in Caldwell's study. 'Even before September 11, 2001, Islam's pretensions to global domination made European television news.'[20] The cause of conflict may be historical, but European miscalculations have played an important part. Muslim cultures 'have historically been Europe's enemies, its overlords, or its underlings. Europe is wagering that attitudes handed down over the centuries, on both sides, have disappeared, or can be made to disappear. That is probably not a wise wager.'[21]

The British scientist and author Kenan Malik refused to use the racist card against the US journalist and bluntly asserted that 'Caldwell is no racist'. But he added that Caldwell confuses diversity of people with diversity of values, as exemplified in the view that 'the presence of too many non-Europeans in Europe is a threat to European values'. Malik also took issue with Caldwell's explanation that Muslim immigration has made Europe less European.

> What has eroded is faith in the idea that it is possible to win peoples of different backgrounds to a common set of secular, humanist, Enlightened values. And that is the real problem: not immigration, nor Muslim immigration, but the lack of conviction in a progressive, secular, humanist project.[22]

Malik was expressing scepticism about multiculturalism's promise – the zeitgeist of a time of European economic decline – but he also was disappointed that the vacuum of ideas it had created was being filled with prejudicial ones like those expressed by Caldwell.

The US-based conservative academic Fouad Ajami was a more vigorous defender of Caldwell's analysis: it was 'subtle, but quite honest and forthright in its reading of history'. Nevertheless Ajami had a far more positive view of Islam than did Caldwell: 'Islam is a magnificent religion that has also been, at times over the centuries, a glorious and generous culture. But, all cant to the contrary, it is in no sense Europe's religion and it is in no sense Europe's culture.'[23] Ajami lent support, then, to Caldwell's view that Islam was alien to Europe.

The difference between Caldwell's analysis and that of Eurabian historical determinists is that he identifies the salience of two contingent factors – ones whose absence would have broken the historical pathway leading to Europe's Islamicisation. These interconnected factors, portrayed by Caldwell as cause and effect, were necessary preconditions for Europe to begin losing control over its culture and identity. The first was a sense of guilt for two historical travesties, colonialism and Nazism, which induced postwar Europe to make acts of atonement and repentance. It was the Holocaust that evoked the greatest guilt: 'Post-Holocaust repentance became a template for regulating the affairs of any minority that could plausibly present itself as seriously aggrieved. Europe's Muslims were a living, thriving, confident European ethnic group with a lot of claims to press.'[24]

The second contingent factor was to make as the most extravagant of acts of atonement an opening up of European borders to immigrants. Caldwell highlighted how Europe became a destination for immigration because of an elite consensus on such atonement policy – even as public opinion expressed opposition to immigration for decade after decade. Without an open-door immigration policy, a product of guilt and elite consensus, therefore, there would be no threat today to Europeanness. Caldwell conjures up the image of a 'bazaar of world cultures' that European citizens were forced to integrate into and he specified that Muslim migration in particular was akin to a form of reverse colonisation of Europe.

An offshoot – or unintended consequence – of these processes of guilt and atonement was a counterintuitive evolution in identity politics. As the identities of Europeans were fragmenting, those of Muslim settlers were gelling – for Caldwell thereby contradicting the assumption of European observers that Muslim diversity was an indisputable fact. The author described how the mantra that 'Muslims suffer the most in the world' was converted into an appeal for unity: 'Conditions are ripe for the various Muslim communities of Europe to coalesce in a unified identity.'[25] The supposed diversity of Islam in Europe was disproved, Caldwell continued, by this regression into a pan-Islamic identity. Such an identity both fed on and contributed to the perceived hostility of the host society.

This shift, for Caldwell, had greater significance than a mere shuffling of identity politics. 'The problem that European Muslims' solidarity creates, at least potentially, is dual loyalty.' And dual loyalty 'can be a vague, dangerous, and constitutionally corrosive thing'. Muslim divergence from earlier immigration waves lay in the ominous fact that 'newly acquired national allegiances were negotiable, revocable, provisional'.[26] He likened the danger of such dubious loyalty to that of having allowed a wave of immigrants from communist countries who were ambivalent about which side they supported to settle in the West at the height of the Cold War. This analogy is unflattering to Muslim migrants. For Europeans, the abrupt appearance of a great number of Muslims who started building their own institutions constituted 'a project to claim territory'.[27] Mosque building showed Europe that Muslims were not establishing a temporary foothold.

At the heart of Caldwell's explanation of Europe's loss of control over its culture and identity is the enabling part played by European elites – not Islam. If Islam has become Europe's first religion measured in terms of the privileges it has gained and the intensity its followers display, it is for Caldwell as a result of the choice European elites made. He asked rhetorically: who would prefer a 'diffident, mocked, and un-chic faith like European Christianity over a dynamic, confident, and streetwise one like European Islam?'[28]

Caldwell's major finding is, then, that Europeans themselves are to blame for the progressive loss of culture and identity caused by so many non-Europeans now residing here. His insight is not original: as we encountered in Chapter 4, Martin Luther concluded in 1518 that the Turk was a scourge sent by God to punish Christians for their sins. Bat Ye'or would put it differently: a culture of *dhimmitude* has emerged, particularly among Europe's ruling elites, with the result that Islam's role has expanded. This submissiveness owes more to European guilt than to Muslim agency. Caldwell contextualises this subservience within the historic confrontation between Muslim and Western civilisations; as a Harvard graduate, his thinking appears influenced by the Huntingtonian paradigm describing the clash of civilisations dominant in international politics today.[29]

Long-shot counterfactuals of the kind identified earlier, for example a different Battle of Poitiers outcome, can challenge a historical determinist analysis. But Caldwell's intriguing referencing of branching points at which immigration policy bringing Muslims to Europe might have taken a different form – producing a much smaller Muslim population – invites an interpolation of short-term counterfactuals. One close-call plausible world counterfactual merits special consideration. Across European democracies, what if greater political weight had been attached in the 1960s and 1970s to the state of public opinion on immigration matters? Could a selective immigration policy have been hammered out decades before it became an official EU approach in 2008? Would defusing anti-immigrant sentiment at an early stage have pre-empted later anti-Muslim attitudes? There is irony in raising the counterfactual proposition that, in a democracy, the public should have more say in policy making.

UNMAKING PUBLIC OPINION ON ISLAM

The simplest way to undo the chain of events that has produced Islamophobia would be to introduce a miracle counterfactual, whereby human nature is altered so that prejudice is absent from people's psychological make-up. Imagining such an alternative world – a long long-shot counterfactual – is not a realistically anchored thought experiment and enters the realm of what can be termed social science fiction. The most credible, vivid, plausible way to unmake this sequence is to turn to close-call counterfactuals. Let me return therefore to the propositions with which this chapter began.

The third statement on the list describes how elite liberalism on immigration policy ran counter to the public's mounting opposition to unmanaged immigration. The fourth observes how the liberal normative regime transitioned to humanitarian arguments supporting continued in-migration after labour needs had been satisfied. This shift in rationale did not go unnoticed by many citizens and led to the first sustained efforts to mobilise anti-immigrant forces. These developments occurred before explicitly anti-Muslim sentiment took off.

The political inefficacy of public opinion in immigration policy formulation emerges as the most plausible factor that, if undone, could have reversed the sequence of events leading to anti-Muslim attitudes. In political science, public opinion is infrequently used as an explanatory variable for policy outcomes. Yet its political salience merits its treatment as at least a context variable shaping policy outcomes.

Public opinion is based on different things: citizens' levels of political knowledge, their political interest, their political sophistication. Important, too, though it is rarely approached this way, is measuring the level of intensity of opinion about an issue. High-intensity opinion typically leads to political organisation for or against a policy. Two political scientists developed a thermostatic model that measured policy responsiveness to public opinion.[30] They found that opinion had a stronger effect on policy than generally assumed. For example, public preferences have been reflected in European legislative behaviour, specifically secondary legislation in the form of regulations and directives, across many policy spheres. While there might not be a 'point landing' leading to congruence of policy with antecedent opinion, the general policy direction is impacted.

Public opinion on valence issues such as immigration offers predictive power of what future policy will be. To be sure, the causal direction may not always lead from public preferences to a consequent policy. Policy decisions may represent 'anticipatory responses' to public opinion by strategic actors like a national legislature or the European Commission. 'Policy entrepreneurship' can tap the state of public opinion.[31] The relevance of such propositions to our counterfactual is straightforward: unmaking the public–elite divide is not the insurmountable task it may appear to be.

Arguments in support of an enhanced role for public opinion in the making of immigration policy have become more forceful as Europe struggles with integration of migrants. An initiative of the Transatlantic Council on Migration, part of the non-partisan and independent Migration Policy Institute, based in Washington, which studies world migration, reflected particular sensitivity to this issue and made a number of recommendations. Four principal addressees of these proposals are explicitly identified.

- '*Governments* must demonstrate to their publics that they are in control of both the composition and scale of immigration.'[32]
- '*Politicians* must acknowledge and address the public's concerns about immigration, such as border control, public security and potential crowding in the labour market. Ignoring these concerns – or worse, suggesting they are evidence of prejudice – will only alienate voters.' One way of doing this is the following: 'Politicians should appeal to values and emotion, not just recite statistics . . . Public opinion is based on (and influenced by) values more than by statistics; therefore addressing a contentious policy issue by "defending facts" can backfire.'[33]
- '*Policymakers* can cull lessons learned from polls to create more effective

narratives and address their constituents' desire for greater control over their lives. The most effective response is to acknowledge people's fear of change, instead of trying to "counter" that fear with facts and statistics.'[34]

- 'Publics want governments to create more stable, predictable and usually smaller flows of legal migrants; to dramatically reduce illegal entry; to prevent unscrupulous employers from undermining wages and work standards; and to ensure that immigrants learn the local language, obey the law, pay taxes and respect a country's civic culture and institutions.'[35]

If we imagine that such recommendations had been implemented in the 1970s, contrary to the facts described in this book, it becomes plausible to undo the sequence of events that led from a dramatic increase in immigration numbers and the disregard of hostile public opinion (arguably a weightier factor than immigrant totals) to the building up of anti-immigration attitudes which eventually were converted principally into anti-Muslim sentiments. The ensuing debates over integration, assimilation and multiculturalism would have been more banal – a desirable outcome that would have replaced highly charged polemics. The evolution of parallel societies, economic and social marginalisation, and the rage of the *banlieue* would have been less intractable challenges because state capacity for absorbing immigrants would have been more closely matched to immigrant numbers.

Would controversies over mosques, minarets, headscarves and burqas not have erupted had this one counterfactual – public preferences are given weight in European democracies – been realised? Many theory-driven explanations highlighting the structural causes of Islamophobia would cite the 1,300 years of supposedly insoluble conflict between Islam and the West to repudiate this imagined outcome. The close-call counterfactual would, by contrast, point to a branching point at which political leaders could choose to 'paint a picture of how society and national identity should look in the longer term, and explain how immigration fits into that construct'.[36] Dialogue in a deliberative democracy conducted in a liberal spirit would likely have reduced prejudice in society and remade a normative consensus in Europe within which Muslims constituted a full-fledged party.

Notes

1. Steven Weber, 'Counterfactuals, Past and Future', in Philip E. Tetlock and Aaron Belkin (eds), *Counterfactual Thought Experiments in World Politics: Logical, Methodological, and Psychological Perspectives* (Princeton, NJ: Princeton University Press, 1996), p. 268.
2. Richard Ned Lebow, *Forbidden Fruit: Counterfactuals and International Relations* (Princeton, NJ: Princeton University Press, 2010), p. 56.

3. Ibid., chapters 3, 7.
4. Ibid., p. 164.
5. Nine criteria determine plausible world counterfactuals. The most important are clarity, completeness, consistency and realism. Lebow, *Forbidden Fruit*, pp. 54–7.
6. Bernard Lewis, *The Crisis of Islam: Holy War and Unholy Terror* (New York: Random House, 2004).
7. Bruce Bawer, *While Europe Slept: How Radical Islam is Destroying the West from Within* (New York: Doubleday, 2006).
8. Bat Ye'or, *Eurabia: The Euro-Arab Axis* (Madison, NJ: Fairleigh Dickinson University Press, 2009), p. 12. Originally, *Eurabia* was the name of a French journal whose first issue was published in 1975 by pro-Arab scholars and essayists.
9. Bat Ye'or, *Eurabia*, p. 75.
10. Ibid., p. 93.
11 Ibid., p. 161.
12. Ibid., p. 9. See also Bat Ye'or, *Islam and Dhimmitude: Where Civilizations Collide* (Madison, NJ: Fairleigh Dickinson University Press, 2001).
13. Bat Ye'or, *Eurabia*, p. 225.
14. Bat Ye'or, *Islam and Dhimmitude*. See also her 'Jihad and Human Rights Today', Islam Review website (undated), http://www.islamreview.com/articles/humanrights.shtml, accessed 8 February 2012.
15. 'The Status of Non-Muslim Minorities under Islamic Rule', Dhimmitude website, http://www.dhimmitude.org/, accessed 8 February 2012.
16. Christopher Caldwell, *Reflections on the Revolution in Europe: Immigration, Islam, and the West* (New York: Doubleday, 2009), p. 11.
17. Ibid., pp. 168–9.
18. Ibid., p. 163.
19. Ibid., p. 189.
20. Ibid., p. 132.
21. Ibid., p. 24.
22. Kenan Malik, review of Caldwell, *Reflections on the Revolution in Europe*, New Humanist website, http://newhumanist.org.uk/2093/book-review-reflections-on-the-revolution-in-europe-immigration-islam-and-europe-by-christopher-caldwell, accessed 8 February 2012.
23. Fouad Ajami, 'Strangers in the Land', *New York Times*, 2 August 2009, p. BR1. For a cross-section of reviews see http://www.neoconeurope.eu/Christopher_Caldwell, accessed 8 February 2012.
24. Caldwell, *Reflections on the Revolution in Europe*, p. 266.
25. Ibid., p. 160.
26. Ibid., pp. 163, 166.
27. Ibid., p. 132.
28. Ibid., p. 190.
29. Paul M. Barrett, 'Cultures in Conflict: On Muslim Immigrants in Europe', *Harvard Magazine*, July–August 2009.
30. For an excellent introduction to the subject, see Mark Franklin and Christopher Wlezien, 'The Responsive Public: Issue Salience, Policy Change, and Preferences for European Unification', *Journal of Theoretical Politics* 9 (1997), pp. 347–63.
31. See Andrew Moravcsik (ed.), *Centralization or Fragmentation? Europe Facing the*

Challenges of Deepening, Diversity, and Democracy (New York: Council on Foreign Relations Press, 1998).

32. Bertelsmann-Stiftung, Migration Policy Institute (eds), *Migration, Public Opinion and Politics: The Transatlantic Council on Migration* (Gütersloh: Bertelsmann-Stiftung, 2009), p. 26. All emphases in this list added.

33. Ibid., p. 21.

34. Ibid., p. 23.

35. Ibid., p. 23

36. Ibid., p. 25.

Select bibliography

James A. Aho, *This Thing of Darkness: A Sociology of the Enemy* (Seattle: University of Washington Press, 1994)

Mikhail A. Alexseev, *Immigration Phobia and the Security Dilemma: Russia, Europe, and the United States* (Cambridge: Cambridge University Press, 2006)

Chris Allen, *Islamophobia* (Farnham: Ashgate, 2010)

Gordon W. Allport, *The Nature of Prejudice* (New York: Basic, 1979)

Ian Almond, *The New Orientalists: Postmodern Representation of Islam from Foucault to Baudrillard* (London: I. B. Tauris, 2007)

At Home in Europe Project, *Muslims in Europe: A Report on 11 EU Cities* (New York & Budapest: Open Society Institute / London: Open Society Foundation, 2009)

F. G. Bailey, *Treasons, Stratagems, and Spoils: How Leaders Make Practical Use of Values and Beliefs* (Boulder, CO: Westview Press, 2001)

Étienne Balibar and Immanuel Wallerstein, *Race, Nation, Class: Ambiguous Identities* (London: Verso, 1991)

Rainer Bauböck, Eva Ersbøll, Kees Groenendijk and Harald Waldrauch (eds), *Acquisition and Loss of Nationality: Policies and Trends in 15 European Countries*, 2 vols (Amsterdam: Amsterdam University Press 2006)

Rainer Bauböck, Bernhard Perchinig and Wiebke Sievers (eds), *Citizenship Policies in the New Europe*, 2nd ed. (Amsterdam: Amsterdam University Press, 2009)

Rainer Bauböck and John Rundell (eds), *Blurred Boundaries: Migration, Ethnicity, Citizenship* (Aldershot: Ashgate, 1998)

Zygmunt Bauman, *Europe: An Unfinished Adventure* (Cambridge: Polity Press, 2004)

Ryan K. Beasley, Juliet Kaarbo, Jeffrey S. Lantis and Michael T. Snarr (eds), *Foreign Policy in Comparative Perspective: Domestic and International Influences on State Behavior* (Washington, DC: CQ Press, 2002)

Tahar Ben Jelloun, *L'Hospitalité française* (Paris: Seuil, 1997)

Latifa Ben Mansour, *Frères musulmans, frères féroces: voyage dans l'enfer du discours islamiste* (Paris: Ramsay, 2002)

Seyla Benhabib, *The Rights of Others: Aliens, Residents and Citizens* (Cambridge: Cambridge University Press, 2003)

Kenneth Benoit and Michael Laver, *Party Policy in Modern Democracies* (Abingdon: Routledge, 2006)

John Berger, *A Seventh Man: Migrant Workers in Europe* (New York: Viking, 1975)

Bertelsmann-Stiftung, Migration Policy Institute (eds), *Migration, Public Opinion and Politics: The Transatlantic Council on Migration* (Gütersloh: Bertelsmann-Stiftung, 2009)

Christophe Bertossi (ed.), *European Anti-discrimination and the Politics of Citizenship: Britain and France* (Basingstoke: Palgrave Macmillan, 2007)

Pascal Blanchard and Nicolas Bancel, *De l'indigène à l'immigré* (Paris: Gallimard, 1998)

Christina Boswell, *European Migration Policies in Flux: Changing Patterns of Inclusion and Exclusion* (Oxford: Blackwell, 2003)

Christina Boswell, *The Political Uses of Expert Knowledge: Immigration Policy and Social Research* (Cambridge: Cambridge University Press, 2009)

Christina Boswell and Andrew Geddes, *Migration and Mobility in the European Union* (Basingstoke: Palgrave Macmillan, 2010)

John R. Bowen, *Can Islam Be French? Pluralism and Pragmatism in a Secular State* (Princeton, NJ: Princeton University Press, 2010)

John R. Bowen, *Why the French Don't Like Headscarves: Islam, the State, and Public Space* (Princeton, NJ: Princeton University Press, 2007)

Alain Boyer, *L'Islam en France* (Paris: Presses Universitaires de France, 1998)

Marijke Breuning, *Foreign Policy Analysis: A Comparative Introduction* (Basingstoke: Palgrave Macmillan, 2007)

Sylvain Brouard, Andrew M. Appleton and Amy G. Mazur (eds), *The French Fifth Republic at Fifty* (Basingstoke: Palgrave Macmillan, 2009)

Matti Bunzl, *Anti-Semitism and Islamophobia: Hatreds Old and New in Europe* (Chicago: Prickly Paradigm Press, 2007)

Christopher Caldwell, *Reflections on the Revolution in Europe: Immigration, Islam, and the West* (New York: Doubleday, 2009)

David Carment and David Bercuson (eds), *The World in Canada: Diaspora, Demography, and Domestic Politics* (Montreal: McGill-Queen's University Press, 2008)

Jocelyne Cesari (ed.), *Muslims in the West after 9/11: Religion, Politics and Law* (London: Routledge, 2010)

Jocelyne Cesari and Seán McLoughlin (eds), *European Muslims and the Secular State* (Aldershot: Ashgate, 2005)

Herrick Chapman and Laura L. Frader (eds), *Race in France: Interdisciplinary Perspectives on the Politics of Difference* (New York: Berghahn, 2004)

Ariane Chebel d'Appollonia, *Les Racismes ordinaries* (Paris: Presses de Sciences Po, 1998)

Ariane Chebel d'Appollonia and Simon Reich (eds), *Immigration, Integration, and Security: America and Europe in Comparative Perspective* (Pittsburgh, PA: University of Pittsburgh Press, 2008)

Jeffrey T. Checkel and Peter J. Katzenstein (eds), *European Identity* (Cambridge: Cambridge University Press, 2009)

Commission Nationale Consultative des Droits de l'Homme, *La Lutte contre le racisme, l'antisémitisme et la xénophobie: année 2007* (Paris: La Documentation Française, 2008)

Congressional Research Service, *Islamist Extremism in Europe* (Washington, DC: Congressional Research Service, 2006)

Wayne Cornelius, Takeyuki Tsuda, Philip L. Martin and James E. Hollifield (eds), *Controlling Immigration: A Global Perspective* (Stanford, CA: Stanford University Press, 1994)

Alastair Crooke, *Resistance: The Essence of the Islamist Revolution* (London: Pluto Press, 2009)

Theodore Dalrymple, *In Praise of Prejudice: The Necessity of Preconceived Ideas* (New York: Encounter, 2007)

Gerard Delanty and Krishan Kumar (eds), *The Sage Handbook of Nations and Nationalism* (London: Sage, 2006)

Thomas Deltombe, *L'Islam imaginaire: la construction médiatique de l'islamophobie en France, 1975–2005* (Paris: La Découverte, 2005)

European Union Monitoring Centre for Racism and Xenophobia, *Muslims in the European Union: Discrimination and Islamophobia* (Vienna: EUMC, 2006)

Adrian Favell, *Eurostars and Eurocities: Free Movement and Mobility in an Integrating Europe* (Oxford: Blackwell, 2008)

Liz Fekete, *A Suitable Enemy: Racism, Migration and Islamophobia in Europe* (London: Pluto Press, 2009)

Joel S. Fetzer and J. Christopher Soper, *Muslims and the State in Great Britain, France, and Germany* (Cambridge: Cambridge University Press, 2005)

Vincent Geisser, *La Nouvelle Islamophobie* (Paris: La Découverte, 2003)

Mérove Gijsberts, Louk Hagendoorn and Peer Scheepers (eds), *Nationalism and Exclusion of Migrants: Cross-national Comparisons* (Aldershot: Ashgate, 2004)

René Girard, *The Girard Reader*, ed. James G. Williams (New York: Crossroad Herder, 1996)

René Girard, *The Scapegoat* (Baltimore, MD: Johns Hopkins University Press, 1986)

Terri E. Givens, Gary P. Freeman and David L. Leal (eds), *Immigration Policy and Security: U.S., European, and Commonwealth Perspectives* (New York: Routledge, 2009)

Ian Goldin, Geoffrey Cameron and Meera Balarajan, *Exceptional People: How*

Immigration Shaped Our World and Will Define Our Future (Princeton, NJ: Princeton University Press, 2011)

Elspeth Guild, *Security and Migration in the 21st Century* (Cambridge: Polity, 2009)

Elspeth Guild, Kees Groenendijk and Sergio Carrera (eds), *Illiberal Liberal States: Immigration, Citizenship and Integration in the EU* (Farnham: Ashgate, 2009)

Virginie Guiraudon and Gallya Lahav (eds), *Immigration Policy in Europe: The Politics of Control* (London: Routledge, 2006)

Yvonne Yazbeck Haddad (ed.), *Muslims in the West: From Sojourners to Citizens* (Oxford: Oxford University Press, 2002)

Alec G. Hargreaves, *Immigration and Identity in Beur Fiction: Voices from the North African Immigrant Community in France* (Oxford: Berg, 1997)

Christopher Hitchens, *God Is Not Great: How Religion Poisons Everything* (New York: Twelve, 2007)

Valerie M. Hudson, *Foreign Policy Analysis: Classic and Contemporary Theory* (Lanham, MD: Rowman and Littlefield, 2006)

Philip Jenkins, *God's Continent: Christianity, Islam, and Europe's Religious Crisis* (New York: Oxford University Press, 2007)

Christian Joppke, *Citizenship and Immigration* (Cambridge: Polity, 2010)

Christian Joppke, *Immigration and the Nation-state: The United States, Germany, and Great Britain* (Oxford: Oxford University Press, 1999)

Christian Joppke and Ewa Morawska (eds), *Toward Assimilation and Citizenship: Immigrants in Liberal Nation-states* (Basingstoke: Palgrave Macmillan, 2003)

Riva Kastoryano, *Etre Turc en France: reflexions sur familles et communauté* (Paris: L'Harmattan, 1986)

Riva Kastoryano (ed.), *An Identity for Europe: The Relevance of Multiculturalism in EU Construction* (Basingstoke: Palgrave Macmillan, 2009)

Riva Kastoryano, *Negotiating Identities: States and Immigrants in France and Germany* (Princeton, NJ: Princeton University Press, 2002)

Peter J. Katzenstein and Robert O. Keohane, *Anti-Americanisms in World Politics* (Ithaca, NY: Cornell University Press, 2006)

Ayhan Kaya, *Islam, Migration and Integration: The Age of Securitisation* (Basingstoke: Palgrave Macmillan, 2009)

Gilles Kepel, *Allah in the West: Islamic Movements in America and Europe* (Cambridge: Polity Press, 1997)

Farhad Khosrokhavar, *Inside Jihadism: Understanding Jihadi Movements Worldwide* (Boulder, CO: Paradigm, 2009)

Pamela Kilpadi (ed.), *Islam and Tolerance in Wider Europe* (New York: Open Society Institute, 2007)

Jytte Klausen, *The Islamic Challenge: Politics and Religion in Western Europe* (Oxford: Oxford University Press, 2005)

Douglas B. Klusmeyer and Demetrios G. Papademetriou, *Immigration Policy in the*

Federal Republic of Germany: Negotiating Membership and Remaking the Nation (New York: Berghahn, 2009)

Julia Kristeva, *Strangers to Ourselves* (New York: Columbia University Press, 1991)

Milja Kurki, *Causation in International Relations: Reclaiming Causal Analysis* (Cambridge: Cambridge University Press, 2008)

Hugues Lagrange, *Le Déni des cultures* (Paris: Seuil, 2010)

Gallya Lahav, *Immigration and Politics in the New Europe: Reinventing Borders* (Cambridge: Cambridge University Press, 2004)

Michèle Lamont, *The Dignity of Working Men: Morality and the Boundaries of Race, Class, and Immigration* (Cambridge, MA: Harvard University Press, 2000)

Walter Laqueur, *The Last Days of Europe: Epitaph for an Old Continent* (New York: Thomas Dunne, 2007)

Jonathan Laurence and Justin Vaisse, *Integrating Islam: Political and Religious Challenges in Contemporary France* (Washington, DC: Brookings Institution Press, 2008)

Richard Ned Lebow, *A Cultural Theory of International Relations* (Cambridge: Cambridge University Press, 2008)

Richard Ned Lebow, *Forbidden Fruit: Counterfactuals and International Relations* (Princeton, NJ: Princeton University Press, 2010)

Rémy Leveau and Khadija Mohsen-Finan (eds), *Musulmans de France et d'Europe* (Paris: CNRS, 2005)

Christina Schori Liang (ed.), *Europe for the Europeans: The Foreign and Security Policy of the Populist Radical Right* (Aldershot: Ashgate, 2007)

Adam Luedtke (ed.), *Migrants and Minorities: the European Response* (Newcastle upon Tyne: Cambridge Scholars, 2010)

Jamal Malik (ed.), *Muslims in Europe: From the Margin to the Centre* (Münster: Lit, 2005).

Ural Manço (ed.), *Reconnaissance et discrimination: présence de l'Islam en Europe occidentale et en Amérique du Nord* (Paris: L'Harmattan, 2004)

Ruth Mandel, *Cosmopolitan Anxieties: Turkish Challenges to Citizenship and Belonging in Germany* (Durham, NC: Duke University Press, 2008)

Philip L. Martin, Susan F. Martin and Patrick Weil, *Managing Migration: The Promise of Cooperation* (Lanham, MD: Lexington, 2006)

Martin E. Marty and R. Scott Appleby (eds), *Religion, Ethnicity, Self-identity* (Hanover, NH: University Press of New England, 1997)

Douglas S. Massey, Graeme Hugo, Joaquin Arango, Ali Kouaouci and Adela Pellegrino, *Worlds in Motion: Understanding International Migration at the End of the Millennium* (Oxford: Clarendon Press, 1998)

Tomaz Mastnak, *Crusading Peace: Christendom, the Muslim World, and Western Political Order* (Berkeley: University of California Press, 2002)

Anthony M. Messina, *The Logics and Politics of Post-WWII Migration to Western Europe* (Cambridge: Cambridge University Press, 2007)

213

Anthony M. Messina (ed.), *Western European Immigration and Integration Policy* (Westport, CT: Praeger, 2002)

Barbara Daly Metcalf (ed.), *Making Muslim Space in North America and Europe* (Berkeley: University of California Press, 1996)

Tariq Modood and Pnina Werbner (eds), *The Politics of Multiculturalism in the New Europe: Racism, Identity and Community* (London: Zed, 1997)

Tariq Modood, Anna Triandafyllidou and Ricard Zapata-Barrero (eds), *Multiculturalism, Muslims and Citizenship: A European Approach* (London: Routledge, 2006)

Jennie Germann Molz and Sarah Gibson (eds), *Mobilizing Hospitality: The Ethics of Social Relations in a Mobile World* (Aldershot: Ashgate, 2007)

Seyyed Hossein Mousavian, *Iran–Europe Relations: Challenges and Opportunities* (London: Routledge, 2008)

Cas Mudde, *Populist Radical Right Parties in Europe* (Cambridge: Cambridge University Press, 2007)

Cas Mudde, *Racist Extremism in Central and Eastern Europe* (London: Routledge, 2005)

Joyce Marie Mushaben, *The Changing Faces of Citizenship: Social Integration and Political Mobilization among Ethnic Minorities in Germany* (New York: Berghahn, 2008)

Amikam Nachmani, *Europe and Its Muslim Minorities: Aspects of Conflict, Attempts at Accord* (Brighton: Sussex Academic Press, 2009)

Lise Noël, *Intolerance: A General Survey* (Montreal: McGill-Queen's University Press, 1994)

Pippa Norris, *Radical Right: Voters and Parties in the Electoral Market* (Cambridge: Cambridge University Press, 2005)

Peter O'Brien, *European Perceptions of Islam and America from Saladin to George W. Bush: Europe's Fragile Ego Uncovered* (New York: Palgrave Macmillan, 2009)

Open Society Justice Initiative, *Ethnic Profiling in the European Union: Pervasive, Ineffective, and Discriminatory* (New York: Open Society Institute, 2009)

Henri Parens, Afaf Mahfouz, Stuart W. Twemlow and David E. Scharff (eds), *The Future of Prejudice: Psychoanalysis and the Prevention of Prejudice* (Lanham, MD: Rowman and Littlefield, 2007)

Craig A. Parsons and Timothy M. Smeeding (eds), *Immigration and the Transformation of Europe* (Cambridge: Cambridge University Press, 2006)

Robert J. Pauly, Jr., *Islam in Europe: Integration or Marginalization?* (Aldershot: Ashgate, 2004)

Nana Poku and David T. Graham (eds), *Redefining Security: Population Movements and National Security* (Westport, CT: Praeger, 1998)

Sandra Ponzanesi and Daniela Merolla (eds), *Migrant Cartographies: New Cultural and Literary Spaces in Post-colonial Europe* (Lanham, MD: Lexington, 2005)

David Pryce-Jones, *Betrayal: France, the Arabs, and the Jews* (New York: Encounter, 2006)

Frederick Quinn, *The Sum of all Heresies: The Image of Islam in Western Thought* (New York: Oxford University Press, 2008)

Emran Qureshi and Michael A. Sells (eds), *The New Crusades: Constructing the Muslim Enemy* (New York: Columbia University Press, 2003)

Tariq Ramadan, *Western Muslims and the Future of Islam* (Oxford: Oxford University Press, 2005)

Tariq Ramadan, *What I Believe* (New York: Oxford University Press, 2009)

Ali Rattansi and Sallie Westwood (eds), *Racism, Modernity and Identity: On the Western Front* (Cambridge: Polity Press, 1994)

Ernest Renan, *L'Islam et la science* (Montpellier: L'Archange Minotaure, 2003)

John E. Roemer, Woojin Lee and Karine Van der Straeten, *Racism, Xenophobia, and Distribution: Multi-issue Politics in Advanced Democracies* (Cambridge, MA: Harvard University Press, 2007)

James Rosenau (ed.), *Linkage Politics: Essays on the Convergence of National and International Systems* (New York: Free Press, 1969)

Olivier Roy, *Globalized Islam: The Search for a New Ummah* (New York: Columbia University Press, 2004)

Runnymede Trust, *Islamophobia: A Challenge for Us All* (London: Runnymede Trust, 1997)

Rosemarie Sackmann, Bernhard Peters and Thomas Faist (eds), *Identity and Integration: Migrants in Western Europe* (Aldershot: Ashgate, 2003)

William Safran, *The French Polity*, 7th ed. (New York: Pearson Longman, 2009)

Thilo Sarrazin, *Deutschland schafft sich ab: Wie wir unser Land aufs Spiel setzen* (Munich: Deutsche Verlags-Anstalt, 2010)

Saskia Sassen, *Guests and Aliens* (New York: New Press, 1999)

Joan Wallach Scott, *The Politics of the Veil* (Princeton, NJ: Princeton University Press, 2007)

Wasif Shadid and Sjoerd van Koningsveld (eds), *Muslims in the Margin: Political Responses to the Presence of Islam in Western Europe* (Kampen, Netherlands: Kok Pharos, 1996)

Idries Shah, *Darkest England* (London: Octagon Press, 1987)

Yasemin Nuhoğlu Soysal, *Limits of Citizenship: Migrants and Postnational Membership in Europe* (Chicago: University of Chicago Press, 1995)

Robert J. Sternberg and Karin Sternberg, *The Nature of Hate* (Cambridge: Cambridge University Press, 2008)

Stephan Stetter, *EU Foreign and Interior Policies: Cross-pillar Politics and the Social Construction of Sovereignty* (London: Routledge, 2007)

David Styan, *France and Iraq: Oil, Arms and French Policy Making in the Middle East* (New York: I. B. Tauris, 2006)

Carol Swain (ed.), *Debating Immigration* (Cambridge: Cambridge University Press, 2007)

Pierre-André Taguieff, *The Force of Prejudice: On Racism and Its Doubles* (Minneapolis: University of Minnesota Press, 2001)

Pierre-André Taguieff, *La Nouvelle Judéophobie* (Paris: Mille et Une Nuits, 2002)

Ray Taras, *Europe Old and New: Transnationalism, Belonging, Xenophobia* (Lanham, MD: Rowman and Littlefield, 2008)

Fabrizio Tassinari, *Why Europe Fears Its Neighbors* (Santa Barbara, CA: Praeger, 2009)

Göran Therborn, *European Modernity and Beyond: The Trajectory of European Societies, 1945–2000* (Thousand Oaks, CA: Sage, 1995)

Bassam Tibi, *Political Islam, World Politics and Europe: Democratic Peace and Euro-Islam versus Global Jihad* (London: Routledge, 2008)

Anna Triandafyllidou (ed.), *Irregular Migration in Europe: Myths and Realities* (Farnham: Ashgate, 2010)

Anna Triandafyllidou (ed.), *Muslims in 21st Century Europe: Structural and Cultural Perspectives* (London: Routledge, 2010)

Steven Vertovec and Alisdair Rogers (eds), *Muslim European Youth: Reproducing Ethnicity, Religion and Culture* (Aldershot: Ashgate, 1998)

Günter Walraff, *Ganz unten* (Cologne: Kiepenheuer und Witsch, 1985)

Patrick Weil, *La France et ses étrangers: l'aventure d'une politique de l'immigration de 1938 à nos jours* (Paris: Calmann-Lévy, 1991)

Patrick Weil, *How to be French: Nationality in the Making since 1789* (Durham, NC: Duke University Press, 2008)

Patrick Weil, *Liberté, Égalité, Discriminations: 'l'identité nationale' au regard de l'histoire* (Paris: Grasset, 2008)

Patrick Weil, *Qu'est-ce qu'un Français? Histoire de la nationalité française depuis la Révolution* (Paris: Gallimard, 2005)

Patrick Weil, *La République et sa diversité: immigration, intégration, discrimination* (Paris: Seuil, 2005)

Michel Wieviorka, *La France raciste* (Paris: Seuil, 1992)

Michel Wieviorka (ed.), *Racisme et xénophobie en Europe: une comparaison internationale* (Paris: La Découverte, 1994)

Catherine Wihtol de Wenden, *Atlas mondial des migrations* (Paris: Autrement, 2009)

Catherine Wihtol de Wenden and Remy Leveau, *La Beurgeoisie: Les trois âges de la vie associative issue de l'immigration* (Paris: CNRS, 2001)

Robert Wistrich, *Demonizing the Other: Anti-Semitism, Racism and Xenophobia* (London: Routledge, 1999)

M. Hakan Yavuz, *Secularism and Muslim Democracy in Turkey* (Cambridge: Cambridge University Press, 2009)

Bat Ye'or, *Eurabia: The Euro-Arab Axis* (Madison, NJ: Fairleigh Dickinson University Press, 2005)

Bat Ye'or, *Islam and Dhimmitude: Where Civilizations Collide* (Madison, NJ: Fairleigh Dickinson University Press, 2001)

Elisabeth Young-Bruehl, *The Anatomy of Prejudices* (Cambridge, MA: Harvard University Press, 1996)

Richard Youngs, *Europe and the Middle East: In the Shadow of September 11* (Boulder, CO: Lynne Rienner, 2006)

Andreas Zick, Beate Küpper, and Andreas Hövermann, *Intolerance, Prejudice and Discrimination: A European Report* (Berlin: Friedrich-Ebert-Stiftung, 2011)

Index